Beginning Programming with Python®

2nd Edition   WITHDRAWN

by John Paul Mueller

for dummies®
A Wiley Brand

Beginning Programming with Python® For Dummies®, 2nd Edition

Published by: **John Wiley & Sons, Inc.**, 111 River Street, Hoboken, NJ 07030-5774, www.wiley.com

Copyright © 2018 by John Wiley & Sons, Inc., Hoboken, New Jersey

Published simultaneously in Canada

For general information on our other products and services, please contact our Customer Care Department within the U.S. at 877-762-2974, outside the U.S. at 317-572-3993, or fax 317-572-4002. For technical support, please visit https://hub.wiley.com/community/support/dummies.

Wiley publishes in a variety of print and electronic formats and by print-on-demand. Some material included with standard print versions of this book may not be included in e-books or in print-on-demand. If this book refers to media such as a CD or DVD that is not included in the version you purchased, you may download this material at http://booksupport.wiley.com. For more information about Wiley products, visit www.wiley.com.

Library of Congress Control Number: 2017964018

ISBN 978-1-119-45789-3; ISBN 978-1-119-45787-9 (ebk); ISBN 978-1-119-45790-9 (ebk)

Manufactured in the United States of America

10 9 8 7 6 5 4 3 2 1

Contents at a Glance

Table of Contents

Introduction

Python is an example of a language that does everything right within the domain of things that it's designed to do. This isn't just me saying it, either: Programmers have voted by using Python enough that it's now the fifth-ranked language in the world (see `https://www.tiobe.com/tiobe-index/` for details). The amazing thing about Python is that you really can write an application on one platform and use it on every other platform that you need to support. In contrast to other programming languages that promised to provide platform independence, Python really does make that independence possible. In this case, the promise is as good as the result you get.

Python emphasizes code readability and a concise syntax that lets you write applications using fewer lines of code than other programming languages require. You can also use a coding style that meets your needs, given that Python supports the functional, imperative, object-oriented, and procedural coding styles (see Chapter 3 for details). In addition, because of the way Python works, you find it used in all sorts of fields that are filled with nonprogrammers. *Beginning Programming with Python for Dummies,* 2nd Edition is designed to help everyone, including nonprogrammers, get up and running with Python quickly.

Some people view Python as a scripted language, but it really is so much more. (Chapter 18 gives you just an inkling of the occupations that rely on Python to make things work.) However, Python it does lend itself to educational and other uses for which other programming languages can fall short. In fact, this book uses Jupypter Notebook for examples, which relies on the highly readable literate programming paradigm advanced by Stanford computer scientist Donald Knuth (see Chapter 4 for details). Your examples end up looking like highly readable reports that almost anyone can understand with ease.

About This Book

Beginning Programming with Python For Dummies, 2nd Edition is all about getting up and running with Python quickly. You want to learn the language fast so that you can become productive in using it to perform your real job, which could be anything. Unlike most books on the topic, this one starts you right at the beginning by showing you what makes Python different from other languages and how it can help you perform useful work in a job other than programming. As a result, you gain an understanding of what you need to do from the start, using hands-on examples and spending a good deal of time performing actually useful tasks. You even get help with installing Python on your particular system.

When you have a good installation on whatever platform you're using, you start with the basics and work your way up. By the time you finish working through the examples in this book, you'll be writing simple programs and performing tasks such as sending an email using Python. No, you won't be an expert, but you will be able to use Python to meet specific needs in the job environment. To make absorbing the concepts even easier, this book uses the following conventions:

>> Text that you're meant to type just as it appears in the book is **bold**. The exception is when you're working through a step list: Because each step is bold, the text to type is not bold.

>> When you see words in *italics* as part of a typing sequence, you need to replace that value with something that works for you. For example, if you see "Type ***Your Name*** and press Enter," you need to replace *Your Name* with your actual name.

>> Web addresses and programming code appear in monofont. If you're reading a digital version of this book on a device connected to the Internet, note that you can click the web address to visit that website, like this: www.dummies.com.

>> When you need to type command sequences, you see them separated by a special arrow, like this: File ➪ New File. In this case, you go to the File menu first and then select the New File entry on that menu. The result is that you see a new file created.

Foolish Assumptions

You might find it difficult to believe that I've assumed anything about you — after all, I haven't even met you yet! Although most assumptions are indeed foolish, I made these assumptions to provide a starting point for the book.

Familiarity with the platform you want to use is important because the book doesn't provide any guidance in this regard. (Chapter 2 does provide Python installation instructions for various platforms, and Chapter 4 tells you how to install Anaconda, which includes Jupyter Notebook — the Integrated Development Environment, or IDE, used for this book.) To provide you with maximum information about Python, this book doesn't discuss any platform-specific issues. You really do need to know how to install applications, use applications, and generally work with your chosen platform before you begin working with this book.

This book also assumes that you can locate information on the Internet. Sprinkled throughout are numerous references to online material that will enhance your learning experience. However, these added sources are useful only if you actually find and use them.

Icons Used in This Book

As you read this book, you see icons in the margins that indicate material of interest (or not, as the case may be). This section briefly describes each icon in this book.

TIP

Tips are nice because they help you save time or perform some task without a lot of extra work. The tips in this book are time-saving techniques or pointers to resources that you should try in order to get the maximum benefit from Python.

WARNING

I don't want to sound like an angry parent or some kind of maniac, but you should avoid doing anything marked with a Warning icon. Otherwise, you could find that your program only serves to confuse users, who will then refuse to work with it.

TECHNICAL STUFF

Whenever you see this icon, think advanced tip or technique. You might find these tidbits of useful information just too boring for words, or they could contain the solution you need to get a program running. Skip these bits of information whenever you like.

REMEMBER

If you don't get anything else out of a particular chapter or section, remember the material marked by this icon. This text usually contains an essential process or a bit of information that you must know to write Python programs successfully.

Beyond the Book

This book isn't the end of your Python programming experience — it's really just the beginning. I provide online content to make this book more flexible and better able to meet your needs. That way, as I receive email from you, I can do things like address questions and tell you how updates to either Python or its associated libraries affect book content. In fact, you gain access to all these cool additions:

>> **Cheat sheet:** You remember using crib notes in school to make a better mark on a test, don't you? You do? Well, a cheat sheet is sort of like that. It provides you with some special notes about tasks that you can do with Python that not every other developer knows. You can find the cheat sheet for this book by going to www.dummies.com and searching Beginning Programming For Dummies, 2nd Edition Cheat Sheet. It contains really neat information like the top ten mistakes developers make when working with Python and some of the Python syntax that gives most developers problems.

>> **Updates:** Sometimes changes happen. For example, I might not have seen an upcoming change when I looked into my crystal ball during the writing of this book. In the past, that simply meant the book would become outdated and less useful, but you can now find updates to the book at by going to `www.dummies.com` and searching this book's title.

In addition to these updates, check out the blog posts with answers to reader questions and demonstrations of useful book-related techniques at `http://blog.johnmuellerbooks.com/`.

>> **Companion files:** Hey! Who really wants to type all the code in the book? Most readers would prefer to spend their time actually working through coding examples, rather than typing. Fortunately for you, the source code is available for download, so all you need to do is read the book to learn Python coding techniques. Each of the book examples even tells you precisely which example project to use. You can find these files at going to `www.dummies.com` and searching this book's title. On the page that appears, scroll down to the graphic of the book's cover and click it; then click More About This Book. Click the Downloads tab on the page that appears.

Where to Go from Here

It's time to start your Programming with Python adventure! If you're a complete programming novice, you should start with Chapter 1 and progress through the book at a pace that allows you to absorb as much of the material as possible.

If you're a novice who's in an absolute rush to get going with Python as quickly as possible, you could skip to Chapter 2 with the understanding that you may find some topics a bit confusing later. Skipping to Chapter 3 is possible if you already have Python installed, but be sure to at least skim Chapter 2 so that you know what assumptions were made when writing this book.

Readers who have some exposure to Python can save time by moving directly to Chapter 4. It's essential to install Anaconda to gain access to Jupyter Notebook, which is the IDE used for this book. Otherwise, you won't be able to use the downloadable source easily. Anaconda is free, so there is no cost involved.

Assuming that you already have Jupyter Notebook installed and know how to use it, you can move directly to Chapter 6. You can always go back to earlier chapters as necessary when you have questions. However, it's important that you understand how each example works before moving to the next one. Every example has important lessons for you, and you could miss vital content if you start skipping too much information.

1

Getting Started with Python

Chapter **1**

Talking to Your Computer

aving a conversation with your computer might sound like the script of a science fiction movie. After all, the members of the *Enterprise* on *Star Trek* regularly talked with their computer. In fact, the computer often talked back. However, with the rise of Apple's Siri (http://www.apple.com/ios/siri/), Amazon's Echo (https://www.amazon.com/dp/B00X4WHP5E/), and other interactive software, perhaps you really don't find a conversation so unbelievable.

REMEMBER

Asking the computer for information is one thing, but providing it with instructions is quite another. This chapter considers why you want to instruct your computer about anything and what benefit you gain from it. You also discover the need for a special language when performing this kind of communication and why you want to use Python to accomplish it. However, the main thing to get out of this chapter is that programming is simply a kind of communication that is akin to other forms of communication you already have with your computer.

Understanding Why You Want to Talk to Your Computer

Talking to a machine may seem quite odd at first, but it's necessary because a computer can't read your mind — yet. Even if the computer did read your mind, it would still be communicating with you. Nothing can occur without an exchange of information between the machine and you. Activities such as

>> Reading your email

>> Writing about your vacation

>> Finding the greatest gift in the world

are all examples of communication that occurs between a computer and you. That the computer further communicates with other machines or people to address requests that you make simply extends the basic idea that communication is necessary to produce any result.

In most cases, the communication takes place in a manner that is nearly invisible to you unless you really think about it. For example, when you visit a chat room online, you might think that you're communicating with another person. However, you're communicating with your computer, your computer is communicating with the other person's computer through the chat room (whatever it consists of), and the other person's computer is communicating with that person. Figure 1-1 gives you an idea of what is actually taking place.

FIGURE 1-1:
Communication with your computer may be invisible unless you really think about it.

Notice the cloud in the center of Figure 1-1. The cloud could contain anything, but you know that it at least contains other computers running other applications. These computers make it possible for your friend and you to chat. Now, think about how easy the whole process seems when you're using the chat application. Even though all these things are going on in the background, it seems as if you're simply chatting with your friend, and the process itself is invisible.

Knowing that an Application is a Form of Communication

Computer communication occurs through the use of applications. You use one application to answer your email, another to purchase goods, and still another to create a presentation. An *application* (sometimes called an *app*) provides the means to express human ideas to the computer in a manner the computer can understand and defines the tools needed to shape the data used for the communication in specific ways. Data used to express the content of a presentation is different from data used to purchase a present for your mother. The way you view, use, and understand the data is different for each task, so you must use different applications to interact with the data in a manner that both the computer and you can understand.

You can obtain applications to meet just about any general need you can conceive of today. In fact, you probably have access to applications for which you haven't even thought about a purpose yet. Programmers have been busy creating millions of applications of all types for many years now, so it may be hard to understand what you can accomplish by creating some new method for talking with your computer through an application. The answer comes down to thinking about the data and how you want to interact with it. Some data simply isn't common enough to have attracted the attention of a programmer, or you may need the data in a format that no application currently supports, so you don't have any way to tell the computer about it unless you create a custom application to do it.

The following sections describe applications from the perspective of working with unique data in a manner that is special in some way. For example, you might have access to a video library database but no method to access it in a way that makes sense to you. The data is unique and your access needs are special, so you may want to create an application that addresses both the data and your needs.

Thinking about procedures you use daily

A *procedure* is simply a set of steps you follow to perform a task. For example, when making toast, you might use a procedure like this:

1. Get the bread and butter from the refrigerator.

2. Open the bread bag and take out two pieces of toast.

3. Remove the cover from the toaster.

4. Place each piece of bread in its own slot.

5. Push the toaster lever down to start toasting the bread.

6. Wait for the toasting process to complete.

7. Remove toast from the toaster.

8. Place toast on a plate.

9. Butter the toast.

Your procedure might vary from the one presented here, but it's unlikely that you'd butter the toast before placing it in the toaster. Of course, you do actually have to remove the bread from the wrapper before you toast it (placing the bread, wrapper and all, into the toaster would likely produce undesirable results). Most people never actually think about the procedure for making toast. However, you use a procedure like this one even though you don't think about it.

REMEMBER

Computers can't perform tasks without a procedure. You must tell the computer which steps to perform, the order in which to perform them, and any exceptions to the rule that could cause failure. All this information (and more) appears within an application. In short, an application is simply a written procedure that you use to tell the computer what to do, when to do it, and how to do it. Because you've been using procedures all your life, all you really need to do is apply the knowledge you already possess to what a computer needs to know about specific tasks.

Writing procedures down

When I was in grade school, our teacher asked us to write a paper about making toast. After we turned in our papers, she brought in a toaster and some loaves of bread. Each paper was read and demonstrated. None of our procedures worked as expected, but they all produced humorous results. In my case, I forgot to tell the teacher to remove the bread from the wrapper, so she dutifully tried to stuff the piece of bread, wrapper and all, into the toaster. The lesson stuck with me. Writing about procedures can be quite hard because we know precisely want we want to do, but often we leave steps out — we assume that the other person also knows precisely what we want to do.

Many experiences in life revolve around procedures. Think about the checklist used by pilots before a plane takes off. Without a good procedure, the plane could crash. Learning to write a great procedure takes time, but it's doable. You may have to try several times before you get a procedure that works completely, but eventually you can create one. Writing procedures down isn't really sufficient, though — you also need to test the procedure by using someone who isn't familiar with the task involved. When working with computers, the computer is your perfect test subject.

Seeing applications as being like any other procedure

A computer acts like the grade school teacher in my example in the previous section. When you write an application, you're writing a procedure that defines a series of steps that the computer should perform to accomplish whatever task you have in mind. If you leave out a step, the results won't be what you expected. The computer won't know what you mean or that you intended for it to perform certain tasks automatically. The only thing the computer knows is that you have provided it with a specific procedure and it needs to perform that procedure.

Understanding that computers take things literally

People eventually get used to the procedures you create. They automatically compensate for deficiencies in your procedure or make notes about things that you left out. In other words, people compensate for problems with the procedures that you write.

REMEMBER

When you begin writing computer programs, you'll get frustrated because computers perform tasks precisely and read your instructions literally. For example, if you tell the computer that a certain value should equal 5, the computer will look for a value of exactly 5. A human might see 4.9 and know that the value is good enough, but a computer doesn't see things that way. It sees a value of 4.9 and decides that it doesn't equal 5 exactly. In short, computers are inflexible, unintuitive, and unimaginative. When you write a procedure for a computer, the computer will do precisely as you ask absolutely every time and never modify your procedure or decide that you really meant for it to do something else.

Defining What an Application Is

As previously mentioned, applications provide the means to define express human ideas in a manner that a computer can understand. To accomplish this goal, the application relies on one or more procedures that tell the computer how to perform the tasks related to the manipulation of data and its presentation. What you see onscreen is the text from your word processor, but to see that information, the computer requires procedures for retrieving the data from disk, putting it into a form you can understand, and then presenting it to you. The following sections define the specifics of an application in more detail.

Understanding that computers use a special language

Human language is complex and difficult to understand. Even applications such as Siri and Alexa have serious limits in understanding what you're saying. Over the years, computers have gained the capability to input human speech as data and to understand certain spoken words as commands, but computers still don't quite understand human speech to any significant degree. The difficulty of human speech is exemplified in the way lawyers work. When you read legalese, it appears as a gibberish of sorts. However, the goal is to state ideas and concepts in a way that isn't open to interpretation. Lawyers seldom succeed in meeting their objective precisely because human speech is imprecise.

Given what you know from previous sections of this chapter, computers could never rely on human speech to understand the procedures you write. Computers always take things literally, so you'd end up with completely unpredictable results if you were to use human language to write applications. That's why humans use special languages, called *programming languages,* to communicate with computers. These special languages make it possible to write procedures that are both specific and completely understandable by both humans and computers.

TECHNICAL STUFF

Computers don't actually speak any language. They use binary codes to flip switches internally and to perform math calculations. Computers don't even understand letters — they understand only numbers. A special application turns the computer-specific language you use to write a procedure into binary codes. For the purposes of this book, you really don't need to worry too much about the low-level specifics of how computers work at the binary level. However, it's interesting to know that computers speak math and numbers, not really a language at all.

Helping humans speak to the computer

It's important to keep the purpose of an application in mind as you write it. An application is there to help humans speak to the computer in a certain way. Every application works with some type of data that is input, stored, manipulated, and output so that the humans using the application obtain a desired result. Whether the application is a game or a spreadsheet, the basic idea is the same. Computers work with data provided by humans to obtain a desired result.

When you create an application, you're providing a new method for humans to speak to the computer. The new approach you create will make it possible for other humans to view data in new ways. The communication between human and computer should be easy enough that the application actually disappears from view. Think about the kinds of applications you've used in the past. The best applications are the ones that let you focus on whatever data you're interacting with.

For example, a game application is considered immersive only if you can focus on the planet you're trying to save or the ship you're trying to fly, rather than the application that lets you do these things.

TIP

One of the best ways to start thinking about how you want to create an application is to look at the way other people create applications. Writing down what you like and dislike about other applications is a useful way to start discovering how you want your applications to look and work. Here are some questions you can ask yourself as you work with the applications:

>> What do I find distracting about the application?

>> Which features were easy to use?

>> Which features were hard to use?

>> How did the application make it easy to interact with my data?

>> How would I make the data easier to work with?

>> What do I hope to achieve with my application that this application doesn't provide?

Professional developers ask many other questions as part of creating an application, but these are good starter questions because they begin to help you think about applications as a means to help humans speak with computers. If you've ever found yourself frustrated by an application you used, you already know how other people will feel if you don't ask the appropriate questions when you create your application. Communication is the most important element of any application you create.

You can also start to think about the ways in which you work. Start writing procedures for the things you do. It's a good idea to take the process one step at a time and write everything you can think of about that step. When you get finished, ask someone else to try your procedure to see how it actually works. You might be surprised to learn that even with a lot of effort, you can easily forget to include steps.

WARNING

The world's worst application usually begins with a programmer who doesn't know what the application is supposed to do, why it's special, what need it addresses, or whom it is for. When you decide to create an application, make sure that you know why you're creating it and what you hope to achieve. Just having a plan in place really helps make programming fun. You can work on your new application and see your goals accomplished one at a time until you have a completed application to use and show off to your friends (all of whom will think you're really cool for creating it).

Understanding Why Python is So Cool

Many programming languages are available today. In fact, a student can spend an entire semester in college studying computer languages and still not hear about them all. (I did just that during my college days.) You'd think that programmers would be happy with all these programming languages and just choose one to talk to the computer, but they keep inventing more.

REMEMBER

Programmers keep creating new languages for good reason. Each language has something special to offer — something it does exceptionally well. In addition, as computer technology evolves, so do the programming languages in order to keep up. Because creating an application is all about efficient communication, many programmers know multiple programming languages so that they can choose just the right language for a particular task. One language might work better to obtain data from a database, and another might create user interface elements especially well.

As with every other programming language, Python does some things exceptionally well, and you need to know what they are before you begin using it. You might be amazed by the really cool things you can do with Python. Knowing a programming language's strengths and weaknesses helps you use it better as well as avoid frustration by not using the language for things it doesn't do well. The following sections help you make these sorts of decisions about Python.

Unearthing the reasons for using Python

Most programming languages are created with specific goals in mind. These goals help define the language characteristics and determine what you can do with the language. There really isn't any way to create a programming language that does everything because people have competing goals and needs when creating applications. When it comes to Python, the main objective was to create a programming language that would make programmers efficient and productive. With that in mind, here are the reasons that you want to use Python when creating an application:

>> **Less application development time:** Python code is usually 2–10 times shorter than comparable code written in languages like C/C++ and Java, which means that you spend less time writing your application and more time using it.

>> **Ease of reading:** A programming language is like any other language — you need to be able to read it to understand what it does. Python code tends to be easier to read than the code written in other languages, which means you spend less time interpreting it and more time making essential changes.

» **Reduced learning time:** The creators of Python wanted to make a programming language with fewer odd rules that make the language hard to learn. After all, programmers want to create applications, not learn obscure and difficult languages.

TIP

Although Python is a popular language, it's not always the most popular language out there (depending on the site you use for comparison). In fact, it currently ranks fifth on sites such as TIOBE (http://www.tiobe.com/index.php/content/paperinfo/tpci/index.html), an organization that tracks usage statistics (among other things). However, if you look at sites such as IEEE Spectrum (https://spectrum.ieee.org/computing/software/the-2017-top-programming-languages), you see that Python is actually the number-one language from that site's perspective. Tech Rapidly has it as the number-three language (see http://techrapidly.com/top-10-best-programming-languages-learn-2018/).

If you're looking for a language solely for the purpose of obtaining a job, Python is a great choice, but Java, C/C++, or C# might be better choices, depending on the kind of job you want to get. Visual Basic is also a great choice, even if it isn't currently quite as popular as Python. Make sure to choose a language you like and one that will address your application-development needs, but also choose on the basis of what you intend to accomplish. Python was the language of the year in both 2007 and 2010 and has ranked as high as the fourth most popular language in February 2011. So it truly is a good choice if you're looking for a job, but not necessarily the best choice. However, you may be surprised to learn that many colleges now use Python to teach coding, and it has become the most popular language in that venue. Check out my blog post at http://blog.johnmuellerbooks.com/2014/07/14/python-as-a-learning-tool for details.

Deciding how you can personally benefit from Python

Ultimately, you can use any programming language to write any sort of application you want. If you use the wrong programming language for the job, the process will be slow, error prone, bug ridden, and you'll absolutely hate it — but you can get the job done. Of course, most of us would rather avoid horribly painful experiences, so you need to know what sorts of applications people typically use Python to create. Here's a list of the most common uses for Python (although people do use it for other purposes):

» **Creating rough application examples:** Developers often need to create a *prototype,* a rough example of an application, before getting the resources to create the actual application. Python emphasizes productivity, so you can use it to create prototypes of an application quickly.

>> **Scripting browser-based applications:** Even though JavaScript is probably the most popular language used for browser-based application scripting, Python is a close second. Python offers functionality that JavaScript doesn't provide (see the comparison at `https://blog.glyphobet.net/essay/2557` for details) and its high efficiency makes it possible to create browser-based applications faster (a real plus in today's fast-paced world).

>> **Designing mathematic, scientific, and engineering applications:** Interestingly enough, Python provides access to some really cool libraries that make it easier to create math, scientific, and engineering applications. The two most popular libraries are NumPy (`http://www.numpy.org/`) and SciPy (`http://www.scipy.org/`). These libraries greatly reduce the time you spend writing specialized code to perform common math, scientific, and engineering tasks.

>> **Working with XML:** The eXtensible Markup Language (XML) is the basis of most data storage needs on the Internet and many desktop applications today. Unlike most languages, where XML is just sort of bolted on, Python makes it a first-class citizen. If you need to work with a Web service, the main method for exchanging information on the Internet (or any other XML-intensive application), Python is a great choice.

>> **Interacting with databases:** Business relies heavily on databases. Python isn't quite a query language, like the Structured Query Language (SQL) or Language INtegrated Query (LINQ), but it does do a great job of interacting with databases. It makes creating connections and manipulating data relatively painless.

>> **Developing user interfaces:** Python isn't like some languages like C# where you have a built-in designer and can drag and drop items from a toolbox onto the user interface. However, it does have an extensive array of graphical user interface (GUI) frameworks — extensions that make graphics a lot easier to create (see `https://wiki.python.org/moin/GuiProgramming` for details). Some of these frameworks do come with designers that make the user interface creation process easier. The point is that Python isn't devoted to just one method of creating a user interface — you can use the method that best suits your needs.

Discovering which organizations use Python

Python really is quite good at the tasks that it was designed to perform. In fact, that's why a lot of large organizations use Python to perform at least some application-creation (development) tasks. You want a programming language that has good support from these large organizations because these organizations tend to spend money to make the language better. Table 1-1 lists the large organizations that use Python the most.

TABLE 1-1 **Large Organizations That Use Python**

Vendor	URL	Application Type
Alice Educational Software – Carnegie Mellon University	(https://www.alice.org/)	Educational applications
Fermilab	(https://www.fnal.gov/)	Scientific applications
Go.com	(http://go.com/)	Browser-based applications
Google	(https://www.google.com/)	Search engine
Industrial Light & Magic	(http://www.ilm.com/)	Just about every programming need
Lawrence Livermore National Library	(https://www.llnl.gov/)	Scientific applications
National Space and Aeronautics Administration (NASA)	(http://www.nasa.gov/)	Scientific applications
New York Stock Exchange	(https://nyse.nyx.com/)	Browser-based applications
Redhat	(http://www.redhat.com/)	Linux installation tools
Yahoo!	(https://www.yahoo.com/)	Parts of Yahoo! mail
YouTube	(http://www.youtube.com/)	Graphics engine
Zope – Digital Creations	(http://www.zope.org/en/latest/)	Publishing application

TIP

These are just a few of the many organizations that use Python extensively. You can find a more complete list of organizations at http://www.python.org/about/ success/. The number of success stories has become so large that even this list probably isn't complete and the people supporting it have had to create categories to better organize it.

Finding useful Python applications

You might have an application written in Python sitting on your machine right now and not even know it. Python is used in a vast array of applications on the market today. The applications range from utilities that run at the console to full-fledged CAD/CAM suites. Some applications run on mobile devices, while others run on the large services employed by enterprises. In short, there is no limit to what you can do with Python, but it really does help to see what others have done. You can find a number of places online that list applications written in Python, but the best place to look is https://wiki.python.org/moin/ Applications.

As a Python programmer, you'll also want to know that Python development tools are available to make your life easier. A *development tool* provides some level of automation in writing the procedures needed to tell the computer what to do. Having more development tools means that you have to perform less work in order to obtain a working application. Developers love to share their lists of favorite tools, but you can find a great list of tools broken into categories at http://www.python.org/about/apps/.

REMEMBER

Of course, this chapter describes a number of tools as well, such as NumPy and SciPy (two scientific libraries). The remainder of the book lists a few other tools; make sure that you copy down your favorite tools for later.

Comparing Python to other languages

Comparing one language to another is somewhat dangerous because the selection of a language is just as much a matter of taste and personal preference as it is any sort of quantifiable scientific fact. So before I'm attacked by the rabid protectors of the languages that follow, it's important to realize that I also use a number of languages and find at least some level of overlap among them all. There is no best language in the world, simply the language that works best for a particular application. With this idea in mind, the following sections provide an overview comparison of Python to other languages. (You can find comparisons to other languages at https://wiki.python.org/moin/LanguageComparisons.)

C#

A lot of people claim that Microsoft simply copied Java to create C#. That said, C# does have some advantages (and disadvantages) when compared to Java. The main (undisputed) intent behind C# is to create a better kind of C/C++ language — one that is easier to learn and use. However, we're here to talk about C# and Python. When compared to C#, Python has these advantages:

>> Significantly easier to learn

>> Smaller (more concise) code

>> Supported fully as open source

>> Better multiplatform support

>> Easily allows use of multiple development environments

>> Easier to extend using Java and C/C++

>> Enhanced scientific and engineering support

Java

For years, programmers looked for a language that they could use to write an application just once and have it run anywhere. Java is designed to work well on any platform. It relies on some tricks that you'll discover later in the book to accomplish this magic. For now, all you really need to know is that Java was so successful at running well everywhere that other languages have sought to emulate it (with varying levels of success). Even so, Python has some important advantages over Java, as shown in the following list:

» Significantly easier to learn

» Smaller (more concise) code

» Enhanced variables (storage boxes in computer memory) that can hold different kinds of data based on the application's needs while running (dynamic typing)

» Faster development times

Perl

Perl was originally an acronym for Practical Extraction and Report Language. Today, people simply call it Perl and let it go at that. However, Perl still shows its roots in that it excels at obtaining data from a database and presenting it in report format. Of course, Perl has been extended to do a lot more than that — you can use it to write all sorts of applications. (I've even used it for a Web service application.) In a comparison with Python, you'll find that Python has these advantages over Perl:

» Simpler to learn

» Easier to read

» Enhanced protection for data

» Better Java integration

» Fewer platform-specific biases

R

Data scientists often have a tough time choosing between R and Python because both languages are adept at statistical analysis and the sorts of graphing that data scientists need to understand data patterns. Both languages are also open source and support a large range of platforms. However, R is a bit more specialized than Python and tends to cater to the academic market. Consequently, Python has these advantages over R in that Python:

>> Emphasizes productivity and code readability

>> Is designed for use by enterprises

>> Offers easier debugging

>> Uses consistent coding techniques

>> Has greater flexibility

>> Is easier to learn

Chapter **2**

Getting Your Own Copy of Python

reating applications requires that you have another application, unless you really want to get low level and write applications in machine code — a decidedly difficult experience that even true programmers avoid if at all possible. If you want to write an application using the Python programming language, you need the applications required to do so. These applications help you work with Python by creating Python code, providing help information as you need it, and letting you run the code you write. This chapter helps you obtain a copy of the Python application, install it on your hard drive, locate the installed applications so that you can use them, and test your installation so that you can see how it works.

Downloading the Version You Need

Every *platform* (combination of computer hardware and operating system software) has special rules that it follows when running applications. The Python application hides these details from you. You type code that runs on any platform that Python supports, and the Python applications translate that code into something the platform can understand. However, in order for the translation to take place, you must have a version of Python that works on your particular platform. Python supports these platforms (and possibly others):

>> Advanced IBM Unix (AIX)

>> Android

>> BeOS

>> Berkeley Software Distribution (BSD)/FreeBSD

>> Hewlett-Packard Unix (HP-UX)

>> IBM i (formerly Application System 400 or AS/400, iSeries, and System i)

>> iPhone Operating System (iOS)

>> Linux

>> Mac OS X (comes pre-installed with the OS)

>> Microsoft Disk Operating System (MS-DOS)

>> MorphOS

>> Operating System 2 (OS/2)

>> Operating System 390 (OS/390) and z/OS

>> PalmOS

>> PlayStation

>> Psion

>> QNX

>> RISC OS (originally Acorn)

>> Series 60

>> Solaris

>> Virtual Memory System (VMS)

>> Windows 32-bit (XP and later)

>> Windows 64-bit

>> Windows CE/Pocket PC

TIP

Wow, that's a lot of different platforms! This book is tested with the Windows, Mac OS X, and Linux platforms. However, the examples could very well work with these other platforms, too, because the examples don't rely on any platform-specific code. Let me know if it works on your non–Windows, Mac, or Linux platform at John@JohnMuellerBooks.com. The current version of Python at the time of this writing is 3.6.2. I'll talk about any Python updates on my blog at http://blog.johnmuellerbooks.com. You can find the answers to your Python book-specific questions there, too.

To get the right version for your platform, you need to go to https://www.python.org/downloads/release/python-362/. The download section is initially hidden from view, so you need to scroll halfway down the page. You see a page similar to the one shown in Figure 2-1. The main part of the page contains links for Windows, Mac OS X, and Linux downloads. These links provide you with the default setup that is used in this book. The platform-specific links on the left side of the page show you alternative Python configurations that you can use when the need arises. For example, you may want to use a more advanced editor than the one provided with the default Python package, and these alternative configurations can provide one for you.

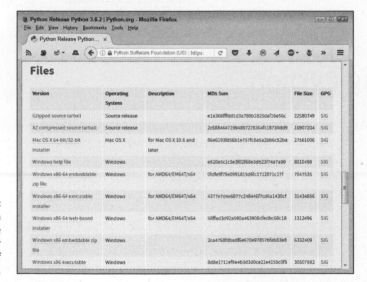

FIGURE 2-1:
The Python download page contains links for all sorts of versions.

If you want to work with another platform, go to https://www.python.org/download/other/ instead. You see a list of Python installations for other platforms, as shown in Figure 2-2. Many of these installations are maintained by volunteers rather than by the people who create the versions of Python for Windows, Mac OS X, and Linux. Make sure you contact these individuals when you have installation questions because they know how best to help you get a good installation on your platform.

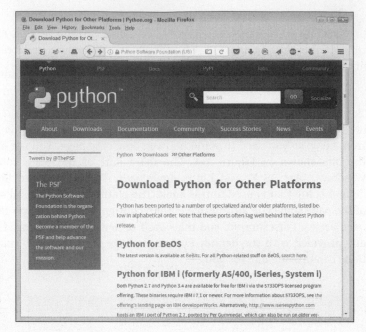

FIGURE 2-2:
Volunteers have
made Python
available on
all sorts of
platforms.

Installing Python

After you download your copy of Python, it's time to install it on your system. The downloaded file contains everything needed to get you started:

>> Python interpreter

>> Help files (documentation)

>> Command-line access

>> Integrated DeveLopment Environment (IDLE) application

>> Preferred Installer Program (pip)

>> Uninstaller (only on platforms that require it)

This book assumes that you're using one of the default Python setups found at `https://www.python.org/downloads/release/python-362/`. If you use a version other than 3.6.2, some of the examples won't work as anticipated. The following sections describe how to install Python on the three platforms directly supported by this book: Windows, Mac OS X, and Linux.

Working with Windows

The installation process on a Windows system follows the same procedure that you use for other application types. The main difference is in finding the file you downloaded so that you can begin the installation process. The following procedure should work fine on any Windows system, whether you use the 32-bit or the 64-bit version of Python.

1. **Locate the downloaded copy of Python on your system.**

The name of this file varies, but normally it appears as python-3.6.2.exe for both 32-bit systems and python-3.6.2-amd64.exe for 64-bit systems. The version number is embedded as part of the filename. In this case, the filename refers to version 3.6.2, which is the version used for this book.

2. **Double-click the installation file.**

(You may see an Open File – Security Warning dialog box that asks whether you want to run this file. Click Run if you see this dialog box pop up.) You see a Python Setup dialog box similar to the one shown in Figure 2-3. The exact dialog box you see depends on which version of the Python installation program you download.

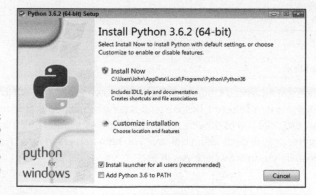

FIGURE 2-3: The setup process begins by asking you who should have access to Python.

3. **Choose a user installation option (the book uses the default setting of Install for All Users).**

Using a personalized installation can make it easier to manage systems that have multiple users. In some cases, the personalized installation also reduces the number of Security Warning dialog boxes you see.

TIP

4. **Select Add Python 3.6 to PATH.**

   Adding this setting enables you to access Python from anywhere on your hard drive. If you don't select this setting, you must manually add Python to the path later.

5. **Click Customize Installation.**

   Install asks you to choose which features to use with your copy of Python, as shown in Figure 2-4. Keep all the features selected for this book. However, for your own installation, you may find that you don't actually require all the Python features.

FIGURE 2-4:
Choose the Python features you want to install.

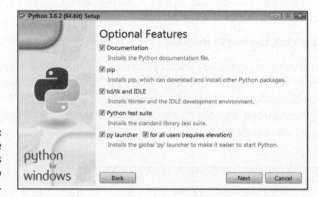

6. **Click Next.**

   You see the Advanced Options dialog box, shown in Figure 2-5. Note that Install for All Users isn't selected, despite your having requested that feature earlier. Install also asks you to provide the name of an installation directory for Python. Using the default destination will save you time and effort later. However, you can install Python anywhere you desire.

FIGURE 2-5:
Decide on an installation location for your copy of Python.

WARNING

Using the Windows \Program Files or \Program Files (x86) folder is problematic for two reasons. First, the folder name has a space in it, which makes it hard to access from within the application. Second, the folder usually requires administrator access, so you'll constantly battle the User Account Control (UAC) feature of Windows if you install Python in either folder.

7. **Select the Install for All Users option to ensure that the installer makes Python accessible to everyone.**

Note that selecting this option automatically selects the Precompile Standard Library option, which you should keep selected.

8. **Type a destination folder name, if necessary.**

This book uses an installation folder of C: \Python36.

9. **Click Install.**

You see the installation process start. At some point, you might see a User Account Control dialog box asking whether you want to perform the install. If you see this dialog box, click Yes. The installation continues and you see an Installation Complete dialog box.

10. **Click Close.**

Python is ready for use.

Working with the Mac

Your Mac system likely already has Python installed on it. However, this installation is normally a few years old — or whatever the age of your system happens to be. For the purposes of this book, the installation will likely work fine. You won't be testing the limits of Python programming technology — just getting a great start using Python.

TECHNICAL STUFF

The Leopard version of OS X (10.5) uses a really old version of Python 2.5.1. This particular version lacks direct access to the IDLE application. As a result, you may find that some book exercises won't work properly. The article at https://wiki. python.org/moin/MacPython/Leopard tells you more about how to overcome this particular issue. The code in this book is tested with OS X version 10.12 that comes with Python 2.7.10, which is just fine for working through the examples in the book. Later versions of OS X and Python will also likely work fine, but you may see warnings about library use or other potential compatibility issues."

Depending on how you use Python, you might want to update your installation at some point. Part of this process involves installing the GNU Compiler Collection (GCC) tools so that Python has access to the low-level resources it needs. The following steps get you started with installing a new version of Python on your Mac OS X 10.6 or above system.

1. **Navigate to** https://www.python.org/downloads/release/python-362/ **with your browser.**

   You see information regarding the latest version of Python, as shown previously in Figure 2-1.

2. **Click the Mac OS X 64-bit/32-bit installer link.**

   The Python disk image begins downloading. Be patient: The disk image requires several minutes to download. Most browsers provide a method for monitoring the download process so that you can easily see how long the download will take.

3. **Double-click** python-3.6.2-macosx10.6.pkg **in the download folder.**

   You see a Welcome dialog box that tells you about this particular Python build.

4. **Click Continue three times.**

   The installation program displays late-breaking notes about Python, licensing information (click Agree when asked about the licensing information), and, finally, a destination dialog box.

5. **Click Install.**

   The installer may request your administrator password. Type the administrator name and password, if required, into the dialog box and click OK. You see an Installing Python dialog box. The contents of this dialog box will change as the installation process proceeds so that you know what part of Python the installer is working with.

   After the installation is completed, you see an Install Succeeded dialog box.

6. **Click Close.**

   Python is ready to use. (You can close the disk image at this point and remove it from your system.)

Working with Linux

Some versions of Linux come with Python installed. For example, if you have a Red Hat Package Manager (RPM)-based distribution (such as SUSE, Red Hat, Yellow Dog, Fedora Core, and CentOS), you likely already have Python on your system and don't need to do anything else.

TECHNICAL STUFF

Depending on which version of Linux you use, the version of Python varies and some systems don't include the Interactive DeveLopment Environment (IDLE) application. If you have an older version of Python (2.5.1 or earlier), you might want to install a newer version so that you have access to IDLE. Many of the book exercises require use of IDLE.

You actually have two techniques to use to install Python on Linux. The following sections discuss both techniques. The first technique works on any Linux distribution; the second technique has special criteria that you must meet.

Using the standard Linux installation

The standard Linux installation works on any system. However, it requires you to work at the Terminal and type commands to complete it. Some of the actual commands may vary by version of Linux. The information at `http://docs.python.org/3/install/` provides some helpful tips that you can use in addition to the procedure that follows.

1. **Navigate to** `https://www.python.org/downloads/release/python-362/` **with your browser.**

You see information regarding the latest version of Python, as shown previously in Figure 2-1.

2. **Click the appropriate link for your version of Linux:**

   a. Gzipped source tarball (any version of Linux)

   b. XZ compressed source tarball (better compression and faster download)

3. **When asked whether you want to open or save the file, choose Save.**

The Python source files begin downloading. Be patient: The source files require a minute or two to download.

4. **Double-click the downloaded file.**

The Archive Manager window opens. After the files are extracted, you see the Python 3.6.2 folder in the Archive Manager window.

5. **Double-click the** Python 3.6.2 folder.

The Archive Manager extracts the files to the Python 3.6.2 subfolder of your home folder.

6. **Open a copy of Terminal.**

The Terminal window appears. If you have never built any software on your system before, you must install the build essentials, SQLite, and bzip2 or the Python installation will fail. Otherwise, you can skip to Step 10 to begin working with Python immediately.

7. **Type** sudo apt-get install build-essential **and press Enter.**

Linux installs the Build Essential support required to build packages (see `https://packages.debian.org/squeeze/build-essential` for details).

8. **Type** sudo apt-get install libsqlite3-dev **and press Enter.**

Linux installs the SQLite support required by Python for database manipulation (see https://packages.debian.org/squeeze/libsqlite3-dev for details).

9. **Type** sudo apt-get install libbz2-dev **and press Enter.**

Linux installs the bzip2 support required by Python for archive manipulation (see https://packages.debian.org/sid/libbz2-dev for details).

10. **Type** CD Python 3.6.2 **in the Terminal window and press Enter.**

Terminal changes directories to the Python 3.6.2 folder on your system.

11. **Type** ./configure **and press Enter.**

The script begins by checking the system build type and then performs a series of tasks based on the system you're using. This process can require a minute or two because there is a large list of items to check.

12. **Type** make **and press Enter.**

Linux executes the make script to create the Python application software. The make process can require up to a minute — it depends on the processing speed of your system.

13. **Type** sudo make altinstall **and press Enter.**

The system may ask you for your administrator password. Type your password and press Enter. At this point, a number of tasks take place as the system installs Python on your system.

Using the graphical Linux installation

All versions of Linux support the standard installation discussed in the "Using the standard Linux installation" section of this chapter. However, a few versions of Debian-based Linux distributions, such as Ubuntu 12.x and later, provide a graphical installation technique as well. You need the administrator group (sudo) password to use this procedure, so having it handy will save you time. The following steps outline the graphical installation technique for Ubuntu, but the technique is similar for other Linux installations:

1. **Open the** Ubuntu Software Center **folder. (The folder may be named** Synaptics **on other platforms.)**

You see a listing of the most popular software available for download and installation.

2. **Select Developer Tools (or Development) from the All Software drop-down list box.**

You see a listing of developer tools, including Python.

3. **Double-click the Python 3.6.2 entry.**

   The Ubuntu Software Center provides details about the Python 3.6.2 entry and offers to install it for you.

4. **Click Install.**

   Ubuntu begins the process of installing Python. A progress bar shows the download and installation status. When the installation is complete, the Install button changes to a Remove button.

5. **Close the** Ubuntu Software Center **folder.**

   You see a Python icon added to the desktop. Python is ready for use.

Accessing Python on Your Machine

After you have Python installed on your system, you need to know where to find it. In some respects, Python does everything it can to make this process easy by performing certain tasks, such as adding the Python path to the machine's path information during installation. Even so, you need to know how to access the installation, which the following sections describe.

A WORD ABOUT THE SCREENSHOTS

As you work your way through the book, you'll use either IDLE or the Python command-line shell to work with Python in the beginning. Later, you use Anaconda because it provides a significantly enhanced and easier-to-use method of interacting with Python. The name of the graphical (GUI) environment, IDLE or Anaconda, is precisely the same across all three platforms, and you won't even see any significant difference in the presentation. The differences you do see are minor, and you should ignore them as you work through the book. With this in mind, the book does rely heavily on Windows screenshots — all the screenshots you see were obtained from a Windows system for the sake of consistency.

The command-line shell also works precisely the same across all three platforms. The presentation may vary a little more than IDLE or Anaconda does simply because the shell used for each platform varies slightly. However, the commands you type for one platform are precisely the same on another platform. The output is the same as well. When viewing the screenshot, look at the content rather than for specific differences in the presentation of the shell.

Using Windows

A Windows installation creates a new folder in the Start menu that contains your Python installation. You can access it by choosing Start ⇨ All Programs ⇨ Python 3.6. The two items of interest in the folder when creating new applications are IDLE (Python GUI) and Python (command line). (Chapter 4 helps you install, configure, and use Anaconda to create your first real application, but you should know how to use both IDLE and the command-line version of Python.)

Clicking IDLE (Python GUI) produces a graphical interactive environment like the one shown in Figure 2-6. When you open this environment, IDLE automatically displays some information so that you know you have the right application open. For example, you see the Python version number (which is 3.6.2 in this case). It also tells you what sort of system you're using to run Python.

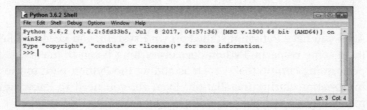

FIGURE 2-6:
Use IDLE when you want the comforts of a graphical environment.

The Python (command line) option opens a command prompt and executes the Python command, as shown in Figure 2-7. Again, the environment automatically displays information such as the Python version and the host platform.

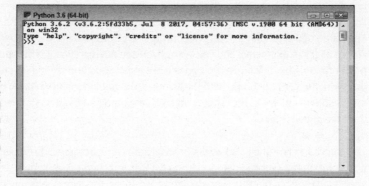

FIGURE 2-7:
Use the command prompt when you want the speed and flexibility of a command-line interface.

A third method to access Python is to open a command prompt, type **Python**, and press Enter. You can use this approach when you want to gain additional flexibility over the Python environment, automatically load items, or execute Python in a higher-privilege environment (in which you gain additional security rights). Python provides a significant array of command-line options that you can see by typing **Python /?** at the command prompt and pressing Enter. Figure 2-8 shows what you typically see. Don't worry too much about these command-line options — you won't need them for this book, but it's helpful to know they exist.

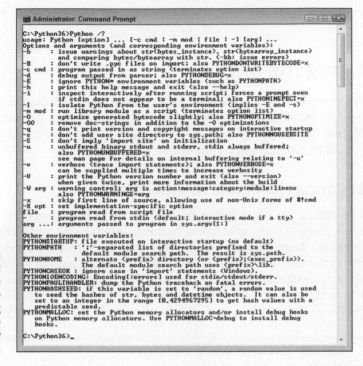

FIGURE 2-8:
Using a standard command line offers the flexibility of using switches to change the way Python works.

REMEMBER

To use this third method of executing Python, you must include Python in the Windows path. This is why you want to choose the Add Python 3.6 to PATH option when installing Python on Windows. If you didn't add the path during installation, you can add it afterward using the instructions found in the Adding a Location to the Windows Path article on my blog at http://blog.johnmuellerbooks. com/2014/02/17/adding-a-location-to-the-windows-path/. This same technique works for adding Python-specific environment variables such as

>> PYTHONSTARTUP

>> PYTHONPATH

>> PYTHONHOME

>> PYTHONCASEOK

>> PYTHONIOENCODING

>> PYTHONFAULTHANDLER

>> PYTHONHASHSEED

None of these environment variables is used in the book. However, you can find out more about them at https://docs.python.org/3.6/using/cmdline. html#environment-variables.

Using the Mac

When working with a Mac, you probably have Python already installed and don't need to install it for this book. However, you still need to know where to find Python. The following sections tell you how to access Python depending on the kind of installation you performed.

Locating the default installation

The default OS X installation doesn't include a Python-specific folder in most cases. Instead, you must open Terminal by choosing Applications➪Utilities➪ Terminal. After Terminal is open, you can type **Python** and press Enter to access the command-line version of Python. The display you see is similar to the one shown previously in Figure 2-7. As with Windows (see the "Using Windows" section of the chapter), using Terminal to open Python offers the advantage of using command-line switches to modify the manner in which Python works.

Locating the updated version of Python you installed

After you perform the installation on your Mac system, open the Applications folder. Within this folder, you find a Python 3.6 folder that contains the following:

>> Extras folder

>> IDLE application (GUI development)

>> Python Launcher (interactive command development)

>> Update Sh. . . command

Double-clicking IDLE application opens a graphical interactive environment that looks similar to the environment shown previously in Figure 2-6. There are some small cosmetic differences, but the content of the window is the same. Double-clicking Python Launcher opens a command-line environment similar to the one shown previously in Figure 2-7. This environment uses all the Python defaults to provide a standard execution environment.

REMEMBER

Even if you install a new version of Python on your Mac, you don't have to settle for using the default environment. It's still possible to open Terminal to gain access to the Python command-line switches. However, when you access Python from the Mac Terminal application, you need to ensure that you're not accessing the default installation. Make sure to add `/usr/local/bin/Python3.6` to your shell search path.

Using Linux

After the installation process is complete, you can find a `Python 3.6` subfolder in your home folder. The physical location of Python 3.6 on your Linux system is normally the `/usr/local/bin/Python3.6` folder. This is important information because you may need to modify the path for your system manually. Linux developers need to type **Python3.6**, rather than just **Python**, when working at the Terminal window to obtain access to the Python 3.6.2 installation.

Testing Your Installation

To ensure that you have a usable installation, you need to test it. It's important to know that your installation will work as expected when you need it. Of course, this means writing your first Python application. To get started, open a copy of IDLE. As previously mentioned, IDLE automatically displays the Python version and host information when you open it (refer to Figure 2-6).

To see Python work, type **print("This is my first Python program.")** and press Enter. Python displays the message you just typed, as shown in Figure 2-9. The `print()` command displays onscreen whatever you tell it to display. You see the `print()` command used quite often in this book to display the results of tasks you ask Python to perform, so this is one of the commands you work with frequently.

FIGURE 2-9:
The `print()` command displays whatever information you tell it to print.

```
Python 3.6.2 Shell
File  Edit  Shell  Debug  Options  Window  Help
Python 3.6.2 (v3.6.2:5fd33b5, Jul  8 2017, 04:57:36) [MSC v.1900 64 bit (AMD64)]
on win32
Type "copyright", "credits" or "license()" for more information.
>>> print("This is my first Python program.")
This is my first Python program.
>>> |
                                                                    Ln: 5  Col: 4
```

Notice that IDLE color codes the various entries for you so that they're easier to see and understand. The colors codes are your indicator that you've done something right. Four color codes are shown in Figure 2-9 (although they're not visible in the print edition of the book):

>> **Purple:** Indicates that you have typed a command

>> **Green:** Specifies the content sent to a command

>> **Blue:** Shows the output from a command

>> **Black:** Defines non-command entries

You know that Python works now because you were able to issue a command to it, and it responded by reacting to that command. It might be interesting to see one more command. Type **3 + 4** and press Enter. Python responds by outputting 7, as shown in Figure 2-10. Notice that 3 + 4 appears in black type because it isn't a command. However, the 7 is still in blue type because it's output.

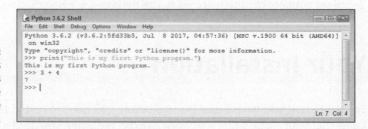

FIGURE 2-10:
Python supports
math directly as
part of the
interactive
environment.

It's time to end your IDLE session. Type **quit( )** and press Enter. IDLE may display a message such as the one shown in Figure 2-11. Well, you never intended to kill anything, but you will now. Click OK, and the session dies.

FIGURE 2-11:
IDLE seems to get
a little dramatic
about ending a
session!

Notice that the `quit()` command has parentheses after it, just as the `print()` command does. All commands have parentheses like these two. That's how you know they're commands. However, you don't need to tell the `quit()` command anything, so you simply leave the area between the parentheses blank.

Chapter **3**

Interacting with Python

U ltimately, any application you create interacts with the computer and the data it contains. The focus is on data because without data, there isn't a good reason to have an application. Any application you use (even one as simple as Solitaire) manipulates data in some way. In fact, the acronym CRUD sums up what most applications do:

» Create

» Read

» Update

» Delete

If you remember CRUD, you'll be able to summarize what most applications do with the data your computer contains (and some applications really are quite cruddy). However, before your application accesses the computer, you have to interact with a programming language that creates a list of tasks to perform in a language the computer understands. That's the purpose of this chapter. You begin interacting with Python. Python takes the list of steps you want to perform on the computer's data and changes those steps into bits the computer understands.

Opening the Command Line

Python offers a number of ways to interact with the underlying language. For example, you worked a bit with the Integrated DeveLopment Environment (IDLE) in Chapter 2. (In Chapter 4, you begin seeing how to use a full-featured Integrated Development Environment, IDE, named Anaconda.) IDLE makes developing full-fledged applications easy. However, sometimes you simply want to experiment or to run an existing application. Often, using the command-line version of Python works better in these cases because it offers better control over the Python environment through command-line switches, uses fewer resources, and relies on a minimalistic interface so that you can focus on trying out code rather than playing with a GUI.

Starting Python

Depending on your platform, you might have multiple ways to start the command line. Here are the methods that are commonly available:

» Select the Python (command-line) option found in the Python36 folder. This option starts a command-line session that uses the default settings.

» Open a command prompt or terminal, type **Python**, and press Enter. Use this option when you want greater flexibility in configuring the Python environment using command-line switches.

UNDERSTANDING THE IMPORTANCE OF THE README FILE

Many applications include a README file. The README file usually provides updated information that didn't make it into the documentation before the application was put into a production status. Unfortunately, most people ignore the README file and some don't even know it exists. As a result, people who should know something interesting about their shiny new product never find out. Python has a NEWS.txt file in the \Python36 directory. When you open this file, you find all sorts of really interesting information, most of which centers on upgrades to Python that you really need to know about.

Opening and reading the README file (named NEWS.txt because people were apparently ignoring the other file) will help you become a Python genius. People will be amazed that you really do know something interesting about Python and will ask you all sorts of questions (deferring to your wisdom). Of course, you could always just sit there, thinking that the README is just too much effort to read.

>> Locate the Python folder, such as C:\Python36 in Windows, and open the Python.exe file directly. This option also opens a command-line session that uses the default settings, but you can do things like open it with increased privileges (for applications that require access to secured resources) or modify the executable file properties (to add command-line switches).

No matter how you start Python at the command line, you eventually end up with a prompt similar to the one shown in Figure 3-1. (Your screen may look slightly different from the one shown in Figure 3-1 if you rely on a platform other than Windows, you're using IDLE instead of the command-line version of Python, your system is configured differently from mine, or you have a different version of Python.) This prompt tells you the Python version, the host operating system, and how to obtain additional information.

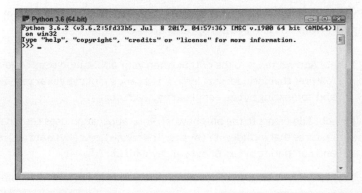

FIGURE 3-1:
The Python command prompt tells you a bit about the Python environment.

Using the command line to your advantage

This section will seem a little complicated at first, and you won't normally need this information when using the book. However, it's still good information, and you'll eventually need it. For now, you can browse the information so that you know what's available and then come back to it later when you really do need the information.

To start Python at a command prompt, type **Python** and press Enter. However, that's not all you can do. You can also provide some additional information to change how Python works:

>> **Options:** An option, or command-line switch, begins with a minus sign followed by one or more letters. For example, if you want to obtain help about Python, you type **Python –h** and press Enter. You see additional information about how to work with Python at the command line. The options are described later in this section.

>> **Filename:** Providing a filename as input tells Python to load that file and run it. You can run any of the example applications from the downloadable code by providing the name of the file containing the example as input. For example, say that you have an example named SayHello.py. To run this example, you type **Python SayHello.py** and press Enter.

>> **Arguments:** An application can accept additional information as input to control how it runs. This additional information is called an argument. Don't worry too much about arguments right now — they appear later in the book.

TECHNICAL
STUFF

Most of the options won't make sense right now. They're here so that you can find them later when you need them (this is the most logical place to include them in the book). Reading through them will help you gain an understanding of what's available, but you can also skip this material until you need it later.

REMEMBER

Python uses case-sensitive options. For example, -s is a completely different option from -S. The Python options are

>> –b: Add warnings to the output when your application uses certain Python features that include: str(bytes_instance), str(bytearray_instance), and comparing bytes or bytearray with str().

>> -bb: Add errors to the output when your application uses certain Python features that include: str(bytes_instance), str(bytearray_instance), and comparing bytes or bytearray with str().

>> –B: Don't write .py or .pyco files when performing a module import.

>> –c *cmd*: Use the information provided by *cmd* to start a program. This option also tells Python to stop processing the rest of the information as options (it's treated as part of the command).

>> –d: Start the debugger (used to locate errors in your application).

>> –E: Ignore all the Python environment variables, such as PYTHONPATH, that are used to configure Python for use.

>> –h: Display help about the options and basic environment variables onscreen. Python always exits after it performs this task without doing anything else so that you can see the help information.

>> –i: Force Python to let you inspect the code interactively after running a script. It forces a prompt even if stdin (the standard input device) doesn't appear to be a terminal.

>> –m *mod*: Run the library module specified by *mod* as a script. This option also tells Python to stop processing the rest of the information as options (the rest of the information is treated as part of the command).

» –O: Optimize the generated bytecode slightly (makes it run faster).

» –OO: Perform additional optimization by removing doc-strings.

» –q: Tell Python not to print the version and copyright messages on interactive startup.

» –s: Force Python not to add the user site directory to sys.path (a variable that tells Python where to find modules).

» –S: Don't run 'import site' on initialization. Using this option means that Python won't look for paths that may contain modules it needs.

» –u: Allow unbuffered binary input for the stdout (standard output) and stderr (standard error) devices. The stdin device is always buffered.

» –v: Place Python in verbose mode so that you can see all the import statements. Using this option multiple times increases the level of verbosity.

» –V: Display the Python version number and exit.

» ––version: Display the Python version number and exit.

» –W *arg*: Modify the warning level so that Python displays more or fewer warnings. The valid *arg* values are

- action
- message
- category
- module
- lineno

» –x: Skip the first line of a source code file, which allows the use of non-Unix forms of #!cmd.

» –X *opt*: Set an implementation-specific option. (The documentation for your version of Python discusses these options, if there are any.)

Using Python environment variables to your advantage

Environment variables are special settings that are part of the command line or terminal environment for your operating system. They serve to configure Python in a consistent manner. Environment variables perform many of the same tasks as do the options that you supply when you start Python, but you can make environment variables permanent so that you can configure Python the same way every time you start it without having to manually supply the option.

As with options, most of these environment variables won't make any sense right now. You can read through them to see what is available. You find some of the environment variables used later in the book. Feel free to skip the rest of this section and come back to it later when you need it.

Most operating systems provide the means to set environment variables temporarily, by configuring them during a particular session, or permanently, by configuring them as part of the operating system setup. Precisely how you perform this task depends on the operating system. For example, when working with Windows, you can use the Set command (see my blog post at http://blog.john muellerbooks.com/2014/02/24/using-the-set-command-to-your-advantage/ for details) or rely on a special Windows configuration feature (see my post at http://blog.johnmuellerbooks.com/2014/02/17/adding-a-location-to-the-windows-path/ for setting the Path environment variable as an example).

Using environment variables makes sense when you need to configure Python the same way on a regular basis. The following list describes the Python environment variables:

- » PYTHONCASEOK=*x*: Forces Python to ignore case when parsing import statements. This is a Windows-only environment variable.

- » PYTHONDEBUG=*x*: Performs the same task as the –d option.

- » PYTHONDONTWRITEBYTECODE=*x*: Performs the same task as the –B option.

- » PYTHONFAULTHANDLER=*x*: Forces Python to dump the Python traceback (list of calls that led to an error) on fatal errors.

- » PYTHONHASHSEED=*arg*: Determines the seed value used to generate hash values from various kinds of data. When this variable is set to random, Python uses a random value to seed the hashes of str, bytes, and datetime objects. The valid integer range is 0 to 4294967295. Use a specific seed value to obtain predictable hash values for testing purposes.

- » PYTHONHOME=*arg*: Defines the default search path that Python uses to look for modules.

- » PYTHONINSPECT=*x*: Performs the same task as the –i option.

- » PYTHONIOENCODING=*arg*: Specifies the encoding[:errors] (such as utf–8) used for the stdin, stdout, and stderr devices.

- » PYTHONNOUSERSITE: Performs the same task as the –s option.

- » PYTHONOPTIMIZE=*x*: Performs the same task as the –O option.

- » PYTHONPATH=*arg*: Provides a semicolon (;) separated list of directories to search for modules. This value is stored in the sys.path variable in Python.

» `PYTHONSTARTUP=`*`arg`*: Defines the name of a file to execute when Python starts. There is no default value for this environment variable.

» `PYTHONUNBUFFERED=`*`x`*: Performs the same task as the –u option.

» `PYTHONVERBOSE=`*`x`*: Performs the same task as the –v option.

» `PYTHONWARNINGS=`*`arg`*: Performs the same task as the –W option.

Typing a Command

After you start the command-line version of Python, you can begin typing commands. Using commands makes it possible to perform tasks, test ideas that you have for writing your application, and discover more about Python. Using the command line lets you gain hands-on experience with how Python actually works — details that could be hidden by an interactive IDE such as IDLE. The following sections get you started using the command line.

Telling the computer what to do

Python, like every other programming language in existence, relies on commands. A *command* is simply a step in a procedure. In Chapter 1, you see how "Get the bread and butter from the refrigerator" is a step in a procedure for making toast. When working with Python, a command, such as `print()`, is simply the same thing: a step in a procedure.

To tell the computer what to do, you issue one or more commands that Python understands. Python translates these commands into instructions that the computer understands, and then you see the result. A command such as `print()` can display the results onscreen so that you get an instant result. However, Python supports all sorts of commands, many of which don't display any results onscreen but still do something important.

As the book progresses, you use commands to perform all sorts of tasks. Each of these tasks will help you accomplish a goal, just as the steps in a procedure do. When it seems as if all the Python commands become far too complex, simply remember to look at them as steps in a procedure. Even human procedures become complex at times, but if you take them one step at a time, you begin to see how they work. Python commands are the same way. Don't get overwhelmed by them; instead, look at them one at a time and focus on just that step in your procedure.

Telling the computer you're done

At some point, the procedure you create ends. When you make toast, the procedure ends when you finish buttering the toast. Computer procedures work precisely the same way. They have a starting and an ending point. When typing commands, the ending point for a particular step is the Enter key. You press Enter to tell the computer that you're done typing the command. As the book progresses, you find that Python provides a number of ways to signify that a step, group of steps, or even an entire application is complete. No matter how the task is accomplished, computer programs always have a distinct starting and stopping point.

Seeing the result

You now know that a command is a step in a procedure and that each command has a distinct starting and ending point. In addition, groups of commands and entire applications also have a distinct starting and ending point. So, take a look at how this works. The following procedure helps you see the result of using a command:

1. **Start a copy of the Python command-line version.**

You see a command prompt where you can type commands, as shown previously in Figure 3-1.

2. **Type** print("This is a line of text.") **at the command line.**

Notice that nothing happens. Yes, you typed a command, but you haven't signified that the command is complete.

3. **Press Enter.**

The command is complete, so you see a result like the one shown in Figure 3-2.

FIGURE 3-2:
Issuing
commands tells
Python what
to tell the
computer to do.

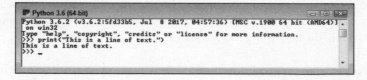

This exercise shows you how things work within Python. Each command that you type performs some task, but only after you tell Python that the command is complete in some way. The print() command displays data onscreen. In this case, you supplied text to display. Notice that the output shown in Figure 3-2 comes immediately after the command because this is an interactive environment — one in which you see the result of any given command immediately after Python performs it. Later, as you start creating applications, you notice that sometimes a result doesn't appear immediately because the application environment delays it. Even so, the command is executed by Python immediately after the application tells Python that the command is complete.

PYTHON'S CODING STYLES

Most programming languages are dedicated to using just one coding style, which reduces flexibility for the programmer. However, Python is different. You can use a number of coding styles to achieve differing effects with Python. The four commonly used Python coding styles are

- **Functional:** Every statement is a kind of math equation. This style lends itself well to use in parallel processing activities.

- **Imperative:** Computations occur as changes to program state. This style is most used for manipulating data structures.

- **Object-oriented:** This is the style commonly used with other languages to simplify the coding environment by using objects to model the real world. Python doesn't fully implement this coding style because it doesn't support features like data hiding, but you can still use this approach to a significant degree. You see this style used later in the book.

- **Procedural:** All the code you've written so far (and much of the initial code in this book) is procedural, meaning that tasks proceed a step at a time. This style is most used for iteration, sequencing, selection, and modularization. It's the simplest form of coding you can use.

Even though this book doesn't cover all these coding styles (and others that Python supports), it's useful to know that you aren't trapped using a particular coding style. Because Python supports multiple coding styles and you can mix and match those styles in a single application, you have the advantage of being able to use Python in the manner that works best for a particular need. You can read more about the coding styles at https://blog.newrelic.com/2015/04/01/python-programming-styles/.

Using Help

Python is a computer language, not a human language. As a result, you won't speak it fluently at first. If you think about it for a moment, it makes sense that you won't speak Python fluently (and as with most human languages, you won't know every command even after you do become fluent). Having to discover Python commands a little at a time is the same thing that happens when you learn to speak another human language. If you normally speak English and try to say something in German, you find that you must have some sort of guide to help you along. Otherwise, anything you say is gibberish and people will look at you quite oddly. Even if you manage to say something that makes sense, it may not be what you want. You might go to a restaurant and order hot hubcaps for dinner when what you really wanted was a steak.

Likewise, when you try to speak Python, you need a guide to help you. Fortunately, Python is quite accommodating and provides immediate help to keep you from ordering something you really don't want. The help provided inside Python works at two levels:

>> **Help mode,** in which you can browse the available commands

>> **Direct help,** in which you ask about a specific command

There isn't a correct way to use help — just the method that works best for you at a particular time. The following sections describe how to obtain help.

Getting into help mode

When you first start Python, you see a display similar to the one shown previously in Figure 3-1. Notice that Python provides you with four commands at the outset (which is actually your first piece of help information):

>> `help`

>> `copyright`

>> `credits`

>> `license`

All four commands provide you with help, of a sort, about Python. For example, the `copyright()` command tells you about who holds the right to copy, license, or otherwise distribute Python. The `credits()` command tells you who put Python together. The `license()` command describes the usage agreement between you and the copyright holder. However, the command you most want to know about is simply `help()`.

To enter help mode, type **help()** and press Enter. Notice that you must include the parentheses after the command even though they don't appear in the help text. Every Python command has parentheses associated with it. After you enter this command, Python goes into help mode and you see a display similar to the one shown in Figure 3-3.

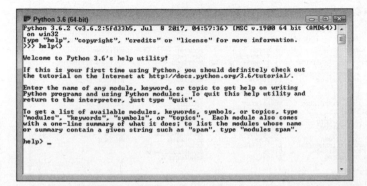

FIGURE 3-3:
You ask Python about other commands in help mode.

REMEMBER

You can always tell that you're in help mode by the help> prompt that you see in the Python window. As long as you see the help> prompt, you know that you're in help mode.

Asking for help

To obtain help, you need to know what question to ask. The initial help message that you see when you go into help mode (refer to Figure 3-3) provides some helpful tips about the kinds of questions you can ask. If you want to explore Python, the four basic topics are

» modules

» keywords

» symbols

» topics

The first two topics won't tell you much for now. You won't need the modules topic until Chapter 10. The keywords topic will begin proving useful in Chapter 4. However, the symbols and topics keywords are already useful because they help you understand where to begin your Python adventure. When you type **symbols** and press Enter, you see a list of symbols used in Python. To see what topics are available, type **topics** and press Enter. You see a list of topics similar to those shown in Figure 3-4.

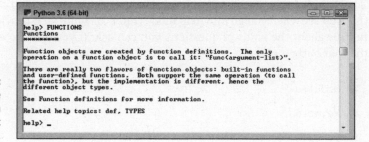

FIGURE 3-4:
The `topics` help
topic provides
you with a
starting point for
your Python
adventure.

REMEMBER

Chapter 7 begins the discussion of `symbols` when you explore the use of operators in Python. When you see a topic that you like, such as FUNCTIONS, simply type that topic and press Enter. To see how this works, type **FUNCTIONS** and press Enter (you must type the word in uppercase — don't worry, Python won't think you're shouting). You see help information similar to that shown in Figure 3-5.

FIGURE 3-5:
You must use
uppercase when
requesting topic
information.

As you work through examples in the book, you use commands that look interesting, and you might want more information about them. For example, in the "Seeing the result" section of this chapter, you use the `print()` command. To see more information about the `print()` command, type **print** and press Enter (notice that you don't include the parentheses this time because you're requesting help about `print()`, not actually using the command). Figure 3-6 shows typical help information for the `print()` command.

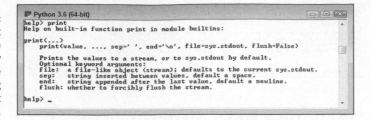

FIGURE 3-6:
Request
command help
information by
typing the
command using
whatever case it
actually uses.

TIP

Unfortunately, reading the help information probably doesn't help much yet because you need to know more about Python. However, you can ask for more information. For example, you might wonder what sys.stdout means — and the help topic certainly doesn't tell you anything about it. Type **sys.stdout** and press Enter. You see the help information shown in Figure 3-7.

FIGURE 3-7:
You can ask for
help on the help
you receive.

You may still not find the information as helpful as you need, but at least you know a little more. In this case, help has a lot to say and it can't all fit on one screen. Notice the following entry at the bottom of the screen:

```
-- More  --
```

To see the additional information, press the spacebar. The next page of help appears. As you read to the bottom of each page of help, you can press the spacebar to see the next page. The pages don't go away — you can scroll up to see previous material.

Leaving help mode

At some point, you need to leave help mode to perform useful work. All you have to do is press Enter without typing anything. When you press Enter, you see a message about leaving help, and then the prompt changes to the standard Python prompt, as shown in Figure 3-8.

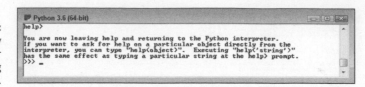

FIGURE 3-8:
Exit help mode by pressing Enter without typing anything.

Obtaining help directly

Entering help mode isn't necessary unless you want to browse, which is always a good idea, or unless you don't actually know what you need to find. If you have a good idea of what you need, all you need to do is ask for help directly (a really nice thing for Python to do). So, instead of fiddling with help mode, you simply type the word *help*, followed by a left parenthesis and single quote, whatever you want to find, another single quote, and the right parenthesis. For example, if you want to know more about the print() command, you type **help('print')** and press Enter. Figure 3-9 shows typical output when you access help this way.

FIGURE 3-9:
Python lets you obtain help whenever you need it without leaving the Python prompt.

You can browse at the Python prompt, too. For example, when you type **help('topics')** and press Enter, you see a list of topics like the one that appears in Figure 3-10. You can compare this list with the one shown in Figure 3-4. The two lists are identical, even though you typed one while in help mode and the other while at the Python prompt.

FIGURE 3-10:
You can browse at the Python prompt if you really want to.

TIP

You might wonder why Python has a help mode at all if you can get the same results at the Python prompt. The answer is convenience. It's easier to browse in the help mode. In addition, even though you don't do a lot of extra typing at the prompt, you do perform less typing while in help mode. Help mode also provides additional helps, such as by listing commands that you can type, as shown previously in Figure 3-3. So you have all kinds of good reasons to enter help mode when you plan to ask Python a lot of help questions.

REMEMBER

No matter where you ask for help, you need to observe the correct capitalization of help topics. For example, if you want general information about functions, you must type **help('FUNCTIONS')** and not help('Functions') or help('functions'). When you use the wrong capitalization, Python will tell you that it doesn't know what you mean or that it couldn't find the help topic. It won't know to tell you that you used the wrong capitalization. Someday computers will know what you meant to type, rather than what you did type, but that hasn't happened yet.

Closing the Command Line

Eventually, you want to leave Python. Yes, it's hard to believe, but people have other things to do besides playing with Python all day long. You have two standard methods for leaving Python and a whole bunch of nonstandard methods. Generally, you want to use one of the standard methods to ensure that Python behaves as you expect it to, but the nonstandard methods work just fine when you simply want to play around with Python and not perform any productive work. The two standard methods are

» `quit()`

» `exit()`

Either of these methods will close the interactive version of Python. The *shell* (the Python program) is designed to allow either command.

Both of these commands can accept an optional argument. For example, you can type **quit(5)** or **exit(5)** and press Enter to exit the shell. The numeric argument sets the command prompt's ERRORLEVEL environment variable, which you can then intercept at the command line or as part of a batch file. Standard practice is to simply use `quit()` or `exit()` when nothing has gone wrong with the application. To see this way of exiting at work, you must

1. **Open a command prompt or terminal.**

   You see a prompt.

2. **Type** Python **and press Enter to start Python.**

   You see the Python prompt.

3. **Type** quit(5) **and press Enter.**

   You see the prompt again.

4. **Type** echo %ERRORLEVEL% **and press Enter.**

   You see the error code, as shown in Figure 3-11. When working with platforms other than Windows, you may need to type something other than echo %ERRORLEVEL%. For example, when working with a bash script, you type **echo $** instead.

```
Administrator: Command Prompt
C:\>Python
Python 3.6.2 (v3.6.2:5fd33b5, Jul  8 2017, 04:57:36) [MSC v.1900 64 bit (AMD64)]
 on win32
Type "help", "copyright", "credits" or "license" for more information.
>>> quit(5)

C:\>echo %ERRORLEVEL%
5

C:\>_
```

One of the most common nonstandard exit methods is to simply click the command prompt's or terminal's Close button. Using this approach means that your application may not have time to perform any required cleanup, which can result in odd behaviors. It's always better to close Python using an expected approach if you've been doing anything more than simply browsing.

TECHNICAL
STUFF

You also have access to a number of other commands for closing the command prompt when needed. In most cases, you won't need these special commands, so you can skip the rest of this section if desired.

When you use quit() or exit(), Python performs a number of tasks to ensure that everything is neat and tidy before the session ends. If you suspect that a session might not end properly anyway, you can always rely on one of these two commands to close the command prompt:

» sys.exit()

» os._exit()

Both of these commands are used in emergency situations only. The first, `sys.exit()`, provides special error-handling features that you discover in Chapter 9. The second, `os._exit()`, exits Python without performing any of the usual cleanup tasks. In both cases, you must import the required module, either `sys` or `os`, before you can use the associated command. Consequently, to use the `sys.exit()` command, you actually use this code:

```
import sys
sys.exit()
```

You must provide an error code when using `os._exit()` because this command is used only when an extreme error has occurred. The call to this command will fail if you don't provide an error code. To use the `os._exit()` command, you actually use this code (where the error code is 5):

```
import os
os._exit(5)
```

Chapter 10 discusses importing modules in detail. For now, just know that these two commands are for special uses only and you won't normally use them in an application.

IN THIS CHAPTER

» Using Jupyter Notebook in Anaconda as an IDE

» Writing and running the first application

» Formatting your application code

» Using comments effectively

» Managing applications using Anaconda

Chapter **4**

Writing Your First Application

M
any people view application development as some sort of magic practiced by wizards called geeks who wave their keyboard to produce software both great and small. However, the truth is a lot more mundane.

Application development follows a number of processes. It's more than a strict procedure, but is most definitely not magic of any sort. As Arthur C. Clark once noted, "Any sufficiently advanced technology is indistinguishable from magic." This chapter is all about removing the magic from the picture and introducing you to the technology. By the time you're finished with this chapter, you too will be able to develop a simple application (and you won't use magic to do it).

As with any other task, people use tools to write applications. In the case of Python, you don't have to use a tool, but using a tool makes the task so much easier that you really will want to use one. In this chapter, you use a commonly available Integrated Development Environment (IDE) named Jupyter Notebook that appears as part of the Anaconda tool collection. An *IDE* is a special kind of application that makes writing, testing, and debugging code significantly easier. In the previous chapter, you use the command-line tool to play around with

Python a little. However, the Anaconda offerings go further than the command-line tool and enables you to write applications with greater ease.

TIP

A vast number of other tools are available for you to use when writing Python applications. This book doesn't tell you much about them because Anaconda performs every task needed and it's readily available free of charge. However, as your skills increase, you might find the features in other tools such as Komodo Edit (`http://www.activestate.com/komodo-edit/downloads`) more to your liking. You can find a great list of these tools at `https://wiki.python.org/moin/IntegratedDevelopmentEnvironments`.

Understanding Why IDEs Are Important

A good question to ask is, why do you need an IDE to work with Python if the command-line tool works fine? For that matter, Python actually comes with a limited IDE called Integrated DeveLopement Environment (IDLE). Most people probably question the need for anything more during the learning process and possibly to develop full-fledged applications. Unfortunately, the tools that come with Python are interesting and even helpful in getting started, but they won't help you create useful applications with any ease. If you choose to work with Python long term, you really need a better tool for the reasons described in the following sections.

Creating better code

A good IDE contains a certain amount of intelligence. For example, the IDE can suggest alternatives when you type the incorrect keyword, or it can tell you that a certain line of code simply won't work as written. The more intelligence that an IDE contains, the less hard you have to work to write better code. Writing better code is essential because no one wants to spend hours looking for errors, called *bugs*.

TIP

IDEs vary greatly in the level and kind of intelligence they provide, which is why so many IDEs exist. You may find the level of help obtained from one IDE to be insufficient to your needs, but another IDE hovers over you like a mother hen. Every developer has different needs and, therefore, different IDE requirements. The point is to obtain an IDE that helps you write clean, efficient code quickly and easily.

Debugging functionality

Finding bugs (errors) in your code is a process called *debugging*. Even the most expert developer in the world spends time debugging. Writing perfect code on the first pass is nearly impossible. When you do, it's cause for celebration because it won't happen often. Consequently, the debugging capabilities of your IDE are critical. Unfortunately, the debugging capabilities of the native Python tools are almost nonexistent. If you spend any time at all debugging, you quickly find the native tools annoying because of what they don't tell you about your code.

TIP

The best IDEs double as training tools. Given enough features, an IDE can help you explore code written by true experts. Tracing through applications is a time-honored method of learning new skills and honing the skills you already possess. A seemingly small advance in knowledge can often become a huge savings in time later. When looking for an IDE, don't just look at debugging features as a means to remove errors — see them also as a means to learn new things about Python.

Defining why notebooks are useful

Most IDEs look like fancy text editors, and that's precisely what they are. Yes, you get all sorts of intelligent features, hints, tips, code coloring, and so on, but at the end of the day, they're all text editors. There's nothing wrong with text editors, and this chapter isn't telling you anything of the sort. However, given that Python developers often focus on scientific applications that require something better than pure text presentation, using notebooks instead can be helpful.

REMEMBER

A *notebook* differs from a text editor in that it focuses on a technique advanced by Stanford computer scientist Donald Knuth called literate programming. You use *literate programming* to create a kind of presentation of code, notes, math equations, and graphics. In short, you wind up with a scientist's notebook full of everything needed to understand the code completely. You commonly see literate programming techniques used in high-priced packages such as Mathematica and MATLAB. Notebook development excels at

>> Demonstration

>> Collaboration

>> Research

>> Teaching objectives

>> Presentation

This book uses the Anaconda tool collection because it provides you with a great Python coding experience, but also helps you discover the enormous potential of literate programming techniques. If you spend a lot of time performing scientific tasks, Anaconda and products like it are essential. In addition, Anaconda is free, so you get the benefits of the literate programming style without the cost of other packages.

Obtaining Your Copy of Anaconda

As mentioned in the previous section, Anaconda doesn't come with your Python installation. You can follow the essential book examples using IDLE if you'd rather, but you really do want to try Anaconda if possible. With this in mind, the following sections help you obtain and install Anaconda on the three major platforms supported by this book.

Obtaining Analytics Anaconda

The basic Anaconda package is a free download that you obtain at `https://store.continuum.io/cshop/anaconda/`. Simply click Download Anaconda to obtain access to the free product. You do need to provide an email address to get a copy of Anaconda. After you put in your email address, you go to another page, where you can choose your platform and the installer for that platform. Anaconda supports the following platforms:

» Windows 32-bit and 64-bit (the installer may offer you only the 64-bit or 32-bit version, depending on which version of Windows it detects)

» Linux 32-bit and 64-bit

» Mac OS X 64-bit

WARNING

This book uses Anaconda version 4.4.0, which supports Python 3.6.2. If you don't use this version of Anaconda, you may find that some examples don't work well and that what you see on your screen doesn't match what you see in the book, even if you're working with Windows. The screenshots in this book are taken using a Windows 64-bit system, but they should be very close to what you see on other platforms when you use Anaconda 4.4.0.

TIP

You can obtain Anaconda with older versions of Python. If you want to use an older version of Python, click the installer archive link near the bottom of the page. You should use an older version of Python only when you have a pressing need to do so.

The Miniconda installer can potentially save time by limiting the number of features you install. However, trying to figure out precisely which packages you do need is an error-prone and time-consuming process. In general, you want to perform a full installation to ensure that you have everything needed for your projects. Even a full install doesn't require much time or effort to download and install on most systems.

The free product is all you need for this book. However, when you look on the site, you see that many other add-on products are available. These products can help you create robust applications. For example, when you add Accelerate to the mix, you obtain the capability to perform multicore and GPU-enabled operations. The use of these add-on products is outside the scope of this book, but the Anaconda site gives you details on using them.

Installing Anaconda on Linux

You have to use the command line to install Anaconda on Linux; you're given no graphical installation option. Before you can perform the install, you must download a copy of the Linux software from the Continuum Analytics site. You can find the required download information in the "Obtaining Analytics Anaconda" section, earlier in this chapter. The following procedure should work fine on any Linux system, whether you use the 32-bit or 64-bit version of Anaconda:

1. Open a copy of Terminal.

The Terminal window appears.

2. Change directories to the downloaded copy of Anaconda on your system.

The name of this file varies, but normally it appears as Anaconda3-4.4.0-Linux-x86.sh for 32-bit systems and Anaconda3-4.4.0-Linux-x86_64.sh for 64-bit systems. The version number is embedded as part of the filename. In this case, the filename refers to version 4.4.0, which is the version used for this book. If you use some other version, you may experience problems with the source code and need to make adjustments when working with it.

3. Type bash Anaconda3-4.4.0-Linux-x86.sh **(for the 32-bit version) or** bash Anaconda3-4.4.0-Linux-x86_64.sh **(for the 64-bit version) and press Enter.**

An installation wizard starts that asks you to accept the licensing terms for using Anaconda.

4. Read the licensing agreement and accept the terms using the method required for your version of Linux.

The wizard asks you to provide an installation location for Anaconda. The book assumes that you use the default location of ~/anaconda. If you choose some other location, you may have to modify some procedures later in the book to work with your setup.

5. Provide an installation location (if necessary) and press Enter (or click Next).

The application extraction process begins. After the extraction is complete, you see a completion message.

6. Add the installation path to your PATH **statement using the method required for your version of Linux.**

You're ready to begin using Anaconda.

Installing Anaconda on MacOS

The Mac OS X installation comes in only one form: 64-bit. Before you can perform the install, you must download a copy of the Mac software from the Continuum Analytics site. You can find the required download information in the "Obtaining Analytics Anaconda" section, earlier in this chapter.

The installation files come in two forms. The first depends on a graphical installer; the second relies on the command line. The command-line version works much like the Linux version described in the "Using the standard Linux installation" section of Chapter 2. The following steps help you install Anaconda 64-bit on a Mac system using the graphical installer:

1. Locate the downloaded copy of Anaconda on your system.

The name of this file varies, but normally it appears as Anaconda3-4.4.0-MacOSX-x86_64.pkg. The version number is embedded as part of the filename. In this case, the filename refers to version 4.4.0, which is the version used for this book. If you use some other version, you may experience problems with the source code and need to make adjustments when working with it.

2. Double-click the installation file.

An introduction dialog box appears.

3. Click Continue.

The wizard asks whether you want to review the Read Me materials. You can read these materials later. For now, you can safely skip the information.

4. Click Continue.

The wizard displays a licensing agreement. Be sure to read through the licensing agreement so that you know the terms of usage.

5. Click I Agree if you agree to the licensing agreement.

The wizard asks you to provide a destination for the installation. The destination controls whether the installation is for an individual user or a group.

WARNING

You may see an error message stating that you can't install Anaconda on the system. The error message occurs because of a bug in the installer and has nothing to do with your system. To get rid of the error message, choose the Install Only for Me option. You can't install Anaconda for a group of users on a Mac system.

6. Click Continue.

The installer displays a dialog box containing options for changing the installation type. Click Change Install Location if you want to modify where Anaconda is installed on your system. (The book assumes that you use the default path of ~/anaconda.) Click Customize if you want to modify how the installer works. For example, you can choose not to add Anaconda to your PATH statement. However, the book assumes that you have chosen the default install options, and no good reason exists to change them unless you have another copy of Python 3.6.2 installed somewhere else.

7. **Click Install.**

The installation begins. A progress bar tells you how the installation process is progressing. When the installation is complete, you see a completion dialog box.

8. **Click Continue.**

You're ready to begin using Anaconda.

Installing Anaconda on Windows

Anaconda comes with a graphical installation application for Windows, so getting a good install means using a wizard, as you would for any other installation. Of course, you need a copy of the installation file before you begin, and you can find the required download information in the "Obtaining Analytics Anaconda" section, earlier in this chapter. The following procedure (which can require a while to complete) should work fine on any Windows system, whether you use the 32-bit or the 64-bit version of Anaconda:

1. **Locate the downloaded copy of Anaconda on your system.**

The name of this file varies, but normally it appears as Anaconda3-4.4.0-Windows-x86.exe for 32-bit systems and Anaconda3-4.4.0-Windows-x86_64.exe for 64-bit systems. The version number is embedded as part of the filename. In this case, the filename refers to version 4.4.0, which is the version used for this book. If you use some other version, you may experience problems with the source code and need to make adjustments when working with it.

2. **Double-click the installation file.**

(You may see an Open File – Security Warning dialog box that asks whether you want to run this file. Click Run if you see this dialog box pop up.) You see an Anaconda3 4.4.0 Setup dialog box similar to the one shown in Figure 4-1. The exact dialog box that you see depends on which version of the Anaconda installation program you download. If you have a 64-bit operating system, using the 64-bit version of Anaconda is always best so that you obtain the best possible performance. This first dialog box tells you when you have the 64-bit version of the product.

FIGURE 4-1:
The setup
process begins by
telling you
whether you have
the 64-bit version.

3. Click Next.

The wizard displays a licensing agreement. Be sure to read through the licensing agreement so that you know the terms of usage.

4. Click I Agree if you agree to the licensing agreement.

You're asked what sort of installation type to perform, as shown in Figure 4-2. In most cases, you want to install the product just for yourself. The exception is if you have multiple people using your system and they all need access to Anaconda.

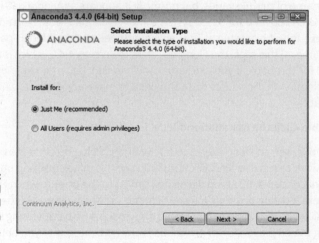

FIGURE 4-2:
Tell the wizard
how to install
Anaconda on
your system.

5. **Choose one of the installation types and then click Next.**

   The wizard asks where to install Anaconda on disk, as shown in Figure 4-3. The book assumes that you use the default location. If you choose some other location, you may have to modify some procedures later in the book to work with your setup.

FIGURE 4-3:
Specify an installation location.

6. **Choose an installation location (if necessary) and then click Next.**

   You see the Advanced Installation Options, shown in Figure 4-4. These options are selected by default, and no good reason exists to change them in most cases. You might need to change them if Anaconda won't provide your default Python 3.6 (or Python 2.7) setup. However, the book assumes that you've set up Anaconda using the default options.

FIGURE 4-4:
Configure the advanced installation options.

7. **Change the advanced installation options (if necessary) and then click Install.**

   You see an Installing dialog box with a progress bar. The installation process can take a few minutes, so get yourself a cup of coffee and read the comics for a while. When the installation process is over, you see a Next button enabled.

8. **Click Next.**

   The wizard tells you that the installation is complete.

9. **Click Finish.**

   You're ready to begin using Anaconda.

Downloading the Datasets and Example Code

This book is about using Python to perform basic programming tasks. Of course, you can spend all your time creating the example code from scratch, debugging it, and only then discovering how it relates to discovering the wonders of Python, or you can take the easy way and download the prewritten code from the Dummies site as described in the book's Introduction so that you can get right to work. The following sections show how to work with Jupyter Notebook, the name of the Anaconda IDE. These sections emphasize the capability to manage application code, including importing the downloadable source and exporting your amazing applications to show friends.

Using Jupyter Notebook

To make working with the code in this book easier, you use Jupyter Notebook. This interface lets you easily create Python notebook files that can contain any number of examples, each of which can run individually. The program runs in your browser, so which platform you use for development doesn't matter; as long as it has a browser, you should be okay.

Starting Jupyter Notebook

Most platforms provide an icon to access Jupyter Notebook. Just click this icon to access Jupyter Notebook. For example, on a Windows system, you choose Start ➪ All Programs ➪ Anaconda 3 ➪ Jupyter Notebook. Figure 4-5 shows how the interface looks when viewed in a Firefox browser. The precise appearance on your system depends on the browser you use and the kind of platform you have installed.

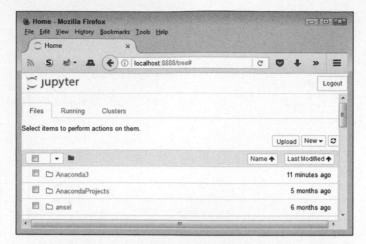

FIGURE 4-5:
Jupyter Notebook provides an easy method to create machine learning examples.

Stopping the Jupyter Notebook server

No matter how you start Jupyter Notebook (or just Notebook, as it appears in the remainder of the book), the system generally opens a command prompt or terminal window to host Jupyter Notebook. This window contains a server that makes the application work. After you close the browser window when a session is complete, select the server window and press Ctrl+C or Ctrl+Break to stop the server.

Defining the code repository

The code you create and use in this book will reside in a repository on your hard drive. Think of a *repository* as a kind of filing cabinet where you put your code. Notebook opens a drawer, takes out the folder, and shows the code to you. You can modify it, run individual examples within the folder, add new examples, and simply interact with your code in a natural manner. The following sections get you started with Notebook so that you can see how this whole repository concept works.

Defining the book's folder

It pays to organize your files so that you can access them more easily later. This book keeps its files in the BPPD (Beginning Programming with Python For Dummies) folder. Use these steps within Notebook to create a new folder:

1. **Choose New ⇨ Folder.**

Notebook creates a new folder named Untitled Folder, as shown in Figure 4-6. The file appears in alphanumeric order, so you may not initially see it. You must scroll down to the correct location.

FIGURE 4-6:
New folders appear with a name of Untitled Folder.

2. **Select the box next to the Untitled Folder entry.**

3. **Click Rename at the top of the page.**

   You see a Rename Directory dialog box like the one shown in Figure 4-7.

FIGURE 4-7:
Rename the folder so that you remember the kinds of entries it contains.

4. **Type** BPPD **and click Rename.**

   Notebook changes the name of the folder for you.

5. **Click the new BPPD entry in the list.**

   Notebook changes the location to the BPPD folder in which you perform tasks related to the exercises in this book.

Creating a new notebook

Every new notebook is like a file folder. You can place individual examples within the file folder, just as you would sheets of paper into a physical file folder. Each example appears in a cell. You can put other sorts of things in the file folder, too, but you see how these things work as the book progresses. Use these steps to create a new notebook:

1. **Click New ⇨ Python 3.**

A new tab opens in the browser with the new notebook, as shown in Figure 4-8. Notice that the notebook contains a cell and that Notebook has highlighted the cell so that you can begin typing code in it. The title of the notebook is Untitled right now. That's not a particularly helpful title, so you need to change it.

FIGURE 4-8: A notebook contains cells that you use to hold code.

2. **Click Untitled on the page.**

Notebook asks what you want to use as a new name, as shown in Figure 4-9.

3. **Type** BPPD_04_Sample **and press Enter.**

The new name tells you that this is a file for *Beginning Programming with Python For Dummies,* Chapter 4, Sample.ipynb. Using this naming convention lets you easily differentiate these files from other files in your repository.

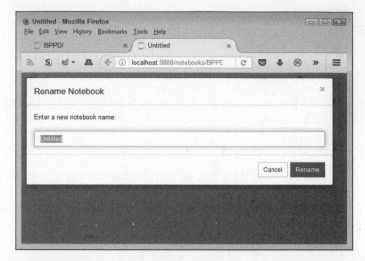

FIGURE 4-9:
Provide a new
name for your
notebook.

Of course, the Sample notebook doesn't contain anything just yet. Place the cursor in the cell, type **print('Python is really cool!')**, and then click the Run button (the button with the right-pointing arrow on the toolbar). You see the output shown in Figure 4-10. The output is part of the same cell as the code (the code resides in a square box and the output resides outside that square box, but both are within the cell). However, Notebook visually separates the output from the code so that you can tell them apart. Notebook automatically creates a new cell for you.

FIGURE 4-10:
Notebook uses
cells to store
your code.

When you finish working with a notebook, shutting it down is important. To close a notebook, choose File ➪ Close and Halt. You return to the Home page, where you can see that the notebook you just created is added to the list, as shown in Figure 4-11.

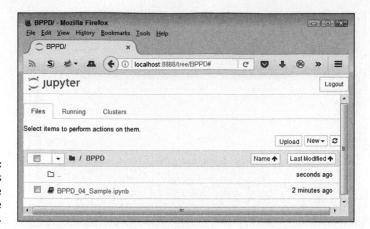

FIGURE 4-11:
Any notebooks
you create
appear in the
repository list.

Exporting a notebook

Creating notebooks and keeping them all to yourself isn't much fun. At some point, you want to share them with other people. To perform this task, you must export your notebook from the repository to a file. You can then send the file to someone else, who will import it into his or her repository.

The previous section shows how to create a notebook named BPPD_04_Sample. ipynb. You can open this notebook by clicking its entry in the repository list. The file reopens so that you can see your code again. To export this code, choose File ⇨ Download As ⇨ Notebook (.ipynb). What you see next depends on your browser, but you generally see some sort of dialog box for saving the notebook as a file. Use the same method for saving the Jupyter Notebook file as you use for any other file you save by using your browser. Remember to choose File ⇨ Close and Halt when you finish so that the application is shut down.

Removing a notebook

Sometimes notebooks get outdated or you simply don't need to work with them any longer. Rather than allow your repository to get clogged with files that you don't need, you can remove these unwanted notebooks from the list. Use these steps to remove the file:

1. **Select the box next to the** BPPD_04_Sample.ipynb **entry.**

2. **Click the trash can icon (Delete) at the top of the page.**

   You see a Delete notebook warning message like the one shown in Figure 4-12.

3. **Click Delete.**

   The file gets removed from the list.

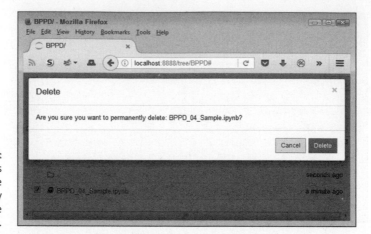

FIGURE 4-12:
Notebook warns
you before
removing any
files from the
repository.

Importing a notebook

To use the source code from this book, you must import the downloaded files into
your repository. The source code comes in an archive file that you extract to a
location on your hard drive. The archive contains a list of `.ipynb` (IPython Notebook) files containing the source code for this book (see the Introduction for
details on downloading the source code). The following steps tell how to import
these files into your repository:

1. **Click Upload at the top of the page.**

    What you see depends on your browser. In most cases, you see some type of
    File Upload dialog box that provides access to the files on your hard drive.

2. **Navigate to the directory containing the files that you want to import
    into Notebook.**

3. **Highlight one or more files to import and click the Open (or other,
    similar) button to begin the upload process.**

    You see the file added to an upload list, as shown in Figure 4-13. The file isn't
    part of the repository yet — you've simply selected it for upload.

4. **Click Upload.**

    Notebook places the file in the repository so that you can begin using it.

FIGURE 4-13:
The files that you want to add to the repository appear as part of an upload list consisting of one or more filenames.

Creating the Application

You've actually created your first Anaconda application by using the steps in the "Creating a new notebook" section, earlier in this chapter. The print() method may not seem like much, but you use it quite often. However, the literate programming approach provided by Anaconda requires a little more knowledge than you currently have. The following sections don't tell you everything about this approach, but they do help you gain an understanding of what literate programming can provide in the way of functionality. However, before you begin, make sure you have the BPPD_04_Sample.ipynb file open for use because you need it to explore Notebook.

Understanding cells

If Notebook were a standard IDE, you wouldn't have cells. What you'd have is a document containing a single, contiguous series of statements. To separate various coding elements, you need separate files. Cells are different because each cell is separate. Yes, the results of things you do in previous cells matter, but if a cell is meant to work alone, you can simply go to that cell and run it. To see how this

works for yourself, type the following code into the next cell of the BPPD_04_
Sample file:

```
myVar = 3 + 4
print(myVar)
```

Now click Run (the right-pointing arrow). The code executes, and you see the output, as shown in Figure 4-14. The output is 7, as expected. However, notice the In [1]: entry. This entry tells you that this is the first cell executed.

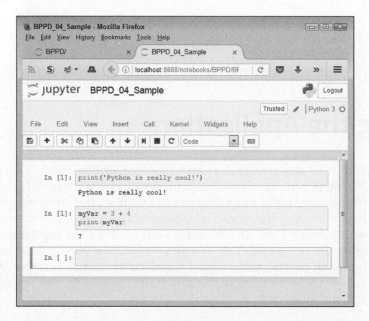

FIGURE 4-14:
Cells execute
individually in
Notebook.

Note that the first cell also has a In [1]: entry. This entry is still from the previous session. Place your cursor in that cell and click Run. Now the cell contains In [2]:, as shown in Figure 4-15. However, note that the next cell hasn't been selected and still contains the In [1]: entry.

Now place the cursor in the third cell — the one that is currently blank — and type print("This is myVar: ", myVar). Click Run. The output in Figure 4-16 shows that the cells have executed in anything but a rigid order, but that myVar is global to the notebook. What you do in other cells with data affects every other cell, no matter what order the execution takes place.

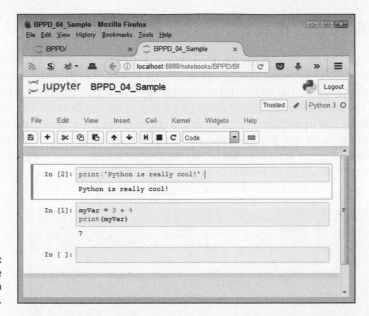

FIGURE 4-15:
Cells can execute in any order in Notebook.

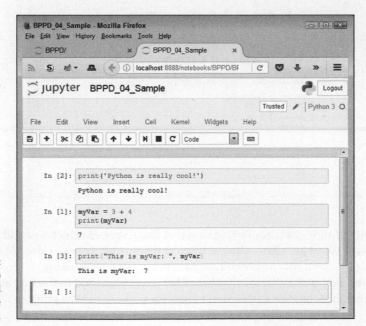

FIGURE 4-16:
Data changes do affect every cell that uses the modified variable.

Adding documentation cells

Cells come in a number of different forms. This book doesn't use them all. However, knowing how to use the documentation cells can come in handy. Select the first cell (the one currently marked with a 2). Choose Insert ⇨ Insert Cell Above. You see a new cell added to the notebook. Note the drop-down list that currently has Code in it. This list allows you to choose the kind of cell to create. Select Markdown from the list and type **# This is a level 1 heading**. Click Run (which may seem like an extremely odd thing to do, but give it a try). You see the text change into a heading, as shown in Figure 4-17.

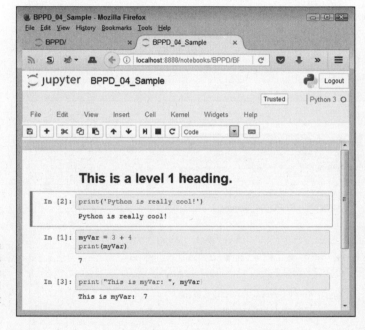

FIGURE 4-17:
Adding headings helps you separate and document your code.

About now, you may be thinking that these special cells act just like HTML pages, and you'd be right. Choose Insert ⇨ Insert Cell Below, select Markdown in the drop-down list, and then type **## This is a level 2 heading**. Click Run. As you can see in Figure 4-18, the number of hashes (#) you add to the text affects the heading level, but the hashes don't show up in the actual heading.

FIGURE 4-18:
Using heading levels provides emphasis for cell content.

Other cell content

This chapter (and book) doesn't demonstrate all the kinds of cell content that you can see by using Notebook. However, you can add things like graphics to your notebooks, too. When the time comes, you can output (print) your notebook as a report and use it in presentations of all sorts. The literate programming technique is different from what you may have used in the past, but it has definite advantages, as you see in upcoming chapters.

Understanding the Use of Indentation

As you work through the examples in this book, you see that certain lines are indented. In fact, the examples also provide a fair amount of white space (such as extra lines between lines of code). Python ignores any indentation in your application. The main reason to add indentation is to provide visual cues about your code. In the same way that indentation is used for book outlines, indentation in code shows the relationships between various code elements.

The various uses of indentation will become more familiar as you work your way through the examples in the book. However, you should know at the outset why indentation is used and how it gets put in place. So it's time for another example. The following steps help you create a new example that uses indentation to make the relationship between application elements a lot more apparent and easier to figure out later.

1. **Choose New ⇨ Python3.**

    Jupyter Notebook creates a new notebook for you. The downloadable source uses the filename BPPD_04_Indentation.ipynb, but you can use any name desired.

2. **Type** print("This is a really long line of text that will" +.

    You see the text displayed normally onscreen, just as you expect. The plus sign (+) tells Python that there is additional text to display. Adding text from multiple lines together into a single long piece of text is called *concatenation*. You learn more about using this feature later in the book, so you don't need to worry about it now.

3. **Press Enter.**

    The insertion point doesn't go back to the beginning of the line, as you might expect. Instead, it ends up directly under the first double quote, as shown in Figure 4-19. This feature is called automatic indention and it's one of the features that differentiates a regular text editor from one designed to write code.

FIGURE 4-19:
The Edit window automatically indents some types of text.

4. **Type** "appear on multiple lines in the source code file.") **and press Enter.**

    Notice that the insertion point goes back to the beginning of the line. When Notebook senses that you have reached the end of the code, it automatically outdents the text to its original position.

5. **Click Run.**

You see the output shown in Figure 4-20. Even though the text appears on multiple lines in the source code file, it appears on just one line in the output. The line does break because of the size of the window, but it's actually just one line.

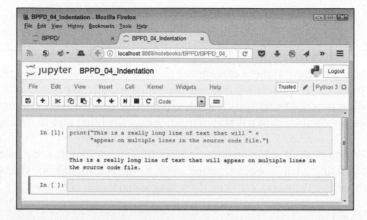

FIGURE 4-20:
Use concatenation to make multiple lines of text appear on a single line in the output.

Adding Comments

People create notes for themselves all the time. When you need to buy groceries, you look through your cabinets, determine what you need, and write it down on a list. When you get to the store, you review your list to remember what you need. Using notes comes in handy for all sorts of needs, such as tracking the course of a conversation between business partners or remembering the essential points of a lecture. Humans need notes to jog their memories. Comments in source code are just another form of note. You add them to the code so that you can remember what task the code performs later. The following sections describe comments in more detail. You can find these examples in the BPPD_04_Comments.ipynb file in the downloadable source.

HEADINGS VERSUS COMMENTS

You may find headings and comments a bit confusing at first. Headings appear in separate cells; comments appear with the source code. They serve different purposes. Headings serve to tell you about an entire code grouping, and individual comments tell you about individual code steps or even lines of code. Even though you use both of them for documentation, each serves a unique purpose. Comments are generally more detailed than headings.

Understanding comments

Computers need some special way to determine that the text you're writing is a comment, not code to execute. Python provides two methods of defining text as a comment and not as code. The first method is the single-line comment. It uses the number sign (#), like this:

```
# This is a comment.
print("Hello from Python!") #This is also a comment.
```

REMEMBER

A single-line comment can appear on a line by itself or it can appear after executable code. It appears on only one line. You typically use a single-line comment for short descriptive text, such as an explanation of a particular bit of code. Notebook shows comments in a distinctive color (usually blue) and in italics.

Python doesn't actually support a multiline comment directly, but you can create one using a triple-quoted string. A multiline comment both starts and ends with three double quotes (""") or three single quotes (''') like this:

```
"""

    Application: Comments.py
    Written by: John
    Purpose: Shows how to use comments.
"""
```

REMEMBER

These lines aren't executed. Python won't display an error message when they appear in your code. However, Notebook treats them differently, as shown in Figure 4-21. Note that the actual Python comments, those preceded by a hash (#) in cell 1, don't generate any output. The triple-quote strings, however, do generate output. If you plan to output your notebook as a report, you need to avoid using triple-quoted strings. (Some IDEs, such as IDLE, ignore the triple-quoted strings completely.)

Unlike standard comments, triple quoted text appears in red, rather than blue and the text isn't in italics. You typically use multiline comments for longer explanations of who created an application, why it was created, and what tasks it performs. Of course, there aren't any hard rules on precisely how you use comments. The main goal is to tell the computer precisely what is and isn't a comment so that it doesn't become confused.

Using comments to leave yourself reminders

A lot of people don't really understand comments — they don't quite know what to do with notes in code. Keep in mind that you might write a piece of code today and then not look at it for years. You need notes to jog your memory so that you remember what task the code performs and why you wrote it. In fact, here are some common reasons to use comments in your code:

>> Reminding yourself about what the code does and why you wrote it

>> Telling others how to maintain your code

>> Making your code accessible to other developers

>> Listing ideas for future updates

>> Providing a list of documentation sources you used to write the code

>> Maintaining a list of improvements you've made

You can use comments in a lot of other ways, too, but these are the most common ways. Look at the way comments are used in the examples in the book, especially as you get to later chapters where the code becomes more complex. As your code becomes more complex, you need to add more comments and make the comments pertinent to what you need to remember about it.

Using comments to keep code from executing

Developers also sometimes use the commenting feature to keep lines of code from executing (referred to as *commenting out*). You might need to do this in order to determine whether a line of code is causing your application to fail. As with any other comment, you can use either single line commenting or multiline commenting. However, when using multiline commenting, you do see the code that isn't executing as part of the output (and it can actually be helpful to see where the code affects the output). Figure 4-22 shows an example of code commenting techniques.

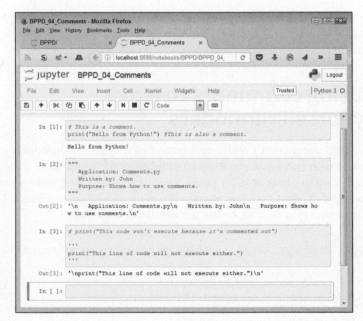

FIGURE 4-22:
Use comments to keep code from executing.

Closing Jupyter Notebook

After you have used the File ➪ Close and Halt command to close each of the notebooks you have open, you can simply close the browser window to end your session. However, the server continues to run in the background. Normally, a Jupyter Notebook window opens, like the one shown in Figure 4-23. This window remains open until you stop the server. Simply press Ctrl+C to end the server session, and the window will close.

FIGURE 4-23:
Make sure to close the server window.

Look again at Figure 4-23 to note a number of commands. These commands tell you what the user interface is doing. By monitoring this window, you can determine what might go wrong during a session. Even though you won't use this feature very often, it's a handy trick to know.

TECHNICAL STUFF

Chapter **5**

Working with Anaconda

naconda provides a powerful Integrated Development Environment (IDE) in the form of Jupyter Notebook. In fact, you can perform every task in this book using just this one utility. That's why this chapter focuses on Jupyter Notebook (simply called Notebook in most places). Unlike most IDEs, Notebook relies on a principle called literate programming that the "Defining why notebooks are useful" section of Chapter 4 describes. This chapter helps you understand how literate programming can help you become more productive when writing Python code.

As part of discovering more about Notebook, you see how to download your code in various forms and how to create code checkpoints to make recovering from errors easier. Working with files effectively is an important part of the development process. Chapter 4 shows only the basics of working with code files; this chapter fills in the details.

Chapter 4 also shows you a few things about cells. You're probably already thinking that cells definitely make certain kinds of coding efforts easier because you can move blocks of code around easily. However, cells can do a lot more, and this chapter tells you about these techniques.

This chapter also helps you understand the mechanics of using Notebook effectively. For example, you might not like how Notebook is configured, so this chapter tells you how to change the configuration. You also need to know how to restart the kernel when things freeze up, and how to obtain help. In addition,

Notebook has features called *magic functions* that really do seem magical. Using these functions doesn't affect your code, but they do affect how you see your code in Notebook and how certain features such as graphics appear. Finally, you need to know how to interact with running processes. In some cases, you need to know what a process is doing in order to make a decision about how to interact with it.

Downloading Your Code

Notebook provides you with a particular kind of coding environment, one that isn't text based, in contrast to many other IDEs. If you were to open an IPython Notebook File (.ipynb, which is the same extension used by Jupyter Notebook), what you would find would be sort of readable, but not really usable. To obtain the special features that Notebook provides, the file must contain additional information not found in a normal text file. Consequently, you find that you must download your code to use it in other environments.

REMEMBER

The "Exporting a notebook" section of Chapter 4 tells how to export your notebook in a form that Notebook understands. However, you may want to download the code into other formats that other applications can use. In fact, the File ⇨ Download As menu contains options for downloading your code in these formats:

>> Python (.py)

>> HTML (.html)

>> Markdown (.md)

>> reST (.rst)

>> LaTeX (.tex)

>> PDF via LaTeX (.pdf)

WARNING

Not all the formats are available all the time. For example, if you want to create a PDF using LaTeX, you must install XeTeX by using the instructions found at https://nbconvert.readthedocs.io/en/latest/install.html#installing-tex. XeTeX provides a rendering engine for creating PDFs.

Depending on your setup, some of the formats might actually open directly in your browser. For example, Figure 5-1 shows how one of the examples from Chapter 4 might look when presented in HTML format. Note that the output will appear precisely as it appears in the file, so what you end up with is a sort of electronic printout. In addition, the content won't always lend itself to modification, such as when using the HTML format.

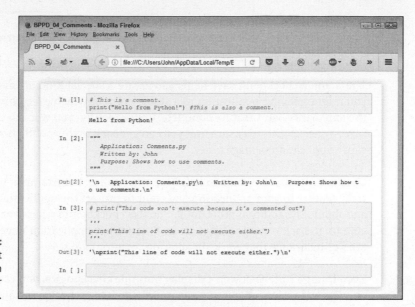

FIGURE 5-1:
Some output formats can open directly in your browser.

Working with Checkpoints

Checkpoints are a Notebook-specific feature that can save you a huge amount of time and embarrassment when used correctly. A *checkpoint* is a kind of interim save and source control combined into a single package. What you get is a picture of your application at a specific point in time.

Defining the uses of checkpoints

Unlike many application saves, a checkpoint is an individual entry. Every time you create a checkpoint, you also create a hidden file. This file resides in a special folder of your project folder. For example, when looking at this book's code, you find the checkpoints in the \BPPD\.ipynb_checkpoints folder. You can go back to this specific checkpoint later, if necessary, to turn back the clock of your development efforts. Checkpoint-type saves occur at these times:

>> **Automatic:** Notebook automatically creates a save for you every 120 seconds by default unless you change this interval using the %autosave magic function (see the "Using the Magic Functions" section of the chapter for details).

>> **Manual checkpoint save:** Generates a separate manually created save file.

All the save options use a single file. Consequently, each save overwrites the previous file. Any save is useful for general backup, ensuring that you have an alternative if an entity damages the original file between occurrences of major events (such as running or closing the application).

The manual checkpoint save helps you create a special kind of save. For example, you might get your application to a stable point at which everything runs, even if the application isn't feature complete. Consequently, you want to create a manual save, a checkpoint, to ensure that you can get back to this point should future edits cause application damage.

Checkpoints can also come in handy at other times. For example, you might add a risky feature to your application and want to protect the application against damage should the addition prove fatal. You use checkpoints whenever you want to be able to go back to a specific point in time during application development. It's a kind of insurance that works in addition to automatic saves.

TIP

Even though Notebook won't display multiple checkpoints, you can keep multiple checkpoints if desired. Simply rename the existing checkpoint and then create a new one. For example, if you name the existing checkpoint BPPD_04_Comments-checkpoint.ipynb, you might rename it to BPPD_04_Comments-checkpoint1.ipynb before you create a new save. To use an older checkpoint, you must rename it back to the original name of checkpoint.ipynb.

Saving a checkpoint

To save a checkpoint, you choose File ⇨ Save and Checkpoint. Notebook automatically saves a copy of the existing notebook in the .ipynb_checkpoints folder using the same name with -checkpoint added. Unless you specifically rename the existing checkpoint, the manual or automatic save will overwrite the existing file. Consequently, all you ever see is a single checkpoint file unless you rename older files manually.

Restoring a checkpoint

To restore a checkpoint, choose the entry found on the File ⇨ Revert to Checkpoint menu. This menu makes it appear that you can have more than one checkpoint file, but the menu never has more than one entry in it. The entry does contain the date and time that you created the checkpoint.

Manipulating Cells

Cells are what make Notebook considerably different from using other IDEs. By using the functionality that cells provide, you can perform all sorts of application manipulations that would otherwise be difficult or error prone using other IDEs, such as moving related code around as a chunk, rather than line-by-line. Chapter 4 shows you a few quick tricks for working with cells. The following sections provide additional techniques that you can use to make cells truly useful.

Adding various cell types

Notebook gives you access to several different cell types. You find out the two types used in this book in Chapter 4. Here's a rundown of all the types that you can use with Notebook:

>> **Code:** Contains interpreted Python code that provides an input and an output area.

>> **Markdown:** Displays special documentation text using the GitHub markup technique, as described at https://help.github.com/categories/writing-on-github/. This book mainly uses markdown cells for headings, but you can include all sorts of information in cells of this type.

>> **Raw NBConvert:** Provides a method for including uninterpreted content within a notebook that affects certain kinds of downloaded output, such as LaTeX. This book doesn't use these kinds of cells because this is a specialty output. You can read more about this topic at https://ipython.org/ipython-doc/3/notebook/nbconvert.html#nbconvert.

>> **Heading (obsolete):** This is an older method of creating headings that you shouldn't use any longer.

Whenever you execute the content of a cell using the Run Cell button or by choosing Cell ⇨ Run Cells and Select Below, and the insertion point is on the last cell, Notebook automatically adds a new cell for you. However, this isn't the only way to add a new cell. For example, you might want to add a new cell in the middle of the notebook. To perform this task, you choose Insert ⇨ Insert Cell Above or Insert ⇨ Insert Cell Below, depending on whether you want to insert a cell above or below the current cell.

Splitting and merging cells

Notebook treats cells as distinct entities. Whatever you do in a cell will affect the application as a whole. However, you can execute or manipulate that individual cell without changing any other cell. In addition, you can execute cells in any order and execute some cells more often than you do others. That's why you need to focus on cell construction: You need to determine whether a cell is independent enough, yet complete enough, to perform a desired task. With this in mind, you may find it necessary to split and merge cells.

Splitting a cell means to create two cells from an existing cell. The split occurs at the current cursor location within the cell. To perform the split, you choose Edit ➪ Split Cell.

Merging a cell means to create a single cell from two existing cells. The cells are merged in the order in which they appear in the notebook, so you must be sure that the cells are in the correct order before you merge them. To perform the merge, you choose Edit ➪ Merge Cell Above or Edit ➪ Merge Cell Below.

Moving cells around

Cells need not stay in the order in which you originally create them. You may find that you need to perform a particular task sooner or later in the process. The simplest way to move a cell is to select the cell and then choose Edit ➪ Move Cell Up or Edit ➪ Move Cell Down. However, these two commands simply move the cells. You might decide to do something completely different.

As do most editors, Notebook comes with a full selection of editing commands. All these commands appear on the Edit menu. Following are editing commands that Notebook provides in addition to the standard movement commands:

- » **Cut Cells:** Removes the selected cell but places it on the Clipboard for later reuse.

- » **Copy Cells:** Places a copy of the selected cell on the Clipboard without removing it.

- » **Paste Cells Above:** Inserts a copy of the cell that appears on the Clipboard above the selected cell.

- » **Paste Cells Below:** Inserts a copy of the cell that appears on the Clipboard below the selected cell.

- » **Delete Cells:** Removes the selected cell without creating any copy.

- » **Undo Delete Cells:** Adds a deleted cell back onto the notebook (there is only one level of undelete, so you must perform this task immediately after a deletion).

Running cells

To see the result of interpreting a cell, even those markdown cells, you need to run the cell. The most common way to perform this task is to click the Run Cell button on the toolbar (the one with the right pointing arrow). However, you might decide that you don't want to run your cells in the default manner. In this case, you have a number of options to choose from on the Cell menu:

>> **Run Cells:** Runs the selected cell while maintaining the current selection.

>> **Run Cells and Select Below (default):** Runs the selected cell and then selects the cell below it. If this is the last cell, Notebook creates a new cell to select.

>> **Run Cells and Insert Below:** Runs the selected cell and then inserts a new cell below it. This is a good option to choose if you're adding new cells in the middle of an application because you get a new cell regardless of whether this is the last cell.

>> **Run All:** Starts at the top and runs every cell in the notebook. When Notebook reaches the bottom, it selects the last cell, but doesn't insert a new one.

>> **Run All Above:** Starts from the current cell and executes all the cells above it in reverse order. You won't find this option in most other IDEs!

>> **Run All Below:** Starts from the current cell and executes all the cells below it in order. When Notebook reaches the bottom, it selects the last cell but doesn't insert a new one.

WARNING

TRUSTING YOUR NOTEBOOK

In the upper-right corner of Notebook, you see a little square box with the words *Not Trusted*. In most cases, it doesn't matter that your notebook is untrusted because of how Python works. However, when dealing with some local or secure resources on a website, you may find that you really do need to place some trust in your notebook.

The fastest, easiest method of overriding the trust issue is to click the Not Trusted button. You see a dialog box that gives you the option of trusting the notebook. Unfortunately, this is also a good way to cause yourself woe with security issues and isn't recommended unless you know that you can trust the source.

Anaconda provides a number of other ways to ensure safe access to secure resources. Performing the extended setup is outside the scope of this book, but you can read about it at https://jupyter-notebook.readthedocs.io/en/latest/security.html. None of the examples in this book require you to run in trusted mode, so you can safely ignore that Not Trusted button for the moment.

Toggling outputs

Sometimes seeing the output from a cell is helpful, but in other cases, the output just gets in the way. In addition, situations that call for starting with a clean output can arise, so you may want to clear the old information. The Cell⇨Current Outputs menu has options that affect just the selected cell, and the Cell⇨All Output menu has options that affect all the cells in the notebook. Here are the options you have for controlling output:

- » **Toggle:** Turns the output on or off, based on a previous condition. The output is still present in its entirety.

- » **Toggle Scrolling:** Reduces the size of long outputs to just the default number of lines. In this way, you can see enough information to know how the cell worked, but not get every detail.

- » **Clear:** Removes the current output. You must rerun the cell in order to generate new output after using this option.

Changing Jupyter Notebook's Appearance

You can modify Notebook's appearance to an extent. In this one respect, you don't get quite as much flexibility with Notebook as you do with other IDEs, but the flexibility is good enough to make the interface usable in most cases. The various options you use are on the View menu:

- » **Toggle Header:** The header is at the top of the display and contains the name of the notebook. (You change the notebook name in the "Creating a new notebook" section of Chapter 4.) It also provides access to the Notebook dashboard when you click Jupyter in the upper left, plus it shows the current save status and lets you log out of Notebook by clicking Logout.

- » **Toggle Toolbar:** The toolbar contains a series of icons that let you perform tasks quickly. The following list describes these icons as they appear from left to right:

  - **Save and Checkpoint:** Saves the current notebook and creates a checkpoint for it.

  - **Insert Cell Below:** Adds a new cell below the selected cell.

  - **Cut Selected Cells:** Removes the current cell and places it on the Clipboard.

- **Copy Selected Cells:** Places a copy of the current cell on the Clipboard without removing it.

- **Paste Cells Below:** Creates a copy of the cell on the Clipboard and places it below the currently selected cell.

- **Move Selected Cells Up:** Moves the selected cell up one position.

- **Move Selected Cells Down:** Moves the selected cell down one position.

- **Run Cell:** Interprets the content of the current cell and selects the next cell. If this is the last cell, Notebook creates a new cell below it. Notebook doesn't interpret Raw NBConvert cells, so nothing happens in this case.

- **Interrupt Kernel:** Stops the kernel from completing the instructions in the current cell.

- **Restart the Kernel:** Stops and then starts the kernel. All variable data is lost during this process.

- **Cell Type Selection:** Chooses one of the cell types described in the "Adding various cell types" section, earlier in this chapter.

- **Open the Command Palette:** Displays the Command Palette dialog box, in which you can search for a particular command. The "Finding commands using the Command Palette" section that follows explains this feature in more detail.

» **Toggle Line Numbers:** Adds or removes line numbers from the code listings. This setting doesn't affect other cell types. The "Working with line numbers" section that follows explains this feature in more detail.

» **Cell Toolbar:** Adds a specific command to the cell toolbar. These commands help you interact in specific ways with the individual cells. The "Using the Cell Toolbar features" section that follows explains this feature in more detail.

Finding commands using the Command Palette

The Command Palette dialog box provides access to the command-mode commands that Notebook supports. Click Open the Command Palette icon on the Toolbar to see the dialog shown in Figure 5-2.

To locate the command you need, simply start typing a phrase that you feel defines the command. For example, you might type **cell** to locate specific cell-related commands. After you find the command you need, you can click it to execute it.

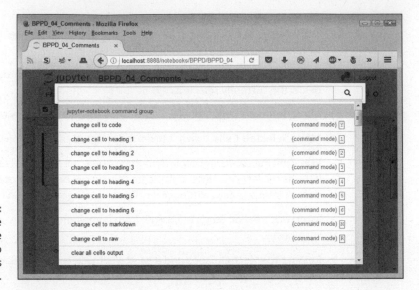

FIGURE 5-2:
Use the
Command Palette
dialog box to
locate commands
you need.

Working with line numbers

Longer listings are hard to work with at times, and when you need to collaborate with others, having a reference can be useful. To display line numbers, choose View ⇨ Toggle Line Numbers. You see line numbers added to all input code cells, as shown in Figure 5-3. Note that the line numbers don't appear in the output.

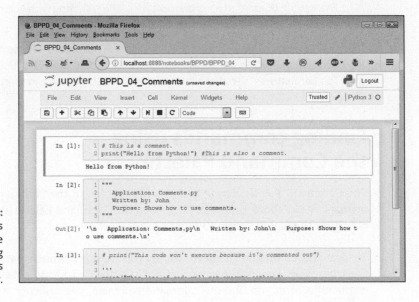

FIGURE 5-3:
Line numbers
make
collaborating
with others
easier.

Using the Cell Toolbar features

Each cell has specific features associated with it. You can add a cell toolbar button to make these features accessibly by using the options on the View ⇨ Cell Toolbar menu. Figure 5-4 shows how a cell appears with the Edit Metadata button in place.

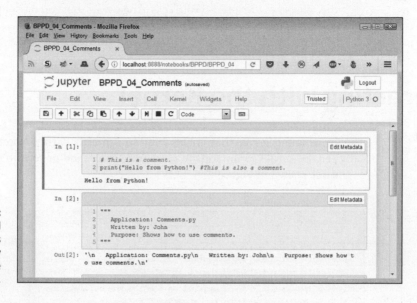

FIGURE 5-4:
Use the cell toolbar buttons to modify underlying code content.

The metadata affects how the cell works. The default settings control both whether the cell is trusted and Notebook will scroll long content. Some of these settings affect only certain kinds of cells. For example, the Raw Cell Format setting affects only Raw NBConvert cells.

You can display only one Cell Toolbar button at a time. So, you can't configure the cells for a slideshow while also adding tags. You must select one feature or the other. Choosing View ⇨ Cell Toolbar ⇨ None removes all the buttons from the display. Here are the Cell Toolbar menu options:

- ≫ **None:** Removes all the Cell Toolbar buttons from the notebook.

- ≫ **Edit Metadata:** Allows configuration of the cell functionality using both standard and custom metadata.

- ≫ **Raw Cell Format:** Selects the kind of data that a Raw NTConvert cell contains. The options include None, LaTeX, reST, HTML, Markdown, Python, and Custom.

- ≫ **Slideshow:** Defines the kind of slide that the cell contains. The options are Slide, Sub-slide, Fragment, Skip, and Notes.

TIP

>> **Attachments:** Presents a list of attachments for the current cell. For example, you can add images or pictures to markdown cells.

>> **Tags:** Manages tags associated with each cell. A *tag* is a piece of information that you provide that helps you understand and classify the cell. The tags are for your use; they mean nothing to Notebook. When you use tags correctly, they enable you to interact with cells in new ways, but you must use the tags consistently to allow tags to work properly.

Interacting with the Kernel

The *kernel* is the server that enables you to run cells within Notebook. You typically see the kernel commands in a separate command or terminal window, such as the one shown in Figure 5-5.

FIGURE 5-5:
The kernel displays its commands in a separate Jupyter Notebook window.

Each entry shows the time the kernel executed the task, which application the command executed, the task it performed, and any resources affected. In most cases, you don't need to do anything with this window, but viewing it can be helpful when you run into problems because you often see error messages that can help you resolve an issue.

You control the kernel in a number of ways. For example, saving a file issues a command to the kernel, which carries the task out for you. However, you also find some kernel-specific commands on the Kernel menu, which are described in the following list:

>> **Interrupt:** Causes the kernel to stop performing the current task without actually shutting the kernel down. You can use this option when you want to do something like stop processing a large dataset.

>> **Restart:** Stops the kernel and starts it again. This option causes you to lose all the variable data. However, in some cases, this is precisely what you need to do when the environment has become dirty with old data.

>> **Restart & Clear Output:** Stops the kernel, starts it again, and clears all the existing cell outputs.

>> **Restart & Run All:** Stops the kernel, starts it again, and then runs every cell starting from the top cell and ending with the last cell. When Notebook reaches the bottom, it selects the last cell but doesn't insert a new one.

>> **Reconnect:** Recreates the connection to the kernel. In some cases, environmental or other issues could cause the application to lose its connection, so you use this option to reestablish the connection without loss of variable data.

>> **Shutdown:** Shuts the kernel down. You may perform this step in preparation for using a different kernel.

>> **Change Kernel:** Selects a different kernel from the list of kernels you have installed. For example, you may want to test an application using various Python versions to ensure that it runs on all of them.

Obtaining Help

The help system in Notebook is designed to provide a certain level of interactivity. For example, when you choose Help ⇨ User Interface Tour, a wizard actually points to various elements of your current notebook and tells you what they are. In this way, you see precisely what each element is used for in a way that also helps you with your current task.

The Help ⇨ Keyboard Shortcuts command provides you with a chart listing the various shortcut commands. To enter command mode, you press Esc first and then type whatever is needed to execute a command. For example, Esc ⇨ F displays the Find and Replace dialog box. As part of using keyboard shortcuts, you can choose Help ⇨ Edit Keyboard Shortcuts to display the Edit Command Mode Shortcuts dialog box, shown in Figure 5-6. You use this dialog box to change how Notebook reacts in command mode.

The Help menu contains two other user interface-specific help entries. The first, Notebook Help, offers extensive online help at http://nbviewer.jupyter.org/ github/ipython/ipython/blob/3.x/examples/Notebook/Index.ipynb. This site contains tutorials and other aids in more effectively using Notebook to perform useful work. The second, Markdown, takes you to https://help.github.com/ articles/getting-started-with-writing-and-formatting-on-github/, where you discover more about formatting the content of markdown cells.

CONSIDERING THE IPYTHON ALTERNATIVE

Chapters 1 through 3 of the book provide insights into using the command-line version of Python. The command shell IPython looks and acts much like the command line provided with Python, but it has a number of interesting add-ons. The most noticeable of these add-ons is the use of color coding for code you type (reducing your chances of making an error). For example, commands appear in green and text appears in yellow. The interface also highlights matching parentheses and other block elements so that you can actually see which block element you're closing.

The help system is another difference between the Python command line and IPython. You get additional access to help, and the information you receive is more detailed. One of the more interesting features in this case is the use of the question mark after the name of any Python object. For example, if you type **print?** and press Enter, you see a quick overview of the print() command. Type **?** and press Enter to see the IPython-specific help overview.

In contrast to the Python command line, IPython also supports many of the Notebook advanced features, such as magic functions, which the "Using the Magic Functions" section of the chapter discusses. These special functions enable you to change how IPython and Notebook display various kinds of Python output, among other things. In sum, when you do need to use a command line, use IPython instead of the command line supplied with Python to obtain added functionality.

TIP

At the bottom of the Help menu, you see the usual About entry. This entry displays a dialog box telling you all about your installation. In some cases, you need this information to obtain help from other Anaconda users. The most important bits of information are the version of Python and Anaconda that you're currently using.

The remainder of the Help menu entries will depend on what you have installed at any given time. Each of these entries is for a specific Python feature (starting with the Python language itself). You generally see all the common libraries as well, such as NumPy and SciPy. All these help entries are designed to make it easier for you to obtain help in creating great code.

Using the Magic Functions

Notebook and its counterpart, IPython, provide you with some special functionality in the form of magic functions. It's kind of amazing to think that these applications offer you magic, but that's precisely what you get with the magic functions. The magic is in the output. For example, instead of displaying graphic output in a separate window, you can chose to display it within the cell, as if by magic (because the cells appear to hold only text). Or you can use magic to check the performance of your application, without all the usual added code that such performance checks require.

A *magic function* begins with either a % or %% sign. Those with a % sign work within the environment and those with a %% sign work at the cell level. For example, if you want to obtain a list of magic functions, type **%lsmagic** and then press Enter in IPython (or run the command in Notebook) to see them, as shown in Figure 5-7. (Note that IPython uses the same input, In, and output, Out, prompts that Notebook uses.)

FIGURE 5-7:
The %lsmagic function displays a list of magic functions for you.

REMEMBER

Not every magic function works with IPython. For example, the %autosave function has no purpose in IPython because IPython doesn't automatically save anything.

Table 5-1 lists a few of the most common magic functions and their purpose. To obtain a full listing, type **%quickref** and press Enter in Notebook (or the IPython console) or check out the full listing at `https://damontallen.github.io/IPython-quick-ref-sheets/`.

TABLE 5-1 ## Common Notebook and IPython Magic Functions

Magic Function	Type Alone Provides Status?	Description
%alias	Yes	Assigns or displays an alias for a system command.
%autocall	Yes	Enables you to call functions without including the parentheses. The settings are Off, Smart (default), and Full. The Smart setting applies the parentheses only if you include an argument with the call.
%automagic	Yes	Enables you to call the line magic functions without including the percent (%) sign. The settings are False (default) and True.
%autosave	Yes	Displays or modifies the intervals between automatic Notebook saves. The default setting is every 120 seconds.
%cd	Yes	Changes directory to a new storage location. You can also use this command to move through the directory history or to change directories to a bookmark.
%cls	No	Clears the screen.
%colors	No	Specifies the colors used to display text associated with prompts, the information system, and exception handlers. You can choose between NoColor (black and white), Linux (default), and LightBG.
%config	Yes	Enables you to configure IPython.
%dhist	Yes	Displays a list of directories visited during the current session.
%file	No	Outputs the name of the file that contains the source code for the object.
%hist	Yes	Displays a list of magic function commands issued during the current session.
%install_ext	No	Installs the specified extension.
%load	No	Loads application code from another source, such as an online example.

Magic Function	Type Alone Provides Status?	Description
%load_ext	No	Loads a Python extension using its module name.
%lsmagic	Yes	Displays a list of the currently available magic functions.
%magic	Yes	Displays a help screen showing information about the magic functions.
%matplotlib	Yes	Sets the backend processor used for plots. Using the inline value displays the plot within the cell for an IPython Notebook file. The possible values are: 'gtk', 'gtk3', 'inline', 'nbagg', 'osx', 'qt', 'qt4', 'qt5', 'tk', and 'wx'.
%paste	No	Pastes the content of the clipboard into the IPython environment.
%pdef	No	Shows how to call the object (assuming that the object is callable).
%pdoc	No	Displays the docstring for an object.
%pinfo	No	Displays detailed information about the object (often more than provided by help alone).
%pinfo2	No	Displays extra detailed information about the object (when available).
%reload_ext	No	Reloads a previously installed extension.
%source	No	Displays the source code for the object (assuming the source is available).
%timeit	No	Calculates the best performance time for an instruction.
%%timeit	No	Calculates the best time performance for all the instructions in a cell, apart from the one placed on the same cell line as the cell magic (which could therefore be an initialization instruction).
%unalias	No	Removes a previously created alias from the list.
%unload_ext	No	Unloads the specified extension.
%%writefile	No	Writes the contents of a cell to the specified file.

Viewing the Running Processes

The main Notebook page, where you choose which notebooks to open, actually has three tabs. You normally interact with the Files tab. The Clusters tab is no longer used, so you don't need to worry about it. However, the Running tab, shown in Figure 5-8, does contain some useful information in the form of terminals and open notebooks.

FIGURE 5-8:
View the terminals connected to your system and the open notebooks.

The terminals' part of the equation only comes into play when you configure your server to allow multiple users. You won't use this feature in this book, so it isn't discussed. However, you can get information about using terminals at sites such as `https://software.intel.com/en-us/dl-training-tool-devguide-using-jupyter-notebook-terminal-console` and `http://jupyter-notebook.readthe docs.io/en/latest/examples/Notebook/Connecting%20with%20the%20Qt%20Console.html`.

The other element on the Running tab is the Notebooks list, shown in Figure 5-8. Whenever you run a new notebook, you see its entry added to the list. In this case, a single notebook is running. You can see that the notebook relies on a Python 3 kernel.

WARNING

You also have the option of shutting the notebook down. Generally, you want to use the File ⇨ Close and Halt command to shut down a notebook instead of closing it this way to prevent data loss, but this option can be helpful when the notebook isn't responding for whatever reason.

2 Talking the Talk

Chapter **6**

Storing and Modifying Information

C hapter 3 introduces you to CRUD, Create, Read, Update, and Delete — not that Chapter 3 contains cruddy material. This acronym provides an easy method to remember precisely what tasks all computer programs perform with information you want to manage. Of course, geeks use a special term for information — data, but either information or data works fine for this book.

REMEMBER

To make information useful, you have to have some means of storing it permanently. Otherwise, every time you turned the computer off, all your information would be gone and the computer would provide limited value. In addition, Python must provide some rules for modifying information. The alternative is to have applications running amok, changing information in any and every conceivable manner. This chapter is about controlling information — defining how information is stored permanently and manipulated by applications you create. You can find the source code for this chapter in the BPPD_06_Storing_And_Modifying_Information.ipynb file provided with the downloadable source code, as described in the book's Introduction.

Storing Information

An application requires fast access to information or else it will take a long time to complete tasks. As a result, applications store information in memory. However, memory is temporary. When you turn off the machine, the information must be stored in some permanent form, such as on your hard drive, a Universal Serial Bus (USB) flash drive, a Secure Digital (SD) card, or on the Internet using something like Anaconda Cloud. In addition, you must also consider the form of the information, such as whether it's a number or text. The following sections discuss the issue of storing information as part of an application in more detail.

Seeing variables as storage boxes

When working with applications, you store information in variables. A *variable* is a kind of storage box. Whenever you want to work with the information, you access it using the variable. If you have new information you want to store, you put it in a variable. Changing information means accessing the variable first and then storing the new value in the variable. Just as you store things in boxes in the real world, so you store things in variables (a kind of storage box) when working with applications.

REMEMBER

Computers are actually pretty tidy. Each variable stores just one piece of information. Using this technique makes it easy to find the particular piece of information you need — unlike in your closet, where things from ancient Egypt could be hidden. Even though the examples you work with in previous chapters don't use variables, most applications rely heavily on variables to make working with information easier.

Using the right box to store the data

People tend to store things in the wrong sort of box. For example, you might find a pair of shoes in a garment bag and a supply of pens in a shoebox. However, Python likes to be neat. As a result, you find numbers stored in one sort of variable and text stored in an entirely different kind of variable. Yes, you use variables in both cases, but the variable is designed to store a particular kind of information. Using specialized variables makes it possible to work with the information inside in particular ways. You don't need to worry about the details just yet — just keep in mind that each kind of information is stored in a special kind of variable.

TECHNICAL STUFF

Python uses specialized variables to store information to make things easy for the programmer and to ensure that the information remains safe. However, computers don't actually know about information types. All that the computer knows about are 0s and 1s, which is the absence or presence of a voltage. At a higher level, computers do work with numbers, but that's the extent of what computers do. Numbers, letters, dates, times, and any other kind of information you can think about all come down to 0s and 1s in the computer system. For example, the letter *A* is actually stored as 01000001 or the number 65. The computer has no concept of the letter *A* or of a date such as 8/31/2017.

Defining the Essential Python Data Types

Every programming language defines variables that hold specific kinds of information, and Python is no exception. The specific kind of variable is called a *data type*. Knowing the data type of a variable is important because it tells you what kind of information you find inside. In addition, when you want to store information in a variable, you need a variable of the correct data type to do it. Python doesn't allow you to store text in a variable designed to hold numeric information. Doing so would damage the text and cause problems with the application. You can generally classify Python data types as numeric, string, and Boolean, although there really isn't any limit on just how you can view them. The following sections describe each of the standard Python data types within these classifications.

Putting information into variables

To place a value into any variable, you make an assignment using the assignment operator (=). Chapter 7 discusses the whole range of basic Python operators in more detail, but you need to know how to use this particular operator to some extent now. For example, to place the number 5 into a variable named myVar, you type **myVar = 5** and press Enter at the Python prompt. Even though Python doesn't provide any additional information to you, you can always type the variable name and press Enter to see the value it contains, as shown in Figure 6-1.

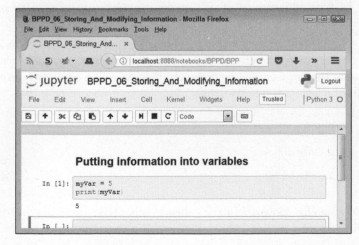

FIGURE 6-1:
Use the assignment operator to place information into a variable.

Understanding the numeric types

Humans tend to think about numbers in general terms. We view 1 and 1.0 as being the same number — one of them simply has a decimal point. However, as far as we're concerned, the two numbers are equal and we could easily use them interchangeably. Python views them as being different kinds of numbers because each form requires a different kind of processing. The following sections describe the integer, floating-point, and complex number classes of data types that Python supports.

Integers

Any whole number is an *integer*. For example, the value 1 is a whole number, so it's an integer. On the other hand, 1.0 isn't a whole number; it has a decimal part to it, so it's not an integer. Integers are represented by the int data type.

REMEMBER

As with storage boxes, variables have capacity limits. Trying to stuff a value that's too large into a storage box results in an error. On most platforms, you can store numbers between −9,223,372,036,854,775,808 and 9,223,372,036,854,775,807 within an int (which is the maximum value that fits in a 64-bit variable). Even though that's a really large number, it isn't infinite.

When working with the int type, you have access to a number of interesting features. Many of them appear later in the book, but one feature is the ability to use different numeric bases:

>> **Base 2:** Uses only 0 and 1 as numbers.

>> **Base 8:** Uses the numbers 0 through 7.

>> **Base 10:** Uses the usual numeric system.

>> **Base 16:** Is also called *hex* and uses the numbers 0 through 9 and the letters A through F to create 16 different possible values.

To tell Python when to use bases other than base 10, you add a 0 and a special letter to the number. For example, 0b100 is the value one-zero-zero in base 2. Here are the letters you normally use:

>> **b:** Base 2

>> **o:** Base 8

>> **x:** Base 16

You can also convert numeric values to other bases by using the bin(), oct(), and hex() commands. So, putting everything together, you can see how to convert between bases using the commands shown in Figure 6-2. Try the command shown in the figure yourself so that you can see how the various bases work. Using a different base actually makes things easier in many situations, and you'll encounter some of those situations later in the book. For now, all you really need to know is that integers support different numeric bases.

FIGURE 6-2:
Integers have many interesting features, including the capability to use different numeric bases.

Understanding the numeric types
Integers

```
In [2]:  Test = 0b100
         print("100 Binary: ", Test)

         Test = 0o100
         print("100 Octal: ", Test)

         Test = 100
         print ("100 Decimal: ", Test)

         Test = 0x100
         print("100 Hexadecimal:", Test)

         print(bin(Test))
         print(oct(Test))
         print(hex(Test))

         100 Binary:  4
         100 Octal:  64
         100 Decimal:  100
         100 Hexadecimal: 256
         0b100000000
         0o400
         0x100
```

Floating-point values

Any number that includes a decimal portion is a floating-point value. For example, 1.0 has a decimal part, so it's a floating-point value. Many people get confused about whole numbers and floating-point numbers, but the difference is easy to remember. If you see a decimal in the number, then it's a floating-point value. Python stores floating-point values in the float data type.

REMEMBER

Floating-point values have an advantage over integer values in that you can store immensely large or incredibly small values in them. As with integer variables, floating-point variables have a storage capacity. In their case, the maximum value that a variable can contain is $\pm 1.7976931348623157 \times 10^{308}$ and the minimum value that a variable can contain is $\pm 2.2250738585072014 \times 10^{-308}$ on most platforms.

When working with floating-point values, you can assign the information to the variable in a number of ways. The two most common methods are to provide the number directly and to use scientific notation. When using scientific notation, an *e* separates the number from its exponent. Figure 6-3 shows both methods of making an assignment. Notice that using a negative exponent results in a fractional value.

UNDERSTANDING THE NEED FOR MULTIPLE NUMBER TYPES

A lot of new developers (and even some older ones) have a hard time understanding why there is a need for more than one numeric type. After all, humans can use just one kind of number. To understand the need for multiple number types, you have to understand a little about how a computer works with numbers.

An integer is stored in the computer as simply a series of bits that the computer reads directly. A value of 0100 in binary equates to a value of 4 in decimal. On the other hand, numbers that have decimal points are stored in an entirely different manner. Think back to all those classes you slept through on exponents in school — they actually come in handy sometimes. A floating-point number is stored as a sign bit (plus or minus), *mantissa* (the fractional part of the number), and *exponent* (the power of 2). (Some texts use the term *significand* in place of mantissa — the terms are interchangeable.) To obtain the floating-point value, you use the equation:

```
Value = Mantissa * 2^Exponent
```

At one time, computers all used different floating-point representations, but they all use the IEEE-754 standard now. You can read about this standard at `http://grouper.ieee.org/groups/754/`. A full explanation of precisely how floating-point numbers work is outside the scope of this book, but you can read a fairly understandable description at `http://www.cprogramming.com/tutorial/floating_point/understanding_floating_point_representation.html`. Nothing helps you understand a concept like playing with the values. You can find a really interesting floating-point number converter at `http://www.h-schmidt.net/FloatConverter/IEEE754.html`, where you can click the individual bits (to turn them off or on) and see the floating-point number that results.

As you might imagine, floating-point numbers tend to consume more space in memory because of their complexity. In addition, they use an entirely different area of the processor — one that works more slowly than the part used for integer math. Finally, integers are precise, as contrasted to floating-point numbers, which can't precisely represent some numbers, so you get an approximation instead. However, floating-point variables can store much larger numbers. The bottom line is that decimals are unavoidable in the real world, so you need floating-point numbers, but using integers when you can reduces the amount of memory your application consumes and helps it work faster. Computer systems have many trade-offs, and this one is unavoidable.

Floating-point values

```
In [3]:  Test = 255.0
         print("Direct Assignment: ", Test)

         Test = 2.55e2
         print("Scientific Notation: ", Test)

         Test = 2.55e-2
         print("Negative Exponent: ", Test)

         Direct Assignment:  255.0
         Scientific Notation:  255.0
         Negative Exponent:  0.0255
```

Complex numbers

You may or may not remember complex numbers from school. A *complex number* consists of a real number and an imaginary number that are paired together. Just in case you've completely forgotten about complex numbers, you can read about them at http://www.mathsisfun.com/numbers/complex-numbers.html. Real-world uses for complex numbers include:

>> Electrical engineering

>> Fluid dynamics

>> Quantum mechanics

>> Computer graphics

>> Dynamic systems

Complex numbers have other uses, too, but this list should give you some ideas. In general, if you aren't involved in any of these disciplines, you probably won't ever encounter complex numbers. However, Python is one of the few languages that provides a built-in data type to support them. As you progress through the book, you find other ways in which Python lends itself especially well to science and engineering.

The imaginary part of a complex number always appears with a *j* after it. So, if you want to create a complex number with 3 as the real part and 4 as the imaginary part, you make an assignment like this:

```
myComplex = 3 + 4j
```

If you want to see the real part of the variable, you simply type **myComplex.real** at the Python prompt and press Enter. Likewise, if you want to see the imaginary part of the variable, you type **myComplex.imag** at the Python prompt and press Enter.

Understanding Boolean values

It may seem amazing, but computers always give you a straight answer! A computer will never provide "maybe" as output. Every answer you get is either True or False. In fact, there is an entire branch of mathematics called Boolean algebra that was originally defined by George Boole (a super-geek of his time) that computers rely upon to make decisions. Contrary to common belief, Boolean algebra has existed since 1854 — long before the time of computers.

When using Boolean value in Python, you rely on the bool type. A variable of this type can contain only two values: True or False. You can assign a value by using the True or False keywords, or you can create an expression that defines a logical idea that equates to true or false. For example, you could say, myBool = 1 > 2, which would equate to False because 1 is most definitely not greater than 2. You see the bool type used extensively in the book, so don't worry about understanding this concept right now.

Understanding strings

Of all the data types, strings are the most easily understood by humans and not understood at all by computers. If you have read the previous chapters in this book, you have already seen strings used quite often. For example, all the example code in Chapter 4 relies on strings. A *string* is simply any grouping of characters you place within double quotes. For example, myString = "Python is a great language." assigns a string of characters to myString.

The computer doesn't see letters at all. Every letter you use is represented by a number in memory. For example, the letter *A* is actually the number 65. To see this for yourself, type **print(ord("A"))** at the Python prompt and press Enter. You see 65 as output. You can convert any single letter to its numeric equivalent by using the ord( ) command.

Because the computer doesn't really understand strings, but strings are so useful in writing applications, you sometimes need to convert a string to a number. You can use the int() and float() commands to perform this conversion. For example, if you type **myInt = int("123")** and press Enter at the Python prompt, you create an int named myInt that contains the value 123. Figure 6-4 shows how you can perform this task and validate the content and type of myInt.

FIGURE 6-4:
Converting a
string to a
number is easy
by using the
int() and
float()
commands.

Understanding strings

```
In [6]: print(ord("A"))

        myInt = int("123")
        print(myInt)

        print(type(myInt))
        65
        123
        <class 'int'>
```

You can convert numbers to a string as well by using the str() command. For example, if you type **myStr = str(1234.56)** and press Enter, you create a string containing the value "1234.56" and assign it to myStr. Figure 6-5 shows this type of conversion and the test you can perform on it. The point is that you can go back and forth between strings and numbers with great ease. Later chapters demonstrate how these conversions make a lot of seemingly impossible tasks quite doable.

FIGURE 6-5:
You can convert
numbers to
strings as well.

```
In [7]: myStr = str(1234.56)
        print(myStr)
        print(type(myStr))
        1234.56
        <class 'str'>
```

Working with Dates and Times

Dates and times are items that most people work with quite a bit. Society bases almost everything on the date and time that a task needs to be or was completed. We make appointments and plan events for specific dates and times. Most of our day revolves around the clock. Because of the time-oriented nature of humans, it's a good idea to look at how Python deals with interacting with dates and time (especially storing these values for later use). As with everything else, computers understand only numbers — the date and time don't really exist.

REMEMBER

To work with dates and times, you need to perform a special task in Python. When writing computer books, chicken-and-egg scenarios always arise, and this is one of them. To use dates and times, you must issue a special `import datetime` command. Technically, this act is called *importing a package,* and you learn more about it in Chapter 11. Don't worry how the command works right now — just use it whenever you want to do something with date and time.

Computers do have clocks inside them, but the clocks are for the humans using the computer. Yes, some software also depends on the clock, but again, the emphasis is on human needs rather than anything the computer might require. To get the current time, you can simply type **datetime.datetime.now()** and press Enter. You see the full date and time information as found on your computer's clock (see Figure 6-6).

FIGURE 6-6:
Get the current date and time by using the now() command.

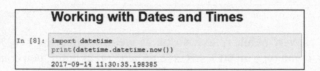

```
Working with Dates and Times
In [8]:   import datetime
          print(datetime.datetime.now())
          2017-09-14 11:30:35.198385
```

You may have noticed that the date and time are a little hard to read in the existing format. Say that you want to get just the current date, in a readable format. It's time to combine a few things you discovered in previous sections to accomplish that task. Type **str(datetime.datetime.now().date())** and press Enter. Figure 6-7 shows that you now have something a little more usable.

FIGURE 6-7:
Make the date and time more readable by using the str() command.

```
In [9]:   print(str(datetime.datetime.now().date()))
          2017-09-14
```

Interestingly enough, Python also has a `time()` command, which you can use to obtain the current time. You can obtain separate values for each of the components that make up date and time by using the `day`, `month`, `year`, `hour`, `minute`, `second`, and `microsecond` values. Later chapters help you understand how to use these various date and time features to keep application users informed about the current date and time on their system.

Chapter **7**

Managing Information

Whether you use the term *information* or *data* to refer to the content that applications manage, the fact is that you must provide some means of working with it or your application really doesn't have a purpose. Throughout the rest of the book, you see *information* and *data* used interchangeably because they really are the same thing, and in real-world situations, you'll encounter them both, so getting used to both is a good idea. No matter which term you use, you need some means of assigning data to variables, modifying the content of those variables to achieve specific goals, and comparing the result you receive with desired results. This chapter addresses all three requirements so that you can start to control data within your applications.

Also essential is to start working through methods of keeping your code understandable. Yes, you could write your application as a really long procedure, but trying to understand such a procedure is incredibly hard, and you'd find yourself repeating some steps because they must be done more than once. Functions are one way for you to package code so that you can more easily understand and reuse as needed.

Applications also need to interact with the user. Yes, some perfectly usable applications are out there that don't really interact with the user, but they're extremely rare and don't really do much, for the most part. In order to provide a useful service, most applications interact with the user to discover how the user wants to manage data. You get an overview of this process in this chapter. Of course, you visit the topic of user interaction quite often throughout the book because it's an important topic.

Controlling How Python Views Data

As discussed in Chapter 6, all data on your computer is stored as 0s and 1s. The computer doesn't understand the concept of letters, Boolean values, dates, times, or any other kind of information except numbers. In addition, a computer's capability to work with numbers is both inflexible and relatively simplistic. When you work with a string in Python, you're depending on Python to translate the concept of a string into a form the computer can understand. The storage containers that your application creates and uses in the form of variables tell Python how to treat the 0s and 1s that the computer has stored. So, you need to understand that the Python view of data isn't the same as your view of data or the computer's view of data — Python acts as an intermediary to make your applications functional.

REMEMBER

To manage data within an application, the application must control the way in which Python views the data. The use of operators, packaging methods such as functions, and the introduction of user input all help applications control data. All these techniques rely, in part, on making comparisons. Determining what to do next means understanding what state the data is in now as compared to some other state. If the variable contains the name John now, but you really want it to contain Mary instead, then you first need to know that it does in fact contain John. Only then can you make the decision to change the content of the variable to Mary.

Making comparisons

Python's main method for making comparisons is through the use of operators. In fact, operators play a major role in manipulating data as well. The upcoming "Working with Operators" section discusses how operators work and how you can use them in applications to control data in various ways. Later chapters use operators extensively as you discover techniques for creating applications that can make decisions, perform tasks repetitively, and interact with the user in interesting ways. However, the basic idea behind operators is that they help applications perform various types of comparisons.

In some cases, you use some fancy methods for performing comparisons in an application. For example, you can compare the output of two functions (as described in the "Comparing function output" section, later in this chapter). With Python, you can perform comparisons at a number of levels so that you can manage data without a problem in your application. Using these techniques hides detail so that you can focus on the point of the comparison and define how to react to that comparison rather than become mired in detail. Your choice of techniques for performing comparisons affects the manner in which Python views the data and determines the sorts of things you can do to manage the data after the comparison is made. All this functionality might seem absurdly complex at the moment, but the important point to remember is that applications require comparisons in order to interact with data correctly.

Understanding how computers make comparisons

Computers don't understand packaging, such as functions, or any of the other structures that you create with Python. All this packaging is for your benefit, not the computer's. However, computers do directly support the concept of operators. Most Python operators have a direct corollary with a command that the computer understands directly. For example, when you ask whether one number is greater than another number, the computer can actually perform this computation directly, using an operator. (The upcoming section explains operators in detail.)

REMEMBER

Some comparisons aren't direct. Computers work only with numbers. So, when you ask Python to compare two strings, what Python actually does is compare the numeric value of each character in the string. For example, the letter *A* is actually the number 65 in the computer. A lowercase letter *a* has a different numeric value — 97. As a result, even though you might see ABC as being equal to abc, the computer doesn't agree — it sees them as different because the numeric values of their individual letters are different.

Working with Operators

Operators are the basis for both control and management of data within applications. You use operators to define how one piece of data is compared to another and to modify the information within a single variable. In fact, operators are essential to performing any sort of math-related task and to assigning data to variables in the first place.

REMEMBER

When using an operator, you must supply either a variable or an expression. You already know that a variable is a kind of storage box used to hold data. An *expression* is an equation or formula that provides a description of a mathematical concept. In most cases, the result of evaluating an expression is a Boolean (true or false) value. The following sections describe operators in detail because you use them everywhere throughout the rest of the book.

Defining the operators

An *operator* accepts one or more inputs in the form of variables or expressions, performs a task (such as comparison or addition), and then provides an output consistent with that task. Operators are classified partially by their effect and partially by the number of elements they require. For example, a unary operator works with a single variable or expression; a binary operator requires two.

REMEMBER

The elements provided as input to an operator are called *operands*. The operand on the left side of the operator is called the left operand, while the operand on the right side of the operator is called the right operand. The following list shows the categories of operators that you use within Python:

>> Unary

>> Arithmetic

>> Relational

>> Logical

>> Bitwise

>> Assignment

>> Membership

>> Identity

Each of these categories performs a specific task. For example, the arithmetic operators perform math-based tasks, while relational operators perform comparisons. The following sections describe the operators based on the category in which they appear.

UNDERSTANDING PYTHON'S ONE TERNARY OPERATOR

A ternary operator requires three elements. Python supports just one such operator, and you use it to determine the truth value of an expression. This ternary operator takes the following form (it apparently has no actual name, but you can call it the if...else operator if desired):

```
TrueValue if Expression else FalseValue
```

When the Expression is true, the operator outputs TrueValue. When the expression is false, it outputs FalseValue. As an example, if you type

```
"Hello" if True else "Goodbye"
```

the operator outputs a response of 'Hello'. However, if you type

```
"Hello" if False else "Goodbye"
```

the operator outputs a response of 'Goodbye'. This is a handy operator for times when you need to make a quick decision and don't want to write a lot of code to do it.

One of the advantages of using Python is that it normally has more than one way to do things. Python has an alternative form of this ternary operator — an even shorter short-cut. It takes the following form:

```
(FalseValue, TrueValue)[Expression]
```

As before, when Expression is true, the operator outputs TrueValue; otherwise, it outputs FalseValue. Notice that the TrueValue and FalseValue elements are reversed in this case. An example of this version is

```
("Hello", "Goodbye")[True]
```

In this case, the output of the operator is 'Goodbye' because that's the value in the True Value position. Of the two forms, the first is a little clearer, while the second is shorter.

Unary

Unary operators require a single variable or expression as input. You often use these operators as part of a decision-making process. For example, you might want to find something that isn't like something else. Table 7-1 shows the unary operators.

TABLE 7-1   Python Unary Operators

Operator	Description	Example
~	Inverts the bits in a number so that all the 0 bits become 1 bits and vice versa.	~4 results in a value of –5
–	Negates the original value so that positive becomes negative and vice versa.	–(–4) results in 4 and –4 results in –4
+	Is provided purely for the sake of completeness. This operator returns the same value that you provide as input.	+4 results in a value of 4

Arithmetic

Computers are known for their capability to perform complex math. However, the complex tasks that computers perform are often based on much simpler math tasks, such as addition. Python provides access to libraries that help you perform complex math tasks, but you can always create your own libraries of math functions using the simple operators found in Table 7-2.

TABLE 7-2   Python Arithmetic Operators

Operator	Description	Example
+	Adds two values together	5 + 2 = 7
–	Subtracts the right operand from the left operand	5 – 2 = 3
*	Multiplies the right operand by the left operand	5 * 2 = 10
/	Divides the left operand by the right operand	5 / 2 = 2.5
%	Divides the left operand by the right operand and returns the remainder	5 % 2 = 1
**	Calculates the exponential value of the right operand by the left operand	5 ** 2 = 25
//	Performs integer division, in which the left operand is divided by the right operand and only the whole number is returned (also called floor division)	5 // 2 = 2

Relational

The relational operators compare one value to another and tell you when the relationship you've provided is true. For example, 1 is less than 2, but 1 is never greater than 2. The truth value of relations is often used to make decisions in your applications to ensure that the condition for performing a specific task is met. Table 7-3 describes the relational operators.

TABLE 7-3 ## Python Relational Operators

Operator	Description	Example
==	Determines whether two values are equal. Notice that the relational operator uses two equals signs. A mistake many developers make is using just one equals sign, which results in one value being assigned to another.	1 == 2 is False
!=	Determines whether two values are not equal. Some older versions of Python allowed you to use the <> operator in place of the != operator. Using the <> operator results in an error in current versions of Python.	1 != 2 is True
>	Verifies that the left operand value is greater than the right operand value.	1 > 2 is False
<	Verifies that the left operand value is less than the right operand value.	1 < 2 is True
>=	Verifies that the left operand value is greater than or equal to the right operand value.	1 >= 2 is False
<=	Verifies that the left operand value is less than or equal to the right operand value.	1 <= 2 is True

Logical

The logical operators combine the true or false value of variables or expressions so that you can determine their resultant truth value. You use the logical operators to create Boolean expressions that help determine whether to perform tasks. Table 7-4 describes the logical operators.

TABLE 7-4 ## Python Logical Operators

Operator	Description	Example
and	Determines whether both operands are true.	True and True is True
		True and False is False
		False and True is False
		False and False is False
or	Determines when one of two operands is true.	True or True is True
		True or False is True
		False or True is True
		False or False is False
not	Negates the truth value of a single operand. A true value becomes false and a false value becomes true.	not True is False
		not False is True

Bitwise

The bitwise operators interact with the individual bits in a number. For example, the number 6 is actually 0b0110 in binary.

TIP

If your binary is a little rusty, you can use the handy Binary to Decimal to Hexadecimal Converter at http://www.mathsisfun.com/binary-decimal-hexadecimal-converter.html. You need to enable JavaScript to make the site work.

A bitwise operator would interact with each bit within the number in a specific way. When working with a logical bitwise operator, a value of 0 counts as false and a value of 1 counts as true. Table 7-5 describes the bitwise operators.

TABLE 7-5   **Python Bitwise Operators**

Operator	Description	Example
& (And)	Determines whether both individual bits within two operators are true and sets the resulting bit to true when they are.	0b1100 & 0b0110 = 0b0100
| (Or)	Determines whether either of the individual bits within two operators is true and sets the resulting bit to true when one of them is.	0b1100 | 0b0110 = 0b1110
^ (Exclusive or)	Determines whether just one of the individual bits within two operators is true and sets the resulting bit to true when one is. When both bits are true or both bits are false, the result is false.	0b1100 ^ 0b0110 = 0b1010
~ (One's complement)	Calculates the one's complement value of a number.	~0b1100 = –0b1101 ~0b0110 = –0b0111
<< (Left shift)	Shifts the bits in the left operand left by the value of the right operand. All new bits are set to 0 and all bits that flow off the end are lost.	0b00110011 << 2 = 0b11001100
>> (Right shift)	Shifts the bits in the left operand right by the value of the right operand. All new bits are set to 0 and all bits that flow off the end are lost.	0b00110011 >> 2 = 0b00001100

Assignment

The assignment operators place data within a variable. The simple assignment operator appears in previous chapters of the book, but Python offers a number of other interesting assignment operators that you can use. These other assignment operators can perform mathematical tasks during the assignment process, which makes it possible to combine assignment with a math operation. Table 7-6 describes the assignment operators. For this particular table, the initial value of MyVar in the Example column is 5.

TABLE 7-6 **Python Assignment Operators**

Operator	Description	Example
=	Assigns the value found in the right operand to the left operand.	MyVar = 5 results in MyVar containing 5
+=	Adds the value found in the right operand to the value found in the left operand and places the result in the left operand.	MyVar += 2 results in MyVar containing 7
−=	Subtracts the value found in the right operand from the value found in the left operand and places the result in the left operand.	MyVar −= 2 results in MyVar containing 3
*=	Multiplies the value found in the right operand by the value found in the left operand and places the result in the left operand.	MyVar *= 2 results in MyVar containing 10
/=	Divides the value found in the left operand by the value found in the right operand and places the result in the left operand.	MyVar /= 2 results in MyVar containing 2.5
%=	Divides the value found in the left operand by the value found in the right operand and places the remainder in the left operand.	MyVar %= 2 results in MyVar containing 1
**=	Determines the exponential value found in the left operand when raised to the power of the value found in the right operand and places the result in the left operand.	MyVar **= 2 results in MyVar containing 25
//=	Divides the value found in the left operand by the value found in the right operand and places the integer (whole number) result in the left operand.	MyVar //= 2 results in MyVar containing 2

Membership

The membership operators detect the appearance of a value within a list or sequence and then output the truth value of that appearance. Think of the membership operators as you would a search routine for a database. You enter a value that you think should appear in the database, and the search routine finds it for you or reports that the value doesn't exist in the database. Table 7-7 describes the membership operators.

TABLE 7-7   Python Membership Operators

Operator	Description	Example
In	Determines whether the value in the left operand appears in the sequence found in the right operand.	"Hello" in "Hello Goodbye" is True
not in	Determines whether the value in the left operand is missing from the sequence found in the right operand.	"Hello" not in "Hello Goodbye" is False

Identity

The identity operators determine whether a value or expression is of a certain class or type. You use identity operators to ensure that you're actually working with the sort of information that you think you are. Using the identity operators can help you avoid errors in your application or determine the sort of processing a value requires. Table 7-8 describes the identity operators.

TABLE 7-8   Python Identity Operators

Operator	Description	Example
Is	Evaluates to true when the type of the value or expression in the right operand points to the same type in the left operand.	type(2) is int is True
is not	Evaluates to true when the type of the value or expression in the right operand points to a different type than the value or expression in the left operand.	type(2) is not int is False

Understanding operator precedence

When you create simple statements that contain just one operator, the order of determining the output of that operator is also simple. However, when you start working with multiple operators, it becomes necessary to determine which operator to evaluate first. For example, you should know whether 1 + 2 * 3 evaluates to 7 (where the multiplication is done first) or 9 (where the addition is done first). An order of operator precedence tells you that the answer is 7 unless you use parentheses to override the default order. In this case, (1 + 2) * 3 would evaluate to 9 because the parentheses have a higher order of precedence than multiplication does. Table 7-9 defines the order of operator precedence for Python.

TABLE 7-9   **Python Operator Precedence**

Operator	Description
( )	You use parentheses to group expressions and to override the default precedence so that you can force an operation of lower precedence (such as addition) to take precedence over an operation of higher precedence (such as multiplication).
**	Exponentiation raises the value of the left operand to the power of the right operand.
~ + -	Unary operators interact with a single variable or expression.
* / % //	Multiply, divide, modulo, and floor division.
+ -	Addition and subtraction.
>> <<	Right and left bitwise shift.
&	Bitwise AND.
^ |	Bitwise exclusive OR and standard OR.
<= < > >=	Comparison operators.
== !=	Equality operators.
= %= /= //= -= += *= **=	Assignment operators.
Is is not	Identity operators.
In not in	Membership operators.
not or and	Logical operators.

Creating and Using Functions

To manage information properly, you need to organize the tools used to perform the required tasks. Each line of code that you create performs a specific task, and you combine these lines of code to achieve a desired result. Sometimes you need to repeat the instructions with different data, and in some cases your code becomes so long that keeping track of what each part does is hard. Functions serve as organization tools that keep your code neat and tidy. In addition, functions make it easy to reuse the instructions you've created as needed with different data. This section of the chapter tells you all about functions. More important, in this section you start creating your first serious applications in the same way that professional developers do.

Viewing functions as code packages

You go to your closet, open the door, and everything spills out. In fact, it's an avalanche, and you're lucky that you've survived. That bowling ball in the top shelf could have done some severe damage! However, you're armed with storage boxes and soon you have everything in the closet in neatly organized boxes. The shoes go in one box, games in another, and old cards and letters in yet another. After you're done, you can find anything you want in the closet without fear of injury. Functions are just like that: They take messy code and place it in packages that make it easy to see what you have and understand how it works.

REMEMBER

Commentaries abound on just what functions are and why they're necessary, but when you boil down all that text, it comes down to a single idea: Functions provide a means of packaging code to make it easy to find and access. If you can think of functions as organizers, you find that working with them is much easier. For example, you can avoid the problem that many developers have of stuffing the wrong items in a function. All your functions will have a single purpose, just like those storage boxes in the closet.

Understanding code reusability

You go to your closet, take out new pants and shirt, remove the labels, and put them on. At the end of the day, you take everything off and throw it in the trash. Hmmm . . . That really isn't what most people do. Most people take the clothes off, wash them, and then put them back into the closet for reuse. Functions are reusable, too. No one wants to keep repeating the same task; it becomes monotonous and boring. When you create a function, you define a package of code that you can use over and over to perform the same task. All you need to do is tell the computer to perform a specific task by telling it which function to use. The computer faithfully executes each instruction in the function absolutely every time you ask it to do so.

REMEMBER

When you work with functions, the code that needs services from the function is named the *caller*, and it calls upon the function to perform tasks for it. Much of the information you see about functions refers to the caller. The caller must supply information to the function, and the function returns information to the caller.

At one time, computer programs didn't include the concept of code reusability. As a result, developers had to keep reinventing the same code. It didn't take long for someone to come up with the idea of functions, though, and the concept has evolved over the years until functions have become quite flexible. You can make functions do anything you want. Code reusability is a necessary part of applications to

>> Reduce development time

>> Reduce programmer error

>> Increase application reliability

>> Allow entire groups to benefit from the work of one programmer

>> Make code easier to understand

>> Improve application efficiency

In fact, functions do a whole list of things for applications in the form of reusability. As you work through the examples in this book, you see how reusability makes your life significantly easier. If not for reusability, you'd still be programming by plugging 0s and 1s into the computer by hand.

Defining a function

Creating a function doesn't require much work. Python tends to make things fast and easy for you. The following steps show you the process of creating a function that you can later access:

1. **Create a new notebook in Notebook.**

   The book uses the filename BPPD_07_Managing_Information.ipynb, which is where you find all the source code for this chapter. See the Introduction for information on using the downloadable source.

2. **Type def Hello(): and press Enter.**

   This step tells Python to define a function named Hello. The parentheses are important because they define any requirements for using the function. (There aren't any requirements in this case.) The colon at the end tells Python that you're done defining the way in which people will access the function. Notice that the insertion pointer is now indented, as shown in Figure 7-1. This indentation is a reminder that you must give the function a task to perform.

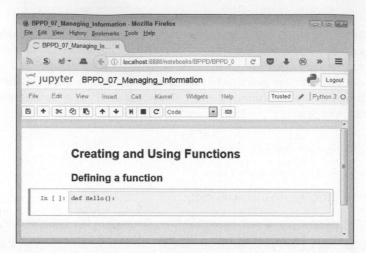

FIGURE 7-1:
Define the name
of your function.

3. **Type** print("This is my first Python function!") **and press Enter.**

   You should notice something special, as shown in Figure 7-2. The insertion
   pointer is still indented because Notebook is waiting for you to provide the
   next step in the function.

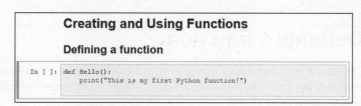

FIGURE 7-2:
Notebook awaits
your next
instruction.

4. **Click Run Cell.**

   The function is now complete.

Even though this is a really simple function, it demonstrates the pattern you use
when creating any Python function. You define a name, provide any requirements
for using the function (none in this case), and provide a series of steps for using
the function. A function ends when the insertion point is at the left side or you
move to the next cell.

Accessing functions

After you define a function, you probably want to use it to perform useful work. Of
course, this means knowing how to access the function. In the previous section,
you create a new function named Hello(). To access this function, you type

Hello() and click Run Cell. Figure 7-3 shows the output you see when you execute this function.

FIGURE 7-3:
Whenever you
type the
function's name,
you get the
output the
function provides.

```
Accessing functions

In [2]:  Hello()

         This is my first Python function!
```

Every function you create will provide a similar pattern of usage. You type the function name, an open parenthesis, any required input, and a close parenthesis; then you press Enter. In this case, you have no input, so all you type is **Hello()**. As the chapter progresses, you see other examples for which input is required.

Sending information to functions

The Hello() example in the previous section is nice because you don't have to keep typing that long string every time you want to say Hello(). However, it's also quite limited because you can use it to say only one thing. Functions should be flexible and allow you to do more than just one thing. Otherwise, you end up writing a lot of functions that vary by the data they use rather than the functionality they provide. Using arguments helps you create functions that are flexible and can use a wealth of data.

Understanding arguments

The term *argument* doesn't mean that you're going to have a fight with the function; it means that you supply information to the function to use in processing a request. Perhaps a better word for it would be input, but the term *input* has been used for so many other purposes that developers decided to use something a bit different: argument. Although the purpose of an argument might not be clear from its name, understanding what it does is relatively straightforward. An argument makes it possible for you to send data to the function so that the function can use it when performing a task. Using arguments makes your function more flexible.

The Hello() function is currently inflexible because it prints just one string. Adding an argument to the function can make it a lot more flexible because you can send strings to the function to say anything you want. To see how arguments work, create a new function in the notebook. This version of Hello(), Hello2(), requires an argument:

```
def Hello2( Greeting ):
    print(Greeting)
```

Notice that the parentheses are no longer empty. They contain a word, Greeting, which is the argument for Hello2(). The Greeting argument is actually a variable that you can pass to print() in order to see it onscreen.

Sending required arguments

You have a new function, Hello2(). This function requires that you provide an argument to use it. At least, that's what you've heard so far. Type **Hello2()** and click Run Cell. You see an error message, as shown in Figure 7-4, telling you that Hello2() requires an argument.

```
In [4]: Hello2()

        --------------------------------------------------------------------------
        ---------
        TypeError                                Traceback (most recent ca
        ll last)
        <ipython-input-4-8edee0424aab> in <module>()
        ----> 1 Hello2()

        TypeError: Hello2() missing 1 required positional argument: 'Greeti
        ng'
```

FIGURE 7-4:
You must supply an argument or you get an error message.

Not only does Python tell you that the argument is missing, it tells you the name of the argument as well. Creating a function the way you have done so far means that you must supply an argument. Type **Hello2("This is an interesting function.")** and click Run Cell. This time, you see the expected output. However, you still don't know whether Hello2() is flexible enough to print multiple messages. Type **Hello2("Another message. . .")** and click Run Cell. You see the expected output again, as shown in Figure 7-5, so Hello2() is indeed an improvement over Hello().

FIGURE 7-5:
Use Hello2() to print any message you desire.

```
In [5]: Hello2("This is an interesting function.")

        This is an interesting function.

In [6]: Hello2("Another message...")

        Another message...
```

You might easily to assume that Greeting will accept only a string from the tests you have performed so far. **Type Hello2(1234)**, click Run Cell, and you see 1234 as the output. Likewise, type **Hello2(5 + 5)** and click Run Cell. This time you see the result of the expression, which is 10.

Sending arguments by keyword

As your functions become more complex and the methods to use them do as well, you may want to provide a little more control over precisely how you call the function and provide arguments to it. Up until now, you have *positional arguments*, which means that you have supplied values in the order in which they appear in the argument list for the function definition. However, Python also has a method for sending arguments by keyword. In this case, you supply the name of the argument followed by an equals sign (=) and the argument value. To see how this works, type the following function in the notebook:

```
def AddIt(Value1, Value2):
    print(Value1, " + ", Value2, " = ", (Value1 + Value2))
```

Notice that the print() function argument includes a list of items to print and that those items are separated by commas. In addition, the arguments are of different types. Python makes it easy to mix and match arguments in this manner.

Time to test AddIt(). Of course, you want to try the function using positional arguments first, so type **AddIt(2, 3)** and click Run Cell. You see the expected output of 2 + 3 = 5. Now type **AddIt(Value2 = 3, Value1 = 2)** and click Run Cell. Again, you receive the output 2 + 3 = 5 even though the position of the arguments has been reversed.

Giving function arguments a default value

Whether you make the call using positional arguments or keyword arguments, the functions to this point have required that you supply a value. Sometimes a function can use default values when a common value is available. Default values make the function easier to use and less likely to cause errors when a developer doesn't provide an input. To create a default value, you simply follow the argument name with an equals sign and the default value. To see how this works, type the following function in the notebook:

```
def Hello3(Greeting = "No Value Supplied"):
    print(Greeting)
```

This is yet another version of the original Hello() and updated Hello2() functions, but Hello3() automatically compensates for individuals who don't supply a value. When someone tries to call Hello3() without an argument, it doesn't raise an error. Type **Hello3()** and press Enter to see for yourself. Type **Hello3("This is a string.")** to see a normal response. Lest you think the function is now unable to use other kinds of data, type **Hello3(5)** and press Enter; then **Hello3(2 + 7)** and press Enter. Figure 7-6 shows the output from all these tests.

FIGURE 7-6:
Supply default
arguments when
possible to make
your functions
easier to use.

```
        Giving function arguments a default value

In [12]:  def Hello3(Greeting = "No Value Supplied"):
              print(Greeting)

In [13]:  Hello3()
          Hello3("This is a string")
          Hello3(5)
          Hello3(2 + 7)

          No Value Supplied
          This is a string
          5
          9
```

Creating functions with a variable number of arguments

In most cases, you know precisely how many arguments to provide with your function. It pays to work toward this goal whenever you can because functions with a fixed number of arguments are easier to troubleshoot later. However, sometimes you simply can't determine how many arguments the function will receive at the outset. For example, when you create a Python application that works at the command line, the user might provide no arguments, the maximum number of arguments (assuming there is more than one), or any number of arguments in between.

Fortunately, Python provides a technique for sending a variable number of arguments to a function. You simply create an argument that has an asterisk in front of it, such as *VarArgs. The usual technique is to provide a second argument that contains the number of arguments passed as an input. Here is an example of a function that can print a variable number of elements. (Don't worry too much if you don't understand it completely now — you haven't seen some of these techniques used before.)

```
def Hello4(ArgCount, *VarArgs):
    print("You passed ", ArgCount, " arguments.")
    for Arg in VarArgs:
        print(Arg)
```

This example uses something called a for loop. You meet this structure in Chapter 9. For now, all you really need to know is that it takes the arguments out of VarArgs one at a time, places the individual argument into Arg, and then prints Arg using print(). What should interest you most is seeing how a variable number of arguments can work.

After you type the function into the notebook, type **Hello4(1, "A Test String.")** and click Run Cell. You should see the number of arguments and the test string as output — nothing too exiting there. However, now type **Hello4(3, "One", "Two", "Three")** and click Run Cell. As shown in Figure 7-7, the function handles the variable number of arguments without any problem at all.

FIGURE 7-7:
Variable
argument
functions can
make your
applications more
flexible.

```
                Creating functions with a variable number of arguments

In [14]:   def Hello4(ArgCount, *VarArgs):
               print("You passed ", ArgCount, " arguments.")
               for Arg in VarArgs:
                   print(Arg)

In [15]:   Hello4(1, "A Test String.")

           You passed  1  arguments.
           A Test String.

In [16]:   Hello4(3, "One", "Two", "Three")

           You passed  3  arguments.
           One
           Two
           Three
```

Returning information from functions

Functions can display data directly or they can return the data to the caller so that the caller can do something more with it. In some cases, a function displays data directly as well as returns data to the caller, but more commonly, a function either displays the data directly or returns it to the caller. Just how functions work depends on the kind of task the function is supposed to perform. For example, a function that performs a math-related task is more likely to return the data to the caller than certain other functions.

To return data to a caller, a function needs to include the keyword `return`, followed by the data to return. You have no limit on what you can return to a caller. Here are some types of data that you commonly see returned by a function to a caller:

>> **Values:** Any value is acceptable. You can return numbers, such as 1 or 2.5; strings, such as "Hello There!"; or Boolean values, such as True or False.

>> **Variables:** The content of any variable works just as well as a direct value. The caller receives whatever data is stored in the variable.

>> **Expressions:** Many developers use expressions as a shortcut. For example, you can simply return A + B rather than perform the calculation, place the result in a variable, and then return the variable to the caller. Using the expression is faster and accomplishes the same task.

>> **Results from other functions:** You can actually return data from another function as part of the return of your function.

It's time to see how return values work. Type the following code into the notebook:

```
def DoAdd(Value1, Value2):
    return Value1 + Value2
```

This function accepts two values as input and then returns the sum of those two values. Yes, you could probably perform this task without using a function, but this is how many functions start. To test this function, type **print("The sum of 3 + 4 is ", DoAdd(3, 4))** and click Run Cell. You see the output shown in Figure 7-8.

FIGURE 7-8:
Return values can make your functions even more useful.

```
Returning information from functions

In [17]:  def DoAdd(Value1, Value2):
              return Value1 + Value2

In [18]:  print "The sum of 3 + 4 is ", DoAdd(3,4)

          The sum of 3 + 4 is  7
```

Comparing function output

You use functions with return values in a number of ways. For example, the previous section of this chapter shows how you can use functions to provide input for another function. You use functions to perform all sorts of tasks. One of the ways to use functions is for comparison purposes. You can actually create expressions from them that define a logical output.

To see how this might work, use the DoAdd() function from the previous section. Type **print("3 + 4 equals 2 + 5 is ", (DoAdd(3, 4) == DoAdd(2, 5)))** and click Run Cell. You see the truth value of the statement that 3 + 4 equals 2 + 5, as shown in Figure 7-9. The point is that functions need not provide just one use or that you view them in just one way. Functions can make your code quite versatile and flexible.

FIGURE 7-9:
Use your functions to perform a wide variety of tasks.

```
Comparing function output

In [19]:  print "3 + 4 equals 2 + 5 is ", (DoAdd(3,4)==DoAdd(2,5))

          3 + 4 equals 2 + 5 is  True
```

Getting User Input

Very few applications exist in their own world — that is, apart from the user. In fact, most applications interact with users in a major way because computers are designed to serve user needs. To interact with a user, an application must provide some means of obtaining user input. Fortunately, the most commonly used technique for obtaining input is also relatively easy to implement. You simply use the input() function to do it.

REMEMBER

The input() function always outputs a string. Even if a user types a number, the output from the input() function is a string. This means that if you are expecting a number, you need to convert it after receiving the input. The input() function also lets you provide a string prompt. This prompt is displayed to tell the user what to provide in the way of information. The following example shows how to use the input() function in a simple way:

```
Name = input("Tell me your name: ")
print("Hello ", Name)
```

In this case, the input() function asks the user for a name. After the user types a name and presses Enter, the example outputs a customized greeting to the user. Try running this example. Figure 7-10 shows typical results when you input John as the username.

FIGURE 7-10:
Provide a username and see a greeting as output.

Getting User Input

```
In [20]:  Name = input("Tell me your name: ")
          print("Hello ", Name)

          Tell me your name: John
          Hello  John
```

You can use input() for other kinds of data; all you need is the correct conversion function. For example, the code in the following example provides one technique for performing such a conversion, as shown here:

```
ANumber = float(input("Type a number: "))
print("You typed: ", ANumber)
```

When you run this example, the application asks for a numeric input. The call to float() converts the input to a number. After the conversion, print() outputs the result. When you run the example using a value such as 5.5, you obtain the desired result.

WARNING

Understand that data conversion isn't without risk. If you attempt to type something other than a number, you get an error message, as shown in Figure 7-11. Chapter 10 helps you understand how to detect and fix errors before they cause a system crash.

FIGURE 7-11:
Data conversion changes the input type to whatever you need, but could cause errors.

```
In [21]:  ANumber = float(input("Type a number: "))
          print("You typed: ", ANumber)

          Type a number: Hello
          ----------------------------------------------------------------
          ValueError                          Traceback (most recent call last)
          <ipython-input-21-5b050a92debd> in <module>()
          ----> 1 ANumber = float(input("Type a number: "))
                2 print("You typed: ", ANumber)

          ValueError: could not convert string to float: 'Hello'
```

Chapter **8**

Making Decisions

The ability to make a decision, to take one path or another, is an essential element of performing useful work. Math gives the computer the capability to obtain useful information. Decisions enable you to do something with the information after obtaining it. Without the capability to make decisions, a computer would be useless. So any language you use will include the capability to make decisions in some manner. This chapter explores the techniques that Python uses to make decisions. You can find the downloadable source code for this chapter in the `BPPD_08_Making_Decisions.ipynb` file, as described in the book's Introduction.

REMEMBER

Think through the process you use when making a decision. You obtain the actual value of something, compare it to a desired value, and then act accordingly. For example, when you see a signal light and see that it's red, you compare the red light to the desired green light, decide that the light isn't green, and then stop. Most people don't take time to consider the process they use because they use it so many times every day. Decision making comes naturally to humans, but computers must perform the following tasks every time:

1. Obtain the actual or current value of something.

2. Compare the actual or current value to a desired value.

3. Perform an action that corresponds to the desired outcome of the comparison.

Making Simple Decisions by Using the if Statement

The if statement is the easiest method for making a decision in Python. It simply states that if something is true, Python should perform the steps that follow. The following sections tell you how you can use the if statement to make decisions of various sorts in Python. You may be surprised at what this simple statement can do for you.

Understanding the if statement

You use if statements regularly in everyday life. For example, you may say to yourself, "If it's Wednesday, I'll eat tuna salad for lunch." The Python if statement is a little less verbose, but it follows precisely the same pattern. Say you create a variable, TestMe, and place a value of 6 in it, like this:

```
TestMe = 6
```

You can then ask the computer to check for a value of 6 in TestMe, like this:

```
if TestMe == 6:
    print("TestMe does equal 6!")
```

Every Python if statement begins, oddly enough, with the word *if*. When Python sees if, it knows that you want it to make a decision. After the word *if* comes a condition. A *condition* simply states what sort of comparison you want Python to make. In this case, you want Python to determine whether TestMe contains the value 6.

REMEMBER

Notice that the condition uses the relational equality operator, ==, and not the assignment operator, =. A common mistake that developers make is to use the assignment operator rather than the equality operator. You can see a list of relational operators in Chapter 7.

The condition always ends with a colon (:). If you don't provide a colon, Python doesn't know that the condition has ended and will continue to look for additional conditions on which to base its decision. After the colon come any tasks you want Python to perform. In this case, Python prints a statement saying that TestMe is equal to 6.

Using the if statement in an application

You can use the if statement in a number of ways in Python. However, you immediately need to know about three common ways to use it:

>> Use a single condition to execute a single statement when the condition is true.

>> Use a single condition to execute multiple statements when the condition is true.

>> Combine multiple conditions into a single decision and execute one or more statements when the combined condition is true.

The following sections explore these three possibilities and provide you with examples of their use. You see additional examples of how to use the if statement throughout the book because it's such an important method of making decisions.

Working with relational operators

A *relational operator* determines how a value on the left side of an expression compares to the value on the right side of an expression. After it makes the determination, it outputs a value of true or false that reflects the truth value of the expression. For example, 6 == 6 is true, while 5 == 6 is false. Table 7-3 in Chapter 7 lists the relational operators. The following steps show how to create and use an if statement.

1. Open a new notebook.

You can also use the downloadable source file, BPPD_08_Making_Decisions. ipynb.

2. Type TestMe = 6 **and press Enter.**

This step assigns a value of 6 to TestMe. Notice that it uses the assignment operator and not the equality operator.

3. Type if TestMe == 6: **and press Enter.**

This step creates an if statement that tests the value of TestMe by using the equality operator. You should notice two features of Notebook at this point:

- The word *if* is highlighted in a different color than the rest of the statement.

- The next line is automatically indented.

4. **Type** print("TestMe does equal 6!") **and press Enter.**

Notice that Python doesn't execute the i f statement yet. It does indent the next line. The word *print* appears in a special color because it's a function name. In addition, the text appears in another color to show you that it's a string value. Color coding makes it much easier to see how Python works.

5. **Click Run Cell.**

Notebook executes the if statement, as shown in Figure 8-1. Notice that the output is in yet another color. Because TestMe contains a value of 6, the if statement works as expected.

FIGURE 8-1:
Simple i f
statements
can help your
application know
what to do
in certain
conditions.

Performing multiple tasks

Sometimes you want to perform more than one task after making a decision. Python relies on indentation to determine when to stop executing tasks as part of an if statement. As long as the next line is indented, it's part of the if statement. When the next line is outdented, it becomes the first line of code outside the if block. A *code block* consists of a statement and the tasks associated with that statement. The same term is used no matter what kind of statement you're working with, but in this case, you're working with an if statement that is part of a code block. The following steps show how to use indentation to execute multiple steps as part of an if statement.

1. **Type the following code into the notebook — pressing Enter after each line:**

```
TestMe = 6
if TestMe == 6:
    print("TestMe does equal 6!")
    print("All done!")
```

Notice that the shell continues to indent lines as long as you continue to type code. Each line you type is part of the current if statement code block.

REMEMBER

When working in the shell, you create a block by typing one line of code after another. If you press Enter twice in a row without entering any text, the code block is ended, and Python executes the entire code block at one time. Of course, when working in Notebook, you must click Run Cell to execute the code within that cell.

2. **Click Run Cell.**

    Python executes the entire code block. You see the output shown in Figure 8-2.

```
                 Performing multiple tasks
In [3]:  TestMe = 6
         if TestMe == 6:
             print "TestMe does equal 6!"
             print("All done!")

         TestMe does equal 6!
         All done!
```

Making multiple comparisons by using logical operators

So far, the examples have all shown a single comparison. Real life often requires that you make multiple comparisons to account for multiple requirements. For example, when baking cookies, if the timer has gone off and the edges are brown, it's time to take the cookies out of the oven.

REMEMBER

To make multiple comparisons, you create multiple conditions by using relational operators and combine them by using logical operators (see Table 7-4 in Chapter 7). A *logical operator* describes how to combine conditions. For example, you might say x == 6 and y == 7 as two conditions for performing one or more tasks. The and keyword is a logical operator that states that both conditions must be true.

One of the most common uses for making multiple comparisons is to determine when a value is within a certain range. In fact, *range checking,* the act of determining whether data is between two values, is an important part of making your application secure and user friendly. The following steps help you see how to perform this task. In this case, you create a file so that you can run the application multiple times.

1. **Type the following code into the notebook — pressing Enter after each line:**

```
Value = int(input("Type a number between 1 and 10: "))
if (Value > 0) and (Value <= 10):
    print("You typed: ", Value)
```

The example begins by obtaining an input value. You have no idea what the user has typed other than that it's a value of some sort. The use of the `int()` function means that the user must type a whole number (one without a decimal portion). Otherwise, the application will raise an *exception* (an error indication; Chapter 10 describes exceptions). This first check ensures that the input is at least of the correct type.

The `if` statement contains two conditions. The first states that `Value` must be greater than 0. You could also present this condition as `Value >= 1`. The second condition states that `Value` must be less than or equal to 10. Only when `Value` meets both of these conditions will the `if` statement succeed and print the value the user typed.

2. **Click Run Cell.**

   Python prompts you to type a number between 1 and 10.

3. **Type 5 and press Enter.**

   The application determines that the number is in the right range and outputs the message shown in Figure 8-3.

```
Making multiple comparisons using logical operators

In [4]:  Value = int(input("Type a number between 1 and 10: "))
         if (Value > 0) and (Value <= 10):
             print "You typed: ", Value

         Type a number between 1 and 10: 5
         You typed:  5
```

4. **Select the cell again. Repeat Steps 2 and 3, but type 22 instead of 5.**

   The application doesn't output anything because the number is in the wrong range. Whenever you type a value that's outside the programmed range, the statements that are part of the `if` block aren't executed.

   Note that the input value updates by one. Each time you execute a cell, the input value will change. Given that the input value is at 4 in Figure 8-3, you now see In [5]: in the Notebook margin.

   REMEMBER

5. **Select the cell again. Repeat Steps 2 and 3, but type 5.5 instead of 5.**

   Python displays the error message shown in Figure 8-4. Even though you may think of 5.5 and 5 as both being numbers, Python sees the first number as a floating-point value and the second as an integer. (Note also that the input value is now at 6.)

Making multiple comparisons using logical operators

```
In [6]:  Value = int(input("Type a number between 1 and 10: "))
         if (Value > 0) and (Value <= 10):
             print("You typed: ", Value)

         Type a number between 1 and 10: 5.5

         ---------------------------------------------------------------------------
         ValueError                                Traceback (most recent call las
         t)
         <ipython-input-6-2a1fe76bbdd9> in <module>()
         ----> 1 Value = int(input("Type a number between 1 and 10: "))
               2 if (Value > 0) and (Value <= 10):
               3     print("You typed: ", Value)

         ValueError: invalid literal for int() with base 10: '5.5'
```

FIGURE 8-4:
Typing the wrong type of information results in an error message.

6. **Repeat Steps 2 and 3, but type** Hello **instead of 5.**

   Python displays about the same error message as before. Python doesn't differentiate between types of wrong input. It knows only that the input type is incorrect and therefore unusable.

TIP

The best applications use various kinds of range checking to ensure that the application behaves in a predictable manner. The more predictable an application becomes, the less the user thinks about the application and the more time the user spends on performing useful work. Productive users tend to be a lot happier than those who constantly fight with their applications.

Choosing Alternatives by Using the if. . .else Statement

Many of the decisions you make in an application fall into a category of choosing one of two options based on conditions. For example, when looking at a signal light, you choose one of two options: press on the brake to stop or press the accelerator to continue. The option you choose depends on the conditions. A green light signals that you can continue on through the light; a red light tells you to stop. The following sections describe how Python makes choosing between two alternatives possible.

Understanding the if. . .else statement

With Python, you choose one of two alternatives by using the else clause of the if statement. A *clause* is an addition to a code block that modifies the way in which it works. Most code blocks support multiple clauses. In this case, the else clause enables you to perform an alternative task, which increases the usefulness of the if statement. Most developers refer to the form of the if statement that has the else clause included as the if...else statement, with the ellipsis implying that something happens between if and else.

Sometimes developers encounter problems with the if...else statement because they forget that the else clause always executes when the conditions for the if statement aren't met. Be sure to think about the consequences of always executing a set of tasks when the conditions are false. Sometimes doing so can lead to unintended consequences.

Using the if. . .else statement in an application

The example in the previous section is a little less helpful than it could be when the user enters a value that's outside the intended range. Even entering data of the wrong type produces an error message, but entering the correct type of data outside the range tells the user nothing. In this example, you discover the means for correcting this problem by using an else clause. The following steps demonstrate just one reason to provide an alternative action when the condition for an if statement is false:

1. **Type the following code into the notebook — pressing Enter after each line:**

```
Value = int(input("Type a number between 1 and 10: "))
if (Value > 0) and (Value <= 10):
    print("You typed: ", Value)
else:
    print("The value you typed is incorrect!")
```

As before, the example obtains input from the user and then determines whether that input is in the correct range. However, in this case, the else clause provides an alternative output message when the user enters data outside the desired range.

Notice that the else clause ends with a colon, just as the if statement does. Most clauses that you use with Python statements have a colon associated with them so that Python knows when the clause has ended. If you receive a coding error for your application, make sure that you check for the presence of the colon as needed.

2. **Click Run Cell.**

Python prompts you to type a number between 1 and 10.

3. **Type 5 and press Enter.**

The application determines that the number is in the right range and outputs the message shown previously in Figure 8-3.

4. **Repeat Steps 2 and 3, but type** 22 **instead of 5.**

This time the application outputs the error message shown in Figure 8-5. The user now knows that the input is outside the desired range and knows to try entering it again.

FIGURE 8-5: Providing feedback for incorrect input is always a good idea.

```
Using the if...else statement in an application

In [8]: Value = int(input("Type a number between 1 and 10: "))
        if (Value > 0) and (Value <= 10):
            print("You typed: ", Value)
        else:
            print("The value you typed is incorrect!")

        Type a number between 1 and 10: 5
        You typed:  5

In [9]: Value = int(input("Type a number between 1 and 10: "))
        if (Value > 0) and (Value <= 10):
            print("You typed: ", Value)
        else:
            print("The value you typed is incorrect!")

        Type a number between 1 and 10: 22
        The value you typed is incorrect!
```

Using the if. . .elif statement in an application

You go to a restaurant and look at the menu. The restaurant offers eggs, pancakes, waffles, and oatmeal for breakfast. After you choose one of the items, the server brings it to you. Creating a menu selection requires something like an if...else statement, but with a little extra oomph. In this case, you use the elif clause to create another set of conditions. The elif clause is a combination of the else clause and a separate if statement. The following steps describe how to use the if...elif statement to create a menu.

1. **Type the following code into the notebook — pressing Enter after each line:**

```
print("1. Red")
print("2. Orange")
print("3. Yellow")
print("4. Green")
print("5. Blue")
print("6. Purple")
Choice = int(input("Select your favorite color: "))
if (Choice == 1):
    print("You chose Red!")
elif (Choice == 2):
    print("You chose Orange!")
```

```
elif (Choice == 3):
    print("You chose Yellow!")
elif (Choice == 4):
    print("You chose Green!")
elif (Choice == 5):
    print("You chose Blue!")
elif (Choice == 6):
    print("You chose Purple!")
else:
    print("You made an invalid choice!")
```

The example begins by displaying a menu. The user sees a list of choices for the application. It then asks the user to make a selection, which it places inside Choice. The use of the int() function ensures that the user can't type anything other than a number.

After the user makes a choice, the application looks for it in the list of potential values. In each case, Choice is compared against a particular value to create a condition for that value. When the user types 1, the application outputs the message "You chose Red!". If none of the options is correct, the else clause is executed by default to tell the user that the input choice is invalid.

2. **Click Run Cell.**

   Python displays the menu. The application asks you to select your favorite color.

3. **Type** 1 **and press Enter.**

   The application displays the appropriate output message, as shown in Figure 8-6.

4. **Repeat Steps 3 and 4, but type** 5 **instead of 1.**

   The application displays a different output message — the one associated with the requested color.

5. **Repeat Steps 3 and 4, but type** 8 **instead of 1.**

   The application tells you that you made an invalid choice.

6. **Repeat Steps 3 and 4, but type** Red **instead of 1.**

   The application displays the expected error message, as shown in Figure 8-7. Any application you create should be able to detect errors and incorrect inputs. Chapter 10 shows you how to handle errors so that they're user friendly.

Using the if...elif statement in an application

```
In [10]:  print("1. Red")
          print("2. Orange")
          print("3. Yellow")
          print("4. Green")
          print("5. Blue")
          print("6. Purple")
          Choice = int(input("Select your favorite color: "))
          if (Choice == 1):
              print("You chose Red!")
          elif (Choice == 2):
              print("You chose Orange!")
          elif (Choice == 3):
              print("You chose Yellow!")
          elif (Choice == 4):
              print("You chose Green!")
          elif (Choice == 5):
              print("You chose Blue!")
          elif (Choice == 6):
              print("You chose Purple!")
          else:
              print("You made an invalid choice!")

          1. Red
          2. Orange
          3. Yellow
          4. Green
          5. Blue
          6. Purple
          Select your favorite color: 1
          You chose Red!
```

FIGURE 8-6: Menus let you choose one option from a list of options.

```
In [13]:  print("1. Red")
          print("2. Orange")
          print("3. Yellow")
          print("4. Green")
          print("5. Blue")
          print("6. Purple")
          Choice = int(input("Select your favorite color: "))
          if (Choice == 1):
              print("You chose Red!")
          elif (Choice == 2):
              print("You chose Orange!")
          elif (Choice == 3):
              print("You chose Yellow!")
          elif (Choice == 4):
              print("You chose Green!")
          elif (Choice == 5):
              print("You chose Blue!")
          elif (Choice == 6):
              print("You chose Purple!")
          else:
              print("You made an invalid choice!")

          1. Red
          2. Orange
          3. Yellow
          4. Green
          5. Blue
          6. Purple
          Select your favorite color: Red

          ---------------------------------------------------------------
          ---
          ValueError                               Traceback (most recent call la
          st)
          <ipython-input-13-7f8bcfa1e0ea> in <module>()
                5 print("5. Blue")
                6 print("6. Purple")
          ----> 7 Choice = int(input("Select your favorite color: "))
                8 if (Choice == 1):
                9     print("You chose Red!")

          ValueError: invalid literal for int() with base 10: 'Red'
```

FIGURE 8-7: Every application you create should include some means of detecting errant input.

Using Nested Decision Statements

The decision-making process often happens in levels. For example, when you go to the restaurant and choose eggs for breakfast, you have made a first-level decision. Now the server asks you what type of toast you want with your eggs. The server wouldn't ask this question if you had ordered pancakes, so the selection of toast becomes a second-level decision. When the breakfast arrives, you decide whether you want to use jelly on your toast. This is a third-level decision. If you had selected a kind of toast that doesn't work well with jelly, you might not have had to make this decision at all. This process of making decisions in levels, with each level reliant on the decision made at the previous level, is called *nesting*. Developers often use nesting techniques to create applications that can make complex decisions based on various inputs. The following sections describe several kinds of nesting you can use within Python to make complex decisions.

Using multiple if or if. . .else statements

The most commonly used multiple selection technique is a combination of `if` and `if...else` statements. This form of selection is often called a *selection tree* because of its resemblance to the branches of a tree. In this case, you follow a particular path to obtain a desired result. The following steps show how to create a selection tree:

1. **Type the following code into the notebook — pressing Enter after each line:**

```
One = int(input("Type a number between 1 and 10: "))
Two = int(input("Type a number between 1 and 10: "))
```

```
if (One >= 1) and (One <= 10):
    if (Two >= 1) and (Two <= 10):
        print("Your secret number is: ", One * Two)
    else:
        print("Incorrect second value!")
else:
    print("Incorrect first value!")
```

This is simply an extension of the example you see in the "Using the if. . .else statement in an application" section of the chapter. However, notice that the indentation is different. The second if. . .else statement is indented within the first if. . .else statement. The indentation tells Python that this is a second-level statement.

2. **Click Run Cell.**

   You see a Python Shell window open with a prompt to type a number between 1 and 10.

3. **Type** 5 **and press Enter.**

   The shell asks for another number between 1 and 10.

4. **Type** 2 **and press Enter.**

   You see the combination of the two numbers as output, as shown in Figure 8-8.

FIGURE 8-8:
Adding multiple levels lets you perform tasks with greater complexity.

Using Nested Decision Statements

Using multiple if or if...else statements

```
In [14]: One = int(input("Type a number between 1 and 10: "))
         Two = int(input("Type a number between 1 and 10: "))
         if (One >= 1) and (One <= 10):
             if (Two >= 1) and (Two <= 10):
                 print("Your secret number is: ", One * Two)
             else:
                 print("Incorrect second value!")
         else:
             print "Incorrect first value!")

Type a number between 1 and 10: 5
Type a number between 1 and 10: 2
Your secret number is:  10
```

This example has the same input features as the previous if. . .else example. For example, if you attempt to provide a value that's outside the requested range, you see an error message. The error message is tailored for either the first or second input value so that the user knows which value was incorrect.

REMEMBER

Providing specific error messages is always useful because users tend to become confused and frustrated otherwise. In addition, a specific error message helps you find errors in your application much faster.

Combining other types of decisions

You can use any combination of if, if...else, and if...elif statements to produce a desired outcome. You can nest the code blocks as many levels deep as needed to perform the required checks. For example, Listing 8-1 shows what you might accomplish for a breakfast menu.

LISTING 8-1: **Creating a Breakfast Menu**

```
print("1. Eggs")
print("2. Pancakes")
print("3. Waffles")
print("4. Oatmeal")
MainChoice = int(input("Choose a breakfast item: "))
if (MainChoice == 2):
   Meal = "Pancakes"
elif (MainChoice == 3):
   Meal = "Waffles"
if (MainChoice == 1):
   print("1. Wheat Toast")
   print("2. Sour Dough")
   print("3. Rye Toast")
   print("4. Pancakes")
   Bread = int(input("Choose a type of bread: "))
   if (Bread == 1):
      print("You chose eggs with wheat toast.")
   elif (Bread == 2):
      print("You chose eggs with sour dough.")
   elif (Bread == 3):
      print("You chose eggs with rye toast.")
   elif (Bread == 4):
      print("You chose eggs with pancakes.")
   else:
      print("We have eggs, but not that kind of bread.")
elif (MainChoice == 2) or (MainChoice == 3):
   print("1. Syrup")
   print("2. Strawberries")
   print("3. Powdered Sugar")
   Topping = int(input("Choose a topping: "))
```

```
    if (Topping == 1):
        print ("You chose " + Meal + " with syrup.")
    elif (Topping == 2):
        print ("You chose " + Meal + " with strawberries.")
    elif (Topping == 3):
        print ("You chose " + Meal + " with powdered sugar.")
    else:
        print ("We have " + Meal + ", but not that topping.")
elif (MainChoice == 4):
    print("You chose oatmeal.")
else:
    print("We don't serve that breakfast item!")
```

This example has some interesting features. For one thing, you might assume that an if...elif statement always requires an else clause. This example shows a situation that doesn't require such a clause. You use an if...elif statement to ensure that Meal contains the correct value, but you have no other options to consider.

The selection technique is the same as you saw for the previous examples. A user enters a number in the correct range to obtain a desired result. Three of the selections require a secondary choice, so you see the menu for that choice. For example, when ordering eggs, it isn't necessary to choose a topping, but you do want a topping for pancakes or waffles.

Notice that this example also combines variables and text in a specific way. Because a topping can apply equally to waffles or pancakes, you need some method for defining precisely which meal is being served as part of the output. The Meal variable that the application defines earlier is used as part of the output after the topping choice is made.

The best way to understand this example is to play with it. Try various menu combinations to see how the application works.

IN THIS CHAPTER

» Performing a task a specific
number of times

» Performing a task until completion

» Placing one task loop within
another

Chapter 9

Performing Repetitive Tasks

All the examples in the book so far have performed a series of steps just one time and then stopped. However, the real world doesn't work this way. Many of the tasks that humans perform are repetitious. For example, the doctor might state that you need to exercise more and tell you to do 100 push-ups each day. If you just do one push-up, you won't get much benefit from the exercise and you definitely won't be following the doctor's orders. Of course, because you know precisely how many push-ups to do, you can perform the task a specific number of times. Python allows the same sort of repetition by using the for statement.

Unfortunately, you don't always know how many times to perform a task. For example, consider needing to check a stack of coins for one of extreme rarity. Taking just the first coin from the top, examining it, and deciding that it either is or isn't the rare coin doesn't complete the task. Instead, you must examine each coin in turn, looking for the rare coin. Your stack may contain more than one. Only after you have looked at every coin in the stack can you say that the task is complete. However, because you don't know how many coins are in the stack, you don't know how many times to perform the task at the outset. You only know the task is done when the stack is gone. Python performs this kind of repetition by using the while statement.

REMEMBER

Most programming languages call any sort of repeating sequence of events a *loop*. The idea is to picture the repetition as a circle, with the code going round and round executing tasks until the loop ends. Loops are an essential part of application elements such as menus. In fact, writing most modern applications without using loops would be impossible.

In some cases, you must create loops within loops. For example, to create a multiplication table, you use a loop within a loop. The inner loop calculates the column values and the outer loop moves between rows. You see such an example later in the chapter, so don't worry too much about understanding precisely how such things work right now. You can find the downloadable source code for this chapter in the BPPD_09_Performing_Repetitive_Tasks.ipynb file, as described in the book's Introduction.

Processing Data Using the for Statement

The first looping code block that most developers encounter is the for statement. It's hard to imagine creating a conventional programming language that lacks such a statement. In this case, the loop executes a fixed number of times, and you know the number of times it will execute before the loop even begins. Because everything about a for loop is known at the outset, for loops tend to be the easiest kind of loop to use. However, in order to use one, you need to know how many times to execute the loop. The following sections describe the for loop in greater detail.

Understanding the for statement

A for loop begins with a for statement. The for statement describes how to perform the loop. The Python for loop works through a sequence of some type. It doesn't matter whether the sequence is a series of letters in a string or items within a collection. You can even specify a range of values to use by specifying the range() function. Here's a simple for statement.

```
for Letter in "Howdy!":
```

The statement begins with the keyword for. The next item is a variable that holds a single element of a sequence. In this case, the variable name is Letter. The in keyword tells Python that the sequence comes next. In this case, the sequence is the string "Howdy". The for statement always ends with a colon, just as the decision-making statements described in Chapter 8 do.

Indented under the for statement are the tasks you want performed within the for loop. Python considers every following indented statement part of the code block that composes the for loop. Again, the for loop works just like the decision-making statements in Chapter 8.

Creating a basic for loop

The best way to see how a for loop actually works is to create one. In this case, the example uses a string for the sequence. The for loop processes each of the characters in the string in turn until it runs out of characters.

1. **Open a new notebook.**

You can also use the downloadable source file, BPPD_09_Performing_Repetitive_Tasks.ipynb.

2. **Type the following code into the notebook — pressing Enter after each line:**

```
LetterNum = 1
for Letter in "Howdy!":
    print("Letter ", LetterNum, " is ", Letter)
    LetterNum+=1
```

The example begins by creating a variable, LetterNum, to track the number of letters that have been processed. Every time the loop completes, LetterNum is updated by 1.

The for statement works through the sequence of letters in the string "Howdy!". It places each letter, in turn, in Letter. The code that follows displays the current LetterNum value and its associated character found in Letter.

3. **Click Run Cell.**

The application displays the letter sequence along with the letter number, as shown in Figure 9-1.

Controlling execution with the break statement

Life is often about exceptions to the rule. For example, you might want an assembly line to produce a number of clocks. However, at some point, the assembly line runs out of a needed part. If the part isn't available, the assembly line must stop in the middle of the processing cycle. The count hasn't completed, but the line must be stopped anyway until the missing part is restocked.

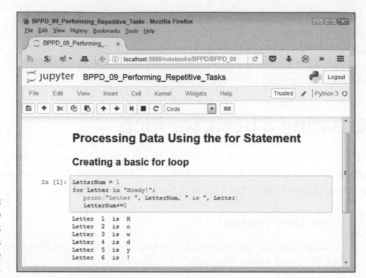

FIGURE 9-1:
Use the for loop
to process
the characters
in a string one
at a time.

Interruptions also occur in computers. You might be streaming data from an online source when a network glitch occurs and breaks the connection; the stream temporarily runs dry, so the application runs out of things to do even though the set number of tasks isn't completed.

REMEMBER

The break clause makes breaking out of a loop possible. However, you don't simply place the break clause in your code — you surround it with an if statement that defines the condition for issuing a break. The statement might say something like this: If the stream runs dry, then break out of the loop.

In this example, you see what happens when the count reaches a certain level when processing a string. The example is a little contrived in the interest of keeping things simple, but it reflects what could happen in the real world when a data element is too long to process (possibly indicating an error condition).

1. Type the following code into the notebook — pressing Enter after each line:

```
Value = input("Type less than 6 characters: ")
LetterNum = 1
for Letter in Value:
    print("Letter ", LetterNum, " is ", Letter)
    LetterNum+=1
    if LetterNum > 6:
        print("The string is too long!")
        break
```

This example builds on the one found in the previous section. However, it lets the user provide a variable-length string. When the string is longer than six characters, the application stops processing it.

The if statement contains the conditional code. When LetterNum is greater than 6, it means that the string is too long. Notice the second level of indentation used for the if statement. In this case, the user sees an error message stating that the string is too long, and then the code executes a break to end the loop.

2. **Click Run Cell.**

   Python displays a prompt asking for input.

3. **Type** Hello **and press Enter.**

   The application lists each character in the string, as shown in Figure 9-2.

Controlling execution with the break statement

```
In [2]:  Value = input("Type less than 6 characters: ")
         LetterNum = 1
         for Letter in Value:
             print("Letter ", LetterNum, " is ", Letter)
             LetterNum+=1
             if LetterNum > 6:
                 print("The string is too long!")
                 break

         Type less than 6 characters: Hello
         Letter  1  is  H
         Letter  2  is  e
         Letter  3  is  l
         Letter  4  is  l
         Letter  5  is  o
```

FIGURE 9-2:
A short string is successfully processed by the application.

4. **Perform Steps 2 and 3 again, but type** I am too long. **instead of Hello.**

   The application displays the expected error message and stops processing the string at character 6, as shown in Figure 9-3.

```
In [3]:  Value = input("Type less than 6 characters: ")
         LetterNum = 1
         for Letter in Value:
             print("Letter ", LetterNum, " is ", Letter)
             LetterNum+=1
             if LetterNum > 6:
                 print("The string is too long!")
                 break

         Type less than 6 characters: I am too long.
         Letter  1  is  I
         Letter  2  is
         Letter  3  is  a
         Letter  4  is  m
         Letter  5  is
         Letter  6  is  t
         The string is too long!
```

FIGURE 9-3:
Long strings are truncated to ensure that they remain a certain size.

TIP

This example adds *length checking* to your repertoire of application data error checks. Chapter 8 shows how to perform range checks, which ensure that a value meets specific limits. The length check is necessary to ensure that data, especially strings, aren't going to overrun the size of data fields. In addition, a small input size makes it harder for intruders to perform certain types of hacks on your system, which makes your system more secure.

Controlling execution with the continue statement

Sometimes you want to check every element in a sequence, but don't want to process certain elements. For example, you might decide that you want to process all the information for every car in a database except brown cars. Perhaps you simply don't need the information about that particular color of car. The break clause simply ends the loop, so you can't use it in this situation. Otherwise, you won't see the remaining elements in the sequence.

REMEMBER

The break clause alternative that many developers use is the continue clause. As with the break clause, the continue clause appears as part of an if statement. However, processing continues with the next element in the sequence rather than ending completely.

The following steps help you see how the continue clause differs from the break clause. In this case, the code refuses to process the letter *w*, but will process every other letter in the alphabet.

1. Type the following code into the notebook — pressing Enter after each line:

```
LetterNum = 1
for Letter in "Howdy!":
    if Letter == "w":
        continue
        print("Encountered w, not processed.")
    print("Letter ", LetterNum, " is ", Letter)
    LetterNum+=1
```

This example is based on the one found in the "Creating a basic for loop" section, earlier in this chapter. However, this example adds an if statement with the continue clause in the if code block. Notice the print() function that is part of the if code block. You never see this string printed because the current loop iteration ends immediately.

2. Click Run Cell.

Python displays the letter sequence along with the letter number, as shown in Figure 9-4. However, notice the effect of the `continue` clause — the letter *w* isn't processed.

```
                Controlling execution with the continue
                statement

In [4]:  LetterNum = 1
         for Letter in "Howdy!":
             if Letter == "w":
                 continue
                 print("Encountered w, not processed.")
             print("Letter ", LetterNum, " is ", Letter)
             LetterNum+=1

         Letter  1  is  H
         Letter  2  is  o
         Letter  3  is  d
         Letter  4  is  y
         Letter  5  is  !
```

Controlling execution with the pass clause

The Python language includes something not commonly found in other languages: a second sort of `continue` clause. The `pass` clause works almost the same way as the `continue` clause does, except that it allows completion of the code in the `if` code block in which it appears. The following steps use an example that is precisely the same as the one found in the previous section, "Controlling execution with the continue statement," except that it uses a `pass` clause instead.

1. Type the following code into the notebook — pressing Enter after each line:

```
LetterNum = 1
for Letter in "Howdy!":
    if Letter == "w":
        pass
        print("Encountered w, not processed.")
    print("Letter ", LetterNum, " is ", Letter)
    LetterNum+=1
```

2. Click Run Cell.

You see a Python Shell window open. The application displays the letter sequence along with the letter number, as shown in Figure 9-5. However, notice the effect of the `pass` clause — the letter *w* isn't processed. In addition, the example displays the string that wasn't displayed for the `continue` clause example.

Controlling execution with the pass clause

```
In [5]: LetterNum = 1
        for Letter in "Howdy!":
            if Letter == "w":
                pass
                print("Encountered w, not processed.")
            print("Letter ", LetterNum, " is ", Letter)
            LetterNum+=1

        Letter  1  is  H
        Letter  2  is  o
        Encountered w, not processed.
        Letter  3  is  w
        Letter  4  is  d
        Letter  5  is  y
        Letter  6  is  !
```

FIGURE 9-5:
Using the pass clause allows for post processing of an unwanted input.

REMEMBER

The `continue` clause enables you to silently bypass specific elements in a sequence and avoid executing any additional code for that element. Use the `pass` clause when you need to perform some sort of post processing on the element, such as logging the element in an error log, displaying a message to the user, or handling the problem element in some other way. The `continue` and `pass` clauses both do the same thing, but they're used in distinctly different situations.

Controlling execution with the else statement

Python has another loop clause that you won't find with other languages: `else`. The `else` clause makes executing code possible even if you have no elements to process in a sequence. For example, you might need to convey to the user that there simply isn't anything to do. In fact, that's what the following example does. This example also appears with the downloadable source code as `ForElse.py`.

1. **Type the following code into the notebook — pressing Enter after each line:**

```
Value = input("Type less than 6 characters: ")
LetterNum = 1
for Letter in Value:
    print("Letter ", LetterNum, " is ", Letter)
    LetterNum+=1
else:
    print("The string is blank.")
```

This example is based on the one found in the "Creating a basic for loop" section, earlier in the chapter. However, when a user presses Enter without typing something, the `else` clause is executed.

2. **Click Run Cell.**

Python displays a prompt asking for input.

3. **Type** Hello **and press Enter.**

The application lists each character in the string, as shown previously in Figure 9-2. However, notice that you also see a statement saying that the string is blank, which seems counterintuitive. When using an else clause with a for loop, the else clause always executes. However, if the iterator isn't valid, then the else clause still executes, so you can use it as an ending statement for any for loop. See the article at http://python-notes.curiousefficiency. org/en/latest/python_concepts/break_else.html for additional details.

4. **Repeat Steps 2 and 3. However, simply press Enter instead of entering any sort of text.**

You see the alternative message shown in Figure 9-6 that tells you the string is blank.

FIGURE 9-6:
The else clause makes it possible to perform tasks based on an empty sequence.

```
In [7]:  Value = input("Type less than 6 characters: ")
         LetterNum = 1
         for Letter in Value:
             print("Letter ", LetterNum, " is ", Letter)
             LetterNum+=1
         else:
             print("The string is blank.")

         Type less than 6 characters:
         The string is blank.
```

WARNING

You can easily misuse the else clause because an empty sequence doesn't always signify a simple lack of input. An empty sequence can also signal an application error or other conditions that need to be handled differently from a simple omission of data. Make sure you understand how the application works with data to ensure that the else clause doesn't end up hiding potential error conditions, rather than making them visible so that they can be fixed.

Processing Data by Using the while Statement

You use the while statement for situations when you're not sure how much data the application will have to process. Instead of instructing Python to process a static number of items, you use the while statement to tell Python to continue processing items until it runs out of items. This kind of loop is useful when you need to perform tasks such as downloading files of unknown size or streaming data from a source such as a radio station. Any situation in which you can't define at the outset how much data the application will process is a good candidate for the while statement, which the following sections describe more fully.

Understanding the while statement

The while statement works with a condition rather than a sequence. The condition states that the while statement should perform a task until the condition is no longer true. For example, imagine a deli with a number of customers standing in front of the counter. The salesperson continues to service customers until no more customers are left in line. The line could (and probably will) grow as the other customers are handled, so it's impossible to know at the outset how many customers will be served. All the salesperson knows is that continuing to serve customers until no more are left is important. Here is how a while statement might look:

```
while Sum < 5:
```

The statement begins with the while keyword. It then adds a condition. In this case, a variable, Sum, must be less than 5 for the loop to continue. Nothing specifies the current value of Sum, nor does the code define how the value of Sum will change. The only thing that is known when Python executes the statement is that Sum must be less than 5 for the loop to continue performing tasks. The statement ends with a colon and the tasks are indented below the statement.

WARNING

Because the while statement doesn't perform a series of tasks a set number of times, creating an *endless loop* is possible, meaning that the loop never ends. For example, say that Sum is set to 0 when the loop begins, and the ending condition is that Sum must be less than 5. If the value of Sum never increases, the loop will continue executing forever (or at least until the computer is shut down). Endless loops can cause all sorts of bizarre problems on systems, such as slowdowns and even computer freezes, so it's best to avoid them. You must always provide a method for the loop to end when using a while loop (contrasted with the for loop, in which the end of the sequence determines the end of the loop). So, when working with the while statement, you must perform three tasks:

1. Create the environment for the condition (such as setting Sum to 0).

2. State the condition within the while statement (such as Sum < 5).

3. Update the condition as needed to ensure that the loop eventually ends (such as adding Sum+=1 to the while code block).

REMEMBER

As with the `for` statement, you can modify the default behavior of the `while` statement. In fact, you have access to the same four clauses to modify the `while` statement behavior:

>> `break`: Ends the current loop.

>> `continue`: Immediately ends processing of the current element.

>> `pass`: Ends processing of the current element after completing the statements in the `if` block.

>> `else`: Provides an alternative processing technique when conditions aren't met for the loop.

Using the while statement in an application

You can use the `while` statement in many ways, but this first example is straightforward. It simply displays a count based on the starting and ending condition of a variable named Sum. The following steps help you create and test the example code.

1. Type the following code into the notebook — pressing Enter after each line:

```
Sum = 0
while Sum < 5:
    print(Sum)
    Sum+=1
```

The example code demonstrates the three tasks you must perform when working with a `while` loop in a straightforward manner. It begins by setting Sum to 0, which is the first step of setting the condition environment. The condition itself appears as part of the `while` statement. The end of the `while` code block accomplishes the third step. Of course, the code displays the current value of Sum before it updates the value of Sum.

REMEMBER

A `while` statement provides flexibility that you don't get with a `for` statement. This example shows a relatively straightforward way to update Sum. However, you can use any update method required to meet the goals of the application. Nothing says that you have to update Sum in a specific manner. In addition, the condition can be as complex as you want it to be. For example, you can track the current value of three or four variables if you want. Of course, the more complex you make the condition, the more likely you are to create an endless loop, so you have a practical limit as to how complex you should make the `while` loop condition.

2. **Click Run Cell.**

Python executes the while loop and displays the numeric sequence shown in Figure 9-7.

Processing Data Using the while Statement

Using the while statement in an application

```
In [8]:   Sum = 0
          while Sum < 5:
              print(Sum)
              Sum+=1

          0
          1
          2
          3
          4
```

Nesting Loop Statements

In some cases, you can use either a for loop or a while loop to achieve the same effect. The loop statements work differently, but the effect is the same. In this example, you create a multiplication table generator by nesting a while loop within a for loop. Because you want the output to look nice, you use a little formatting as well. (Chapter 12 gives you the details.)

1. **Type the following code into the notebook — pressing Enter after each line:**

```
X = 1
Y = 1
print ('{:>4}'.format(' '), end= ' ')
for X in range(1, 11):
    print('{:>4}'.format(X), end=' ')
print()
for X in range(1,11):
    print('{:>4}'.format(X), end=' ')
    while Y <= 10:
        print('{:>4}'.format(X * Y), end=' ')
        Y+=1
    print()
    Y=1
```

This example begins by creating two variables, X and Y, to hold the row and column value of the table. X is the row variable and Y is the column variable.

To make the table readable, this example must create a heading at the top and another along the side. When users see a 1 at the top and a 1 at the side, and follow these values to where they intersect in the table, they can see the value of the two numbers when multiplied.

The first print() statement adds a space (because nothing appears in the corner of the table; see Figure 9-8 to more easily follow this discussion). All the formatting statement says is to create a space 4 characters wide and place a space within it. The {:>4} part of the code determines the size of the column. The format(' ') function determines what appears in that space. The end attribute of the print() statement changes the ending character from a carriage return to a simple space.

The first for loop displays the numbers 1 through 10 at the top of the table. The range() function creates the sequence of numbers for you. When using the range() function, you specify the starting value, which is 1 in this case, and one more than the ending value, which is 11 in this case.

At this point, the cursor is sitting at the end of the heading row. To move it to the next line, the code issues a print() call with no other information.

Even though the next bit of code looks quite complex, you can figure it out if you look at it a line at a time. The multiplication table shows the values from 1 * 1 to 10 * 10, so you need ten rows and ten columns to display the information. The for statement tells Python to create ten rows.

Look again at Figure 9-8 to note the row heading. The first print() call displays the row heading value. Of course, you have to format this information, and the code uses a space of four characters that end with a space, rather than a carriage return, in order to continue printing information in that row.

The while loop comes next. This loop prints the columns in an individual row. The column values are the multiplied values of X * Y. Again, the output is formatted to take up four spaces. The while loop ends when Y is updated to the next value by using Y+=1.

Now you're back into the for loop. The print() statement ends the current row. In addition, Y must be reset to 1 so that it's ready for the beginning of the next row, which begins with 1.

2. Click Run Cell.

You see the multiplication table shown in Figure 9-8.

Nesting Loop Statements

```
In [9]:  X = 1
         Y = 1
         print ('{:>4}'.format(' '), end= ' ')
         for X in range(1, 11):
             print('{:>4}'.format(X), end=' ')
         print()
         for X in range(1,11):
             print('{:>4}'.format(X), end=' ')
             while Y <= 10:
                 print('{:>4}'.format(X * Y), end=' ')
                 Y+=1
             print()
             Y=1
```

```
         1    2    3    4    5    6    7    8    9   10
    1    1    2    3    4    5    6    7    8    9   10
    2    2    4    6    8   10   12   14   16   18   20
    3    3    6    9   12   15   18   21   24   27   30
    4    4    8   12   16   20   24   28   32   36   40
    5    5   10   15   20   25   30   35   40   45   50
    6    6   12   18   24   30   36   42   48   54   60
    7    7   14   21   28   35   42   49   56   63   70
    8    8   16   24   32   40   48   56   64   72   80
    9    9   18   27   36   45   54   63   72   81   90
   10   10   20   30   40   50   60   70   80   90  100
```

FIGURE 9-8: The multiplication table is pleasing to the eye thanks to its formatting.

IN THIS CHAPTER

» **Understanding error sources**

» **Handling error conditions**

» **Specifying that an error has occurred**

» **Developing your own error indicators**

» **Performing tasks even after an error occurs**

Chapter **10**

Dealing with Errors

M ost application code of any complexity has errors in it. When your application suddenly freezes for no apparent reason, that's an error. Seeing one of those obscure message dialog boxes is another kind of error. However, errors can occur that don't provide you with any sort of notification. An application might perform the wrong computation on a series of numbers you provide, resulting in incorrect output that you may never know about unless someone tells you that something is wrong or you check for the issue yourself. Errors need not be consistent, either. You may see them on some occasions and not on others. For example, an error can occur only when the weather is bad or the network is overloaded. In short, errors occur in all sorts of situations and for all sorts of reasons. This chapter tells you about various kinds of errors and what to do when your application encounters them.

It shouldn't surprise you that errors occur. Applications are written by humans, and humans make mistakes. Most developers call application errors *exceptions,* meaning that they're the exception to the rule. Because exceptions do occur in applications, you need to detect and do something about them whenever possible. The act of detecting and processing an exception is called *error handling* or *exception handling.* To properly detect errors, you need to know about error sources and why errors occur in the first place. When you do detect the error, you must process it by *catching* the exception. Catching an exception means examining it and possibly doing something about it. So, another part of this chapter is about discovering how to perform exception handling in your own application.

Sometimes your code detects an error in the application. When this happens, you need to *raise* or *throw* an exception. You see both terms used for the same thing, which simply means that your code encountered an error it couldn't handle, so it passed the error information onto another piece of code to *handle* (interpret, process, and, with luck, fix the exception). In some cases, you use custom error message objects to pass on the information. Even though Python has a wealth of generic message objects that cover most situations, some situations are special. For example, you might want to provide special support for a database application, and Python won't normally cover that contingency with a generic message object. You need to know when to handle exceptions locally, when to send them to the code that called your code, and when to create special exceptions so that every part of the application knows how to handle the exception — all of which are topics covered by this chapter.

Sometimes you also must ensure that your application handles an exception gracefully, even if that means shutting the application down. Fortunately, Python provides the `finally` clause, which always executes, even when an exception occurs. You can place code to close files or perform other essential tasks in the code block associated with this clause. Even though you won't perform this task all the time, it's the last topic discussed in the chapter. You can find the downloadable source code for this chapter in the `BPPD_10_Dealing_with_Errors.ipynb` file, as described in the book's Introduction.

Knowing Why Python Doesn't Understand You

Developers often get frustrated with programming languages and computers because they seemingly go out of their way to cause communication problems. Of course, programming languages and computers are both inanimate — they don't "want" anything. Programming languages and computers also don't think; they literally accept whatever the developer says. Therein lies the problem.

REMEMBER

Neither Python nor the computer will "know what you mean" when you type instructions as code. Both follow whatever instructions you provide to the letter and literally as you provide them. You may not have meant to tell Python to delete a data file unless some absurd condition occurred. However, if you don't make the conditions clear, Python will delete the file whether the condition exists or not. When an error of this sort happens, people commonly say that the application has a *bug* in it. Bugs are simply coding errors that you can remove by using a debugger.

(A *debugger* is a special kind of tool that lets you stop or pause application execution, examine the content of variables, and generally dissect the application to see what makes it tick.)

Errors occur in many cases when the developer makes assumptions that simply aren't true. Of course, this includes assumptions about the application user, who probably doesn't care about the extreme level of care you took when crafting your application. The user will enter bad data. Again, Python won't know or care that the data is bad and will process it even when your intent was to disallow the bad input. Python doesn't understand the concepts of good or bad data; it simply processes incoming data according to any rules you set, which means that you must set rules to protect users from themselves.

Python isn't proactive or creative — those qualities exist only in the developer. When a network error occurs or the user does something unexpected, Python doesn't create a solution to fix the problem. It only processes code. If you don't provide code to handle the error, the application is likely to fail and crash ungracefully — possibly taking all of the user's data with it. Of course, the developer can't anticipate every potential error situation, either, which is why most complex applications have errors in them — errors of omission, in this case.

WARNING

Some developers out there think they can create bulletproof code, despite the absurdity of thinking that such code is even possible. Smart developers assume that some number of bugs will get through the code-screening process, that nature and users will continue to perform unexpected actions, and that even the smartest developer can't anticipate every possible error condition. Always assume that your application is subject to errors that will cause exceptions; that way, you'll have the mindset required to actually make your application more reliable. Keeping Murphy's Law, "If anything can go wrong, it will" in mind will help more than you think. (See more about Murphy's laws at `http://www.murphys-laws.com/`.)

Considering the Sources of Errors

You might be able to divine the potential sources of error in your application by reading tea leaves, but that's hardly an efficient way to do things. Errors actually fall into well-defined categories that help you predict (to some degree) when and where they'll occur. By thinking about these categories as you work through your application, you're far more likely to discover potential errors sources before they occur and cause potential damage. The two principle categories are

>> Errors that occur at a specific time

>> Errors that are of a specific type

The following sections discuss these two categories in greater detail. The overall concept is that you need to think about error classifications in order to start finding and fixing potential errors in your application before they become a problem.

Classifying when errors occur

Errors occur at specific times. The two major time frames are

» Compile time

» Runtime

No matter when an error occurs, it causes your application to misbehave. The following sections describe each time frame.

Compile time

A compile time error occurs when you ask Python to run the application. Before Python can run the application, it must interpret the code and put it into a form that the computer can understand. A computer relies on machine code that is specific to that processor and architecture. If the instructions you write are malformed or lack needed information, Python can't perform the required conversion. It presents an error that you must fix before the application can run.

Fortunately, compile-time errors are the easiest to spot and fix. Because the application won't run with a compile-time error in place, user never sees this error category. You fix this sort of error as you write your code.

TIP

The appearance of a compile-time error should tell you that other typos or omissions could exist in the code. It always pays to check the surrounding code to ensure that no other potential problems exist that might not show up as part of the compile cycle.

Runtime

A runtime error occurs after Python compiles the code you write and the computer begins to execute it. Runtime errors come in several different types, and some are harder to find than others. You know you have a runtime error when the application suddenly stops running and displays an exception dialog box or when the user complains about erroneous output (or at least instability).

REMEMBER

Not all runtime errors produce an exception. Some runtime errors cause instability (the application freezes), errant output, or data damage. Runtime errors can affect other applications or create unforeseen damage to the platform on which the application is running. In short, runtime errors can cause you quite a bit of grief, depending on precisely the kind of error you're dealing with at the time.

Many runtime errors are caused by errant code. For example, you can misspell the name of a variable, preventing Python from placing information in the correct variable during execution. Leaving out an optional but necessary argument when calling a method can also cause problems. These are examples of *errors of commission,* which are specific errors associated with your code. In general, you can find these kinds of errors by using a debugger or by simply reading your code line by line to check for errors.

Runtime errors can also be caused by external sources not associated with your code. For example, the user can input incorrect information that the application isn't expecting, causing an exception. A network error can make a required resource inaccessible. Sometimes even the computer hardware has a glitch that causes a nonrepeatable application error. These are all examples of *errors of omission,* from which the application might recover if your application has error-trapping code in place. It's important that you consider both kinds of runtime errors — errors of commission and omission — when building your application.

Distinguishing error types

You can distinguish errors by type, that is, by how they're made. Knowing the error types helps you understand where to look in an application for potential problems. Exceptions work like many other things in life. For example, you know that electronic devices don't work without power. So, when you try to turn your television on and it doesn't do anything, you might look to ensure that the power cord is firmly seated in the socket.

TIP

Understanding the error types helps you locate errors faster, earlier, and more consistently, resulting in fewer misdiagnoses. The best developers know that fixing errors while an application is in development is always easier than fixing it when the application is in production because users are inherently impatient and want errors fixed immediately and correctly. In addition, fixing an error earlier in the development cycle is always easier than fixing it when the application nears completion because less code exists to review.

The trick is to know where to look. With this in mind, Python (and most other programming languages) breaks errors into the following types:

>> Syntactical

>> Semantic

>> Logical

The following sections examine each of these error types in more detail. I've arranged the sections in order of difficulty, starting with the easiest to find. A syntactical error is generally the easiest; a logical error is generally the hardest.

Syntactical

Whenever you make a typo of some sort, you create a syntactical error. Some Python syntactical errors are quite easy to find because the application simply doesn't run. The interpreter may even point out the error for you by highlighting the errant code and displaying an error message. However, some syntactical errors are quite hard to find. Python is case sensitive, so you may use the wrong case for a variable in one place and find that the variable isn't quite working as you thought it would. Finding the one place where you used the wrong capitalization can be quite challenging.

REMEMBER

Most syntactical errors occur at compile time and the interpreter points them out for you. Fixing the error is made easy because the interpreter generally tells you what to fix, and with considerable accuracy. Even when the interpreter doesn't find the problem, syntactical errors prevent the application from running correctly, so any errors the interpreter doesn't find show up during the testing phase. Few syntactical errors should make it into production as long as you perform adequate application testing.

Semantic

When you create a loop that executes one too many times, you don't generally receive any sort of error information from the application. The application will happily run because it thinks that it's doing everything correctly, but that one additional loop can cause all sorts of data errors. When you create an error of this sort in your code, it's called a *semantic error.*

REMEMBER

Semantic errors occur because the meaning behind a series of steps used to perform a task is wrong — the result is incorrect even though the code apparently runs precisely as it should. Semantic errors are tough to find, and you sometimes need some sort of debugger to find them. (Chapter 20 provides a discussion of tools that you can use with Python to perform tasks such as debugging applications. You can also find blog posts about debugging on my blog at `http://blog.johnmuellerbooks.com`.)

Logical

Some developers don't create a division between semantic and logical errors, but they are different. A semantic error occurs when the code is essentially correct but the implementation is wrong (such as having a loop execute once too often). Logical errors occur when the developer's thinking is faulty. In many cases, this sort of error happens when the developer uses a relational or logical operator incorrectly. However, logical errors can happen in all sorts of other ways, too. For example, a developer might think that data is always stored on the local hard drive, which means that the application may behave in an unusual manner when it attempts to load data from a network drive instead.

REMEMBER

Logical errors are quite hard to fix because the problem isn't with the actual code, yet the code itself is incorrectly defined. The thought process that went into creating the code is faulty; therefore, the developer who created the error is less likely to find it. Smart developers use a second pair of eyes to help spot logical errors. Having a formal application specification also helps because the logic behind the tasks the application performs is usually given a formal review.

Catching Exceptions

Generally speaking, a user should never see an exception dialog box. Your application should always catch the exception and handle it before the user sees it. Of course, the real world is different — users do see unexpected exceptions from time to time. However, catching every potential exception is still the goal when developing an application. The following sections describe how to catch exceptions and handle them.

Basic exception handling

To handle exceptions, you must tell Python that you want to do so and then provide code to perform the handling tasks. You have a number of ways in which you can perform this task. The following sections start with the simplest method first and then move on to more complex methods that offer added flexibility.

UNDERSTANDING THE BUILT-IN EXCEPTIONS

Python comes with a host of built-in exceptions — far more than you might think possible. You can see a list of these exceptions at `https://docs.python.org/3.6/library/exceptions.html`. The documentation breaks the exception list down into categories. Here is a brief overview of the Python exception categories that you work with regularly:

- **Base classes:** The base classes provide the essential building blocks (such as the `Exception` exception) for other exceptions. However, you might actually see some of these exceptions, such as the `ArithmeticError` exception, when working with an application.

- **Concrete exceptions:** Applications can experience hard errors — errors that are hard to overcome because there really isn't a good way to handle them or they signal an event that the application must handle. For example, when a system runs out of memory, Python generates a `MemoryError` exception. Recovering from this error is hard because it isn't always possible to release memory from other uses. When the user presses an interrupt key (such as Ctrl+C or Delete), Python generates a `KeyboardInterrupt` exception. The application must handle this exception before proceeding with any other tasks.

- **OS exceptions:** The operating system can generate errors that Python then passes along to your application. For example, if your application tries to open a file that doesn't exist, the operating system generates a `FileNotFoundError` exception.

- **Warnings:** Python tries to warn you about unexpected events or actions that could result in errors later. For example, if you try to inappropriately use a resource, such as an icon, Python generates a `ResourceWarning` exception. You want to remember that this particular category is a warning and not an actual error: Ignoring it can cause you woe later, but you can ignore it.

Handling a single exception

In Chapter 8, the `IfElse.py` and other examples have a terrible habit of spitting out exceptions when the user inputs unexpected values. Part of the solution is to provide range checking. However, range checking doesn't overcome the problem of a user typing text such as Hello in place of an expected numeric value. Exception handling provides a more complex solution to the problem, as described in the following steps.

1. **Open a new notebook.**

You can also use the downloadable source file, BPPD_10_Dealing_with_Errors.ipynb.

2. **Type the following code into the notebook — pressing Enter after each line:**

```
try:
    Value = int(input("Type a number between 1 and 10: "))
except ValueError:
    print("You must type a number between 1 and 10!")
else:
    if (Value > 0) and (Value <= 10):
        print("You typed: ", Value)
    else:
        print("The value you typed is incorrect!")
```

The code within the try block has its exceptions handled. In this case, handling the exception means getting input from the user by using the int(input()) calls. If an exception occurs outside this block, the code doesn't handle it. With reliability in mind, the temptation might be to enclose all the executable code in a try block so that every exception would be handled. However, you want to make your exception handling small and specific to make locating the problem easier.

REMEMBER

The except block looks for a specific exception in this case: ValueError. When the user creates a ValueError exception by typing Hello instead of a numeric value, this particular exception block is executed. If the user were to generate some other exception, this except block wouldn't handle it.

The else block contains all the code that is executed when the try block code is successful (doesn't generate an exception). The remainder of the code is in this block because you don't want to execute it unless the user does provide valid input. When the user provides a whole number as input, the code can then range check it to ensure that it's correct.

3. **Click Run Cell.**

Python asks you to type a number between 1 and 10.

4. **Type** Hello **and press Enter.**

The application displays an error message, as shown in Figure 10-1.

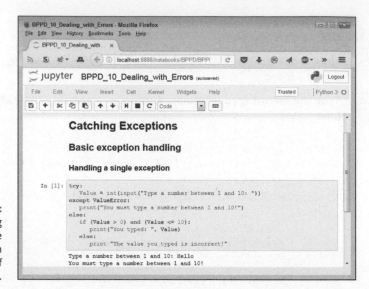

FIGURE 10-1:
Typing the wrong
input type
generates an
error instead of
an exception.

5. **Perform Steps 3 and 4 again, but type** 5.5 **instead of Hello.**

The application generates the same error message, as shown in Figure 10-1.

6. **Perform Steps 3 and 4 again, but type** 22 **instead of Hello.**

The application outputs the expected range error message, as shown in Figure 10-2. Exception handling doesn't weed out range errors. You must still check for them separately.

```
In [3]: try:
            Value = int(input("Type a number between 1 and 10: "))
        except ValueError:
            print("You must type a number between 1 and 10!")
        else:
            if (Value > 0) and (Value <= 10):
                print("You typed: ", Value)
            else:
                print "The value you typed is incorrect!"

        Type a number between 1 and 10: 22
        The value you typed is incorrect!
```

FIGURE 10-2:
Exception
handling doesn't
ensure that the
value is in the
correct range.

7. **Perform Steps 3 and 4 again, but type** 7 **instead of Hello.**

This time, the application finally reports that you've provided a correct value of 7. Even though it seems like a lot of work to perform this level of checking, you can't really be certain that your application is working correctly without it.

TECHNICAL STUFF

You may have to check for other sorts of issues, depending on the environment you choose to use for testing. For example, if you had been using IDLE instead of Notebook for testing purposes, pressing a Ctrl+C, Cmd+C, or an alternative type of unexpected interrupt would have resulted in a KeyboardInterrupt exception. Because Notebook automatically checks for this sort of exception, nothing happens when you press these interrupt keys, so you're saved from having to perform yet another check. Obviously, this strategy works only when everyone uses an IDE, such as Notebook, that provides the required built-in protection.

Using the except clause without an exception

You can create an exception handling block in Python that's generic because it doesn't look for a specific exception. In most cases, you want to provide a specific exception when performing exception handling for these reasons:

>> To avoid hiding an exception you didn't consider when designing the application

>> To ensure that others know precisely which exceptions your application will handle

>> To handle the exceptions correctly by using specific code for that exception

However, sometimes you may need a generic exception-handling capability, such as when you're working with third-party libraries or interacting with an external service. The following steps demonstrate how to use an except clause without a specific exception attached to it.

1. **Type the following code into the notebook — pressing Enter after each line:**

```
try:
    Value = int(input("Type a number between 1 and 10: "))
except:
    print("This is the generic error!")
except ValueError:
    print("You must type a number between 1 and 10!")
else:
    if (Value > 0) and (Value <= 10):
        print("You typed: ", Value)
    else:
        print("The value you typed is incorrect!")
```

The only difference between this example and the previous example is that the except clause doesn't have the ValueError exception specifically associated with it. The result is that this except clause will also catch any other exception that occurs.

2. **Click Run Cell.**

You see the error message shown in Figure 10-3. Python automatically detects that you have placed the exception handlers in the wrong order. (You discover more about this issue in the "Handling more specific to less specific exceptions" section later in the chapter.) Reverse the order of the two exceptions so that they appear like this:

```
try:
    Value = int(input("Type a number between 1 and 10: "))
except ValueError:
    print("You must type a number between 1 and 10!")
except:
    print("This is the generic error!")
else:
    if (Value > 0) and (Value <= 10):
        print("You typed: ", Value)
    else:
        print("The value you typed is incorrect!")
```

Using the except clause without an exception

```
In [5]: try:
            Value = int(input("Type a number between 1 and 10: "))
        except:
            print("This is the generic error!")
        except ValueError:
            print("You must type a number between 1 and 10!")
        else:
            if (Value > 0) and (Value <= 10):
                print("You typed: ", Value)
            else:
                print("The value you typed is incorrect!")

          File "<ipython-input-5-587f65f032cf>", line 2
            Value = int(input("Type a number between 1 and 10: "))
                ^
        SyntaxError: default 'except:' must be last
```

FIGURE 10-3:
The exception handlers are in the wrong order.

3. Click Run Cell.

Python asks you to type a number between 1 and 10.

4. Type Hello and press Enter.

The application displays an error message (refer to Figure 10-1). When the exceptions are in the right order, the code detects specific errors first and then uses less specific handlers only when necessary.

5. Click Run Cell.

Python asks you to type a number between 1 and 10.

6. Choose Kernel ➪ Interrupt.

This act is akin to pressing Ctrl+C or Cmd+C in other IDEs. However, nothing actually appears to happen. Look at the server window, however, and you see a `Kernel Interrupted` message.

7. **Type** 5.5 **and press Enter.**

You see the generic error message shown in Figure 10-4 because Notebook is reacting to the interrupt, rather than the incorrect input; the reason is that the interrupt came first. Python queues errors in the order in which it receives them. Consequently, you may find that an application outputs what appears to be the wrong error message at times.

FIGURE 10-4:
Generic exception
handling traps
the Keyboard
Interrupt
exception.

```
In [7]: try:
            Value = int(input("Type a number between 1 and 10: "))
        except ValueError:
            print("You must type a number between 1 and 10!")
        except:
            print("This is the generic error!")
        else:
            if (Value > 0) and (Value <= 10):
                print("You typed: ", Value)
            else:
                print("The value you typed is incorrect!")

        Type a number between 1 and 10: 5.5
        This is the generic error!
```

8. **Perform Steps 3 and 4 again, but type** 5.5 **instead of Hello.**

The application generates the same error message as before (again, refer to Figure 10-1). In this case, no interrupt occurred, so you see the error message you expected.

Working with exception arguments

Most exceptions don't provide arguments (a list of values that you can check for additional information). The exception either occurs or it doesn't. However, a few exceptions do provide arguments, and you see them used later in the book. The arguments tell you more about the exception and provide details that you need to correct it.

**TECHNICAL
STUFF**

For the sake of completeness, this chapter includes a simple example that generates an exception with an argument. You can safely skip the remainder of this section if desired because the information is covered in more detail later in the book.

1. **Type the following code into the notebook — pressing Enter after each line:**

```
import sys
try:
    File = open('myfile.txt')
```

```
except IOError as e:
    print("Error opening file!\r\n" +
        "Error Number: {0}\r\n".format(e.errno) +
        "Error Text: {0}".format(e.strerror))
else:
    print("File opened as expected.")
    File.close();
```

This example uses some advanced features. The import statement obtains code from another file. Chapter 11 tells you how to use this Python feature.

The open() function opens a file and provides access to the file through the File variable. Chapter 16 tells you how file access works. Given that myfile.txt doesn't exist in the application directory, the operating system can't open it and will tell Python that the file doesn't exist.

Trying to open a nonexistent file generates an IOError exception. This particular exception provides access to two arguments:

- errno: Provides the operating system error number as an integer

- strerror: Contains the error information as a human-readable string

The as clause places the exception information into a variable, e, that you can access as needed for additional information. The except block contains a print() call that formats the error information into an easily read error message.

If you should decide to create the myfile.txt file, the else clause executes. In this case, you see a message stating that the file opened normally. The code then closes the file without doing anything with it.

2. **Click Run Cell.**

    The application displays the Error opening file information, as shown in Figure 10-5.

FIGURE 10-5:
Attempting
to open a
nonexistent file
never works.

Working with exception arguments

```
In [9]: import sys
        try:
            File = open('myfile.txt')
        except IOError as e:
            print("Error opening file!\r\n" +
                "Error Number: {0}\r\n".format(e.errno) +
                "Error Text: {0}".format(e.strerror))
        else:
            print("File opened as expected.")
            File.close();

        Error opening file!
        Error Number: 2
        Error Text: No such file or directory
```

OBTAINING A LIST OF EXCEPTION ARGUMENTS

The list of arguments supplied with exceptions varies by exception and by what the sender provides. It isn't always easy to figure out what you can hope to obtain in the way of additional information. One way to handle the problem is to simply print everything by using code like this:

```python
import sys
try:
    File = open('myfile.txt')
except IOError as e:
    for Arg in e.args:
        print(Arg)
else:
    print("File opened as expected.")
    File.close();
```

The args property always contains a list of the exception arguments in string format. You can use a simple for loop to print each of the arguments. The only problem with this approach is that you're missing the argument names, so you know the output information (which is obvious in this case), but you don't know what to call it.

A more complex method of dealing with the issue is to print both the names and the contents of the arguments. The following code displays both the names and the values of each of the arguments:

```python
import sys
try:
    File = open('myfile.txt')
except IOError as e:
    for Entry in dir(e):
        if (not Entry.startswith("_")):
            try:
                print(Entry, " = ", e.__getattribute__(Entry))
            except AttributeError:
                print("Attribute ", Entry, " not accessible.")
else:
    print("File opened as expected.")
    File.close();
```

In this case, you begin by getting a listing of the attributes associated with the error argument object using the dir() function. The output of the dir() function is a list of

(continued)

(continued)

strings containing the names of the attributes that you can print. Only those arguments that don't start with an underscore (_) contain useful information about the exception. However, even some of those entries are inaccessible, so you must encase the output code in a second try . . . except block (see the "Nested exception handling" section, later in the chapter, for details).

The attribute name is easy because it's contained in Entry. To obtain the value associated with that attribute, you must use the __getattribute() function and supply the name of the attribute you want. When you run this code, you see both the name and the value of each of the attributes supplied with a particular error argument object. In this case, the actual output is as follows:

```
args  =  (2, 'No such file or directory')
Attribute  characters_written  not accessible.
errno  =  2
filename  =  myfile.txt
filename2 = None
strerror  =  No such file or directory
winerror  =  None
with_traceback  =  <built-in method with_traceback of
    FileNotFoundError object at 0x0000000003416DC8>
```

Handling multiple exceptions with a single except clause

Most applications can generate multiple exceptions for a single line of code. This fact demonstrated in the "Using the except clause without an exception" section of the chapter. How you handle the multiple exceptions depends on your goals for the application, the types of exceptions, and the relative skill of your users. Sometimes when working with a less skilled user, it's simply easier to say that the application experienced a nonrecoverable error and then log the details into a log file in the application directory or a central location.

REMEMBER

Using a single except clause to handle multiple exceptions works only when a common source of action fulfills the needs of all the exception types. Otherwise, you need to handle each exception individually. The following steps show how to handle multiple exceptions by using a single except clause.

1. **Type the following code into the notebook — pressing Enter after each line:**

```
try:
    Value = int(input("Type a number between 1 and 10: "))
except (ValueError, KeyboardInterrupt):
    print("You must type a number between 1 and 10!")
else:
    if (Value > 0) and (Value <= 10):
        print("You typed: ", Value)
    else:
        print("The value you typed is incorrect!")
```

REMEMBER

Note that the except clause now sports both a ValueError and a Keyboard Interrupt exception. These exceptions appear within parentheses and are separated by commas.

2. **Click Run Cell.**

   Python asks you to type a number between 1 and 10.

3. **Type** Hello **and press Enter.**

   The application displays an error message (refer to Figure 10-1).

4. **Click Run Cell.**

   Python asks you to type a number between 1 and 10.

5. **Choose Kernel ⇨ Interrupt.**

   This act is akin to pressing Ctrl+C or Cmd+C in other IDEs.

6. **Type** 5.5 **and press Enter.**

   The application displays an error message (refer to Figure 10-1).

7. **Perform Steps 2 and 3 again, but type** 7 **instead of Hello.**

   This time, the application finally reports that you've provided a correct value of 7.

Handling multiple exceptions with multiple except clauses

When working with multiple exceptions, it's usually a good idea to place each exception in its own except clause. This approach allows you to provide custom handling for each exception and makes it easier for the user to know precisely what went wrong. Of course, this approach is also a lot more work. The following steps demonstrate how to perform exception handling by using multiple except clauses.

1. **Type the following code into the window — pressing Enter after each line:**

```
try:
    Value = int(input("Type a number between 1 and 10: "))
except ValueError:
    print("You must type a number between 1 and 10!")
except KeyboardInterrupt:
    print("You pressed Ctrl+C!")
else:
    if (Value > 0) and (Value <= 10):
        print("You typed: ", Value)
    else:
        print("The value you typed is incorrect!")
```

REMEMBER

Notice the use of multiple except clauses in this case. Each except clause handles a different exception. You can use a combination of techniques, with some except clauses handling just one exception and other except clauses handling multiple exceptions. Python lets you use the approach that works best for the error-handling situation.

2. **Click Run Cell.**

Python asks you to type a number between 1 and 10.

3. **Type** Hello **and press Enter.**

The application displays an error message (refer to Figure 10-1).

4. **Perform Steps 2 and 3 again, but type** 22 **instead of Hello.**

The application outputs the expected range error message (refer to Figure 10-2).

5. **Perform Steps 2 and 3 again, but choose Kernel ➪ Interrupt, and then type** 5.5 **and press Enter.**

The application outputs a specific message that tells the user what went wrong, as shown in Figure 10-6.

FIGURE 10-6:
Using multiple
except clauses
makes specific
error messages
possible.

```
In [17]:  try:
              Value = int(input("Type a number between 1 and 10: "))
          except ValueError:
              print("You must type a number between 1 and 10!")
          except KeyboardInterrupt:
              print("You pressed Ctrl+C!")
          else:
              if (Value > 0) and (Value <= 10):
                  print("You typed: ", Value)
              else:
                  print("The value you typed is incorrect!")

          Type a number between 1 and 10: 5.5
          You pressed Ctrl+C!
```

6. **Perform Steps 2 and 3 again, but type** 7 **instead of Hello.**

This time, the application finally reports that you've provided a correct value of 7.

Handling more specific to less specific exceptions

One strategy for handling exceptions is to provide specific except clauses for all known exceptions and generic except clauses to handle unknown exceptions. You can see the exception hierarchy that Python uses at https://docs.python. org/3/library/exceptions.html#exception-hierarchy. When viewing this chart, BaseException is the uppermost exception. Most exceptions are derived from Exception. When working through math errors, you can use the generic ArithmeticError or a more specific ZeroDivisionError exception.

Python evaluates except clauses in the order in which they appear in the source code file. The first clause is examined first, the second clause is examined second, and so on. The following steps help you examine an example that demonstrates the importance of using the correct exception order. In this case, you perform tasks that result in math errors.

1. **Type the following code into the notebook — pressing Enter after each line:**

```
try:
    Value1 = int(input("Type the first number: "))
    Value2 = int(input("Type the second number: "))
    Output = Value1 / Value2
except ValueError:
    print("You must type a whole number!")
except KeyboardInterrupt:
    print("You pressed Ctrl+C!")
except ArithmeticError:
    print("An undefined math error occurred.")
except ZeroDivisionError:
    print("Attempted to divide by zero!")
else:
    print(Output)
```

The code begins by obtaining two inputs: Value1 and Value2. The first two except clauses handle unexpected input. The second two except clauses handle math exceptions, such as dividing by zero. If everything goes well with the application, the else clause executes, which prints the result of the operation.

2. Click Run Cell.

Python asks you to type the first number.

3. Type Hello and press Enter.

As expected, Python displays the `ValueError` exception message. However, it always pays to check for potential problems.

4. Click Run Cell again.

Python asks you to type the first number.

5. Type 8 and press Enter.

The application asks you to enter the second number.

6. Type 0 and press Enter.

You see the error message for the `ArithmeticError` exception, as shown in Figure 10-7. What you should actually see is the `ZeroDivisionError` exception because it's more specific than the `ArithmeticError` exception.

```
In [20]:  try:
              Value1 = int(input("Type the first number: "))
              Value2 = int(input("Type the second number: "))
              Output = Value1 / Value2
          except ValueError:
              print("You must type a whole number!")
          except KeyboardInterrupt:
              print("You pressed Ctrl+C!")
          except ArithmeticError:
              print("An undefined math error occurred.")
          except ZeroDivisionError:
              print("Attempted to divide by zero!")
          else:
              print(Output)

          Type the first number: 8
          Type the second number: 0
          An undefined math error occurred.
```

FIGURE 10-7: The order in which Python processes exceptions is important.

7. Reverse the order of the two exceptions so that they look like this:

```
except ZeroDivisionError:
    print("Attempted to divide by zero!")
except ArithmeticError:
    print("An undefined math error occurred.")
```

8. Perform Steps 4 through 6 again.

This time, you see the `ZeroDivisionError` exception message because the exceptions appear in the correct order.

9. **Perform Steps 4 through 5 again, but type** 2 **for the second number instead of 0.**

This time, the application finally reports an output value of 4.0, as shown in Figure 10-8.

```
In [22]: try:
             Value1 = int(input("Type the first number: "))
             Value2 = int(input("Type the second number: "))
             Output = Value1 / Value2
         except ValueError:
             print("You must type a whole number!")
         except KeyboardInterrupt:
             print("You pressed Ctrl+C!")
         except ZeroDivisionError:
             print("Attempted to divide by zero!")
         except ArithmeticError:
             print("An undefined math error occurred.")
         else:
             print(Output)

         Type the first number: 8
         Type the second number: 2
         4.0
```

FIGURE 10-8:
Providing usable
input results in a
usable output.

REMEMBER

Notice that the output shown in Figure 10-8 is a floating-point value. Division results in a floating-point value unless you specify that you want an integer output by using the floor division operator (//).

Nested exception handling

Sometimes you need to place one exception-handling routine within another in a process called *nesting.* When you nest exception-handling routines, Python tries to find an exception handler in the nested level first and then moves to the outer layers. You can nest exception-handling routines as deeply as needed to make your code safe.

One of the more common reasons to use a dual layer of exception-handling code is when you want to obtain input from a user and need to place the input code in a loop to ensure that you actually get the required information. The following steps demonstrate how this sort of code might work.

1. **Type the following code into the notebook — pressing Enter after each line:**

```
TryAgain = True
while TryAgain:
    try:
        Value = int(input("Type a whole number. "))
    except ValueError:
        print("You must type a whole number!")
```

```
    try:
        DoOver = input("Try again (y/n)? ")
    except:
        print("OK, see you next time!")
        TryAgain = False
    else:
        if (str.upper(DoOver) == "N"):
            TryAgain = False
except KeyboardInterrupt:
    print("You pressed Ctrl+C!")
    print("See you next time!")
    TryAgain = False
else:
    print(Value)
    TryAgain = False
```

The code begins by creating an input loop. Using loops for this type of purpose is actually quite common in applications because you don't want the application to end every time an input error is made. This is a simplified loop, and normally you create a separate function to hold the code.

When the loop starts, the application asks the user to type a whole number. It can be any integer value. If the user types any non-integer value or presses Ctrl+C, Cmd+C, or another interrupt key combination, the exception-handling code takes over. Otherwise, the application prints the value that the user supplied and sets TryAgain to False, which causes the loop to end.

A ValueError exception can occur when the user makes a mistake. Because you don't know why the user input the wrong value, you have to ask if the user wants to try again. Of course, getting more input from the user could generate another exception. The inner try...except code block handles this secondary input.

Notice the use of the str.upper() function when getting character input from the user. This function makes it possible to receive y or Y as input and accept them both. Whenever you ask the user for character input, converting lowercase characters to uppercase is a good idea so that you can perform a single comparison (reducing the potential for error).

The KeyboardInterrupt exception displays two messages and then exits automatically by setting TryAgain to False. The KeyboardInterrupt occurs only when the user presses a specific key combination designed to end the application. The user is unlikely to want to continue using the application at this point.

2. **Click Run Cell.**

Python asks the user to input a whole number.

3. **Type** Hello **and press Enter.**

The application displays an error message and asks whether you want to try again.

4. **Type** Y **and press Enter.**

The application asks you to input a whole number again, as shown in Figure 10-9.

Nested exception handling

```
In [*]: TryAgain = True
        while TryAgain:
            try:
                Value = int(input("Type a whole number. "))
            except ValueError:
                print("You must type a whole number!")
                try:
                    DoOver = input("Try again (y/n)? ")
                except:
                    print("OK, see you next time!")
                    TryAgain = False
                else:
                    if (str.upper(DoOver) == "N"):
                        TryAgain = False
            except KeyboardInterrupt:
                print("You pressed Ctrl+C!")
                print("See you next time!")
                TryAgain = False
            else:
                print(Value)
                TryAgain = False

        Type a whole number. Hello
        You must type a whole number!
        Try again (y/n)? Y

        Type a whole number.
```

FIGURE 10-9: Using a loop means that the application can recover from the error.

5. **Type** 5.5 **and press Enter.**

The application again displays the error message and asks whether you want to try again.

6. **Choose Kernel ⇨ Interrupt to interrupt the application, type** Y, **and then press Enter.**

The application ends, as shown in Figure 10-10. Notice that the message is the one from the inner exception. The application never gets to the outer exception because the inner exception handler provides generic exception handling.

Nested exception handling

```
In [23]: TryAgain = True
         while TryAgain:
             try:
                 Value = int(input("Type a whole number. "))
             except ValueError:
                 print("You must type a whole number!")
                 try:
                     DoOver = input("Try again (y/n)? ")
                 except:
                     print("OK, see you next time!")
                     TryAgain = False
                 else:
                     if (str.upper(DoOver) == "N"):
                         TryAgain = False
             except KeyboardInterrupt:
                 print("You pressed Ctrl+C!")
                 print("See you next time!")
                 TryAgain = False
             else:
                 print(Value)
                 TryAgain = False

Type a whole number. Hello
You must type a whole number!
Try again (y/n)? Y
Type a whole number. 5.5
You must type a whole number!
Try again (y/n)? Y
OK, see you next time!
```

FIGURE 10-10:
The inner exception handler provides secondary input support.

7. **Click Run Cell.**

Python asks the user to input a whole number.

8. **Choose Kernel ⇨ Interrupt to interrupt the application, type** 5.5, **and then press Enter.**

The application ends, as shown in Figure 10-11. Notice that the message is the one from the outer exception. In Steps 6 and 8, the user ends the application by pressing an interrupt key. However, the application uses two different exception handlers to address the problem.

```
In [24]: TryAgain = True
         while TryAgain:
             try:
                 Value = int(input("Type a whole number. "))
             except ValueError:
                 print("You must type a whole number!")
                 try:
                     DoOver = input("Try again (y/n)? ")
                 except:
                     print("OK, see you next time!")
                     TryAgain = False
                 else:
                     if (str.upper(DoOver) == "N"):
                         TryAgain = False
             except KeyboardInterrupt:
                 print("You pressed Ctrl+C!")
                 print("See you next time!")
                 TryAgain = False
             else:
                 print(Value)
                 TryAgain = False

Type a whole number. 5.5
You pressed Ctrl+C!
See you next time!
```

FIGURE 10-11:
The outer exception handler provides primary input support.

Raising Exceptions

So far, the examples in this chapter have reacted to exceptions. Something happens and the application provides error-handling support for that event. However, situations arise for which you may not know how to handle an error event during the application design process. Perhaps you can't even handle the error at a particular level and need to pass it up to some other level to handle. In short, in some situations, your application must generate an exception. This act is called *raising* (or sometimes *throwing*) the exception. The following sections describe common scenarios in which you raise exceptions in specific ways.

Raising exceptions during exceptional conditions

The example in this section demonstrates how you raise a simple exception — that it doesn't require anything special. The following steps simply create the exception and then handle it immediately.

1. **Type the following code into the notebook — pressing Enter after each line:**

```
try:
    raise ValueError
except ValueError:
    print("ValueError Exception!")
```

You wouldn't ever actually create code that looks like this, but it shows you how raising an exception works at its most basic level. In this case, the raise call appears within a try...except block. A basic raise call simply provides the name of the exception to raise (or throw). You can also provide arguments as part of the output to provide additional information.

REMEMBER

Notice that this try...except block lacks an else clause because there is nothing to do after the call. Although you rarely use a try...except block in this manner, you can. You may encounter situations like this one sometimes and need to remember that adding the else clause is purely optional. On the other hand, you must add at least one except clause.

2. **Click Run Cell.**

Python displays the expected exception text, as shown in Figure 10-12.

FIGURE 10-12:
Raising an
exception
requires only a
call to raise.

Raising Exceptions

Raising exceptions during exceptional conditions

```
In [25]:  try:
              raise ValueError
          except ValueError:
              print ("ValueError Exception!")

          ValueError Exception!
```

Passing error information to the caller

Python provides exceptionally flexible error handling in that you can pass information to the *caller* (the code that is calling your code) no matter which exception you use. Of course, the caller may not know that the information is available, which leads to a lot of discussion on the topic. If you're working with someone else's code and don't know whether additional information is available, you can always use the technique described in the "Obtaining a list of exception arguments" sidebar earlier in this chapter to find it.

You may have wondered whether you could provide better information when working with a ValueError exception than with an exception provided natively by Python. The following steps show that you can modify the output so that it does include helpful information.

1. **Type the following code into the notebook — pressing Enter after each line:**

```
try:
    Ex = ValueError()
    Ex.strerror = "Value must be within 1 and 10."
    raise Ex
except ValueError as e:
    print("ValueError Exception!", e.strerror)
```

The ValueError exception normally doesn't provide an attribute named strerror (a common name for string error), but you can add it simply by assigning a value to it as shown. When the example raises the exception, the except clause handles it as usual but obtains access to the attributes using e. You can then access the e.strerror member to obtain the added information.

2. **Click Run Cell.**

Python displays an expanded ValueError exception, as shown in Figure 10-13.

FIGURE 10-13:
You can add error
information to
any exception.

```
                 Passing error information to the caller
In [26]:  try:
              Ex = ValueError()
              Ex.strerror = "Value must be within 1 and 10."
              raise Ex
          except ValueError as e:
              print "ValueError Exception!", e.strerror

          ValueError Exception! Value must be within 1 and 10.
```

Creating and Using Custom Exceptions

Python provides a wealth of standard exceptions that you should use whenever possible. These exceptions are incredibly flexible, and you can even modify them as needed (within reason) to meet specific needs. For example, the "Passing error information to the caller" section of this chapter demonstrates how to modify a ValueError exception to allow for additional data. However, sometimes you simply must create a custom exception because none of the standard exceptions will work. Perhaps the exception name just doesn't tell the viewer the purpose that the exception serves. You may need a custom exception for specialized database work or when working with a service.

WARNING

The example in this section is going to seem a little complicated for now because you haven't worked with classes before. Chapter 15 introduces you to classes and helps you understand how they work. If you want to skip this section until after you read Chapter 15, you can do so without any problem.

The example in this section shows a quick method for creating your own exceptions. To perform this task, you must create a class that uses an existing exception as a starting point. To make things a little easier, this example creates an exception that builds upon the functionality provided by the ValueError exception. The advantage of using this approach rather than the one shown in the "Passing error information to the caller" section, the preceding section in this chapter, is that this approach tells anyone who follows you precisely what the addition to the ValueError exception is; additionally, it makes the modified exception easier to use.

1. Type the following code into the notebook — pressing Enter after each line:

```
class CustomValueError(ValueError):
    def __init__(self, arg):
        self.strerror = arg
        self.args = {arg}
try:
    raise CustomValueError("Value must be within 1 and 10.")
except CustomValueError as e:
    print("CustomValueError Exception!", e.strerror)
```

This example essentially replicates the functionality of the example in the "Passing error information to the caller" section of the chapter. However, it places the same error in both strerror and args so that the developer has access to either (as would normally happen).

The code begins by creating the CustomValueError class that uses the ValueError exception class as a starting point. The __init__() function provides the means for creating a new instance of that class. Think of the class as a blueprint and the instance as the building created from the blueprint.

REMEMBER

Notice that the strerror attribute has the value assigned directly to it, but args receives it as an array. The args member normally contains an array of all the exception values, so this is standard procedure, even when args contains just one value as it does now.

The code for using the exception is considerably easier than modifying ValueError directly. All you do is call raise with the name of the exception and the arguments you want to pass, all on one line.

2. **Click Run Cell.**

The application displays the letter sequence, along with the letter number, as shown in Figure 10-14.

FIGURE 10-14: Custom exceptions can make your code easier to read.

Creating and Using Custom Exceptions

```
In [27]: class CustomValueError(ValueError):
             def __init__(self, arg):
                 self.strerror = arg
                 self.args = (arg)
         try:
             raise CustomValueError("Value must be within 1 and 10.")
         except CustomValueError as e:
             print "CustomValueError Exception!", e.strerror

         CustomValueError Exception! Value must be within 1 and 10.
```

Using the finally Clause

Normally you want to handle any exception that occurs in a way that doesn't cause the application to crash. However, sometimes you can't do anything to fix the problem, and the application is most definitely going to crash. At this point, your goal is to cause the application to crash gracefully, which means closing files so that the user doesn't lose data and performing other tasks of that nature. Anything you can do to keep damage to data and the system to a minimum is an essential part of handling data for a crashing application.

The `finally` clause is part of the crashing-application strategy. You use this clause to perform any required last-minute tasks. Normally, the `finally` clause is quite short and uses only calls that are likely to succeed without further problem. It's essential to close the files, log the user off, and perform other required tasks, and then let the application crash before something terrible happens (such as a total system failure). With this necessity in mind, the following steps show a simple example of using the `finally` clause.

1. **Type the following code into the notebook — pressing Enter after each line:**

```
import sys
try:
    raise ValueError
    print("Raising an exception.")
except ValueError:
    print("ValueError Exception!")
    sys.exit()
finally:
    print("Taking care of last minute details.")
print("This code will never execute.")
```

In this example, the code raises a `ValueError` exception. The `except` clause executes as normal when this happens. The call to `sys.exit()` means that the application exits after the exception is handled. Perhaps the application can't recover in this particular instance, but the application normally ends, which is why the final `print()` function call won't ever execute.

The `finally` clause code always executes. It doesn't matter whether the exception happens or not. The code you place in this block needs to be common code that you always want to execute. For example, when working with a file, you place the code to close the file into this block to ensure that the data isn't damaged by remaining in memory rather than going to disk.

2. **Click Run Cell.**

The application displays the `except` clause message and the `finally` clause message, as shown in Figure 10-15. The `sys.exit()` call prevents any other code from executing.

Note that this isn't a normal exit, so Notepad displays additional information for you. When you use some other IDEs, such as IDLE, the application simply exits without displaying any additional information.

Using the finally Clause

```
In [1]:  import sys
         try:
             raise ValueError
             print("Raising an exception.")
         except ValueError:
             print("ValueError Exception!")
             sys.exit()
         finally:
             print("Taking care of last minute details.")
         print("This code will never execute.")

ValueError Exception!
Taking care of last minute details.

An exception has occurred, use %tb to see the full traceback.

SystemExit

C:\Users\John\Anaconda3\lib\site-packages\IPython\core\interactiveshell.p
y:2889: UserWarning: To exit: use 'exit', 'quit', or Ctrl-D.
  warn("To exit: use 'exit', 'quit', or Ctrl-D.", stacklevel=1)
```

FIGURE 10-15:
Use the finally
clause to ensure
specific actions
take place
before the
application ends.

3. **Comment out the** `raise ValueError` **call by preceding it with two pound signs, like this:**

```
##raise ValueError
```

Removing the exception will demonstrate how the finally clause actually works.

4. **Click Run Cell.**

The application displays a series of messages, including the finally clause message, as shown in Figure 10-16. This part of the example shows that the finally clause always executes, so you need to use it carefully.

```
In [2]:  import sys
         try:
             ## raise ValueError
             print "Raising an exception."
         except ValueError:
             print("ValueError Exception!")
             sys.exit()
         finally:
             print("Taking care of last minute details.")
         print("This code will never execute.")

Raising an exception.
Taking care of last minute details.
This code will never execute.
```

FIGURE 10-16:
Be sure to
remember that
the finally
clause always
executes.

3

Performing Common Tasks

Import and use packages.

Use strings to display data in human-readable form.

Create and manage lists of objects.

Use collections to enhance list capabilities.

Develop and use classes.

Chapter **11**

Interacting with Packages

The examples in this book are small, but the functionality of the resulting applications is extremely limited as well. Even tiny real-world applications contain thousands of lines of code. In fact, applications that contain millions of lines of code are somewhat common. Imagine trying to work with a file large enough to contain millions of lines of code — you'd never find anything. In short, you need some method to organize code into small pieces that are easier to manage, much like the examples in this book. The Python solution is to place code in separate code groupings called *packages*. (In some sources, you may see *modules* used in place of packages; the two terms are used interchangeably.) Commonly used packages that contain source code for generic needs are called *libraries.*

REMEMBER

Packages are contained in separate files. To use the package, you must tell Python to grab the file and read it into the current application. The process of obtaining code found in external files is called *importing.* You import a package or library to use the code it contains. A few examples in the book have already shown the import statement in use, but this chapter explains the import statement in detail so that you know how to use it.

As part of the initial setup, Python created a pointer to the general-purpose libraries that it uses. That's why you can simply add an import statement with the name of the library and Python can find it. However, it pays to know how to locate the files on disk in case you ever need to update them or you want to add your own packages and libraries to the list of files that Python can use.

The library code is self-contained and well documented (at least in most cases it is). Some developers might feel that they never need to look at the library code, and they're right to some degree — you never have to look at the library code in order to use it. You might want to view the library code, though, to ensure that you understand how the code works. In addition, the library code can teach you new programming techniques that you might not otherwise discover. So, viewing the library code is optional, but it can be helpful.

The one thing you do need to know how to do is obtain and use the Python library documentation. This chapter shows you how to obtain and use the library documentation as part of the application-creation process. You can find the downloadable source code for the client code examples this chapter in the BPPD_11_Interacting_with_Packages.ipynb file, as described in the book's Introduction. The package examples appear in the BPPD_11_Packages.ipynb file.

Creating Code Groupings

Grouping like pieces of code together is important to make the code easier to use, modify, and understand. As an application grows, managing the code found in a single file becomes harder and harder. At some point, the code becomes impossible to manage because the file has become too large for anyone to work with.

REMEMBER

The term *code* is used broadly in this particular case. Code groupings can include:

>> Classes

>> Functions

>> Variables

>> Runnable code

The collection of classes, functions, variables, and runnable code within a package is known as *attributes*. A package has attributes that you access by that attribute's name. Later sections in this chapter discuss precisely how package access works.

TECHNICAL
STUFF

The runnable code can actually be written in a language other than Python. For example, it's somewhat common to find packages that are written in C/C++ instead of Python. The reason that some developers use runnable code is to make the Python application faster, less resource intensive, and better able to use a particular platform's resources. However, using runnable code comes with the downside of making your application less portable (able to run on other platforms) unless you have runnable code packages for each platform that you want to support. In addition, dual-language applications can be harder to maintain because you must have developers who can speak each of the computer languages used in the application.

The most common way to create a package is to define a separate file containing the code you want to group separately from the rest of the application. For example, you might want to create a print routine that an application uses in a number of places. The print routine isn't designed to work on its own but is part of the application as a whole. You want to separate it because the application uses it in numerous places and you could potentially use the same code in another application. The ability to reuse code ranks high on the list of reasons to create packages.

To make things easier to understand, the examples in this chapter use a common package. The package doesn't do anything too amazing, but it demonstrates the principles of working with packages. Open a Python 3 Notebook project, name it BPPD_11_Packages, and create the code shown in Listing 11-1. After you complete this task, download the code as a new Python file named BPPD_11_Packages.py by choosing File ⇨ Download As ⇨ Python (.py) in Notebook.

LISTING 11-1: **A Simple Demonstration Package**

```python
def SayHello(Name):
    print("Hello ", Name)
    return
def SayGoodbye(Name):
    print("Goodbye ", Name)
    return
```

You may need to copy the resulting file to your existing BPPD folder, depending on where your browser normally downloads files. When done correctly, your Notebook dashboard should contain a copy of the file, as shown in Figure 11-1. Using the Notebook's Import feature, described in the "Importing a notebook" section of Chapter 4, makes things considerably easier.

The example code contains two simple functions named SayHello() and SayGoodbye(). In both cases, you supply a Name to print and the function prints it onscreen along with a greeting for you. At that point, the function returns control to the caller. Obviously, you normally create more complicated functions, but these functions work well for the purposes of this chapter.

FIGURE 11-1:
Make sure you
place a copy of
the package in
your BPPD folder.

Understanding the package types

The Python support system is immense. In fact, you'll likely never use more than a small fraction of it for even the most demanding applications. It's not that Python itself is all that huge; the language is actually somewhat concise compared to many other languages out there. The immensity comes from the Python system of packages that perform everything from intense scientific work, to AI, to space exploration, to biologic modeling, to anything else you can imagine and many things you can't. However, not all those packages are available all the time, so you need some idea of what sort of packages Python supports and where you might find them (in order of preference):

>> **Built-in:** The built-in packages address most common needs. You find them in the Adaconda3\Lib folder on your system, and all you need to do to use them is import them into your application.

>> **Custom:** As demonstrated in this chapter, you can create your own packages and use them as needed. They appear on your hard drive, normally in the same directory as your project code, and you simply import them into your application.

>> **Conda:** You can find a wealth of packages specifically designed for Anaconda. Many of these packages appear at http://conda.anaconda.org/mutirri. Before you can use these packages, you must install them by using the conda utility at the Anaconda command line, as described in the "Installing conda packages" section of this chapter. After you have the package installed, you use it as you would any built-in package.

>> **Non-conda:** Just because a package isn't specifically designed for use with Anaconda doesn't mean that you can't use it. You can find a great wealth of packages from third parties that provide significant functionality. To install these packages, you use the pip utility at the Anaconda command line, as described in the "Installing packages by using pip" section, later in this chapter. After you have the package installed, you may have to perform additional configuration as described by the party who created the package. Generally, when the package is configured, you use it as you would any built-in package.

Considering the package cache

Anaconda provides a package cache that resides outside the Python library. This package cache lets you easily interact with the Anaconda-specific packages by using the conda command-line utility. To see how you use this package cache, open an Anaconda command prompt or terminal window. You get access to this feature through the Anaconda Prompt entry in the Anaconda3 folder on your system. Type **conda list** and press Enter to see a list of the packages that you have installed now. Figure 11-2 shows typical results.

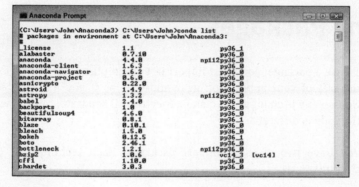

FIGURE 11-2: Obtain a list of Anaconda-specific packages by using the conda utility.

REMEMBER

Note that the output displays the package name as you would access it from within Anaconda, the package version, and the associated Python version. All this information is helpful in managing the packages. The following list provides the essential conda commands for managing your packages:

>> conda clean: Removes packages that you aren't using.

>> conda config: Configures the package cache setup.

>> conda create: Defines a new conda environment that contains a specific list of packages, which makes it easier to manage the packages and can improve application speed.

>> `conda help`: Displays a complete list of conda commands.

>> `conda info`: Displays the conda configuration information, which includes details on where conda stores packages and where it looks for new packages.

>> `conda install`: Installs one or more packages into the default or specified conda environment.

>> `conda list`: Outputs a list of conda packages with varying levels of detail. You can specify which packages to list and in which environments to look.

>> `conda remove`: Removes one or more packages from the package cache.

>> `conda search`: Looks for specific packages by using the search criteria you provide.

>> `conda update`: Updates some or all of the packages in the package cache.

TIP

These commands can do a lot more than you might think. Of course, it's impossible to memorize all that information, so you can rely on the `--help` command-line switch to obtain full details on using a particular command. For example, to learn more about conda list, type **conda list --help** and press Enter.

Importing Packages

To use a package, you must import it. Python places the package code inline with the rest of your application in memory — as if you had created one huge file. Neither file is changed on disk — they're still separate, but the way Python views the code is different.

REMEMBER

You have two ways to import packages. Each technique is used in specific circumstances:

>> `import`: You use the import statement when you want to import an entire package. This is the most common method that developers use to import packages because it saves time and requires only one line of code. However, this approach also uses more memory resources than does the approach of selectively importing the attributes you need, which the next paragraph describes.

>> `from...import`: You use the from...import statement when you want to selectively import individual package attributes. This method saves resources, but at the cost of complexity. In addition, if you try to use an attribute that you didn't import, Python registers an error. Yes, the package still contains the attribute, but Python can't see it because you didn't import it.

INTERACTING WITH THE CURRENT PYTHON DIRECTORY

The directory that Python is using to access code affects which packages you can load. The Python library files are always included in the list of locations that Python can access, but Python knows nothing of the directory you use to hold your source code unless you tell it to look there. Of course, you need to know how to interact with the directory functions in order to tell Python where to look for specific bits of code. You can find this example in the BPPD_11_Directory.ipynb file, as described in the book's Introduction.

1. **Open a new notebook.**

2. **Type** import os **and press Enter.**

    This action imports the Python os library. You need to import this library to change the directory (the location Python sees on disk) to the working directory for this book.

3. **Type** print(os.getcwd()) **and click Run Cell.**

    You see the current working directory (cwd) that Python uses to obtain local code.

4. **In a new cell, type** for entry in os.listdir(): print(entry) **and click Run Cell.**

    You see a listing of the directory entries. The listing lets you determine whether the file you need is in the cwd. If not, you need to change directories to a location that does contain the required file.

To change directories to a new location, you use the os.chdir() method and include the new location as a string, such as os.chdir('C:\MyDir'). However, you normally find with Notebook that the cwd does contain the files for your current project.

Now that you have a better idea of how to import packages, it's time to look at them in detail. The following sections help you work through importing packages using the two techniques available in Python.

Using the import statement

The import statement is the most common method for importing a package into Python. This approach is fast and ensures that the entire package is ready for use. The following steps get you started using the import statement.

1. **Open a new notebook.**

   You can also use the downloadable source file, BPPD_11_Interacting_with_
   Packages.ipynb.

2. **Change directories, if necessary, to the downloadable source code
   directory.**

   Generally, Notebook places you in the correct directory to use the source code
   files, so you won't need to perform this step. See the instructions found in the
   "Interacting with the current Python directory" sidebar.

3. **Type** import BPPD_11_Packages **and press Enter.**

   This instruction tells Python to import the contents of the BPPD_11_Packages.
   py file that you created in the "Creating Code Groupings" section of the
   chapter. The entire library is now ready for use.

WARNING

   It's important to know that Python also creates a cache of the package in the
   __pycache__ subdirectory. If you look into your source code directory after you
   import BPPD_11_Packages for the first time, you see the new __pycache__
   directory. If you want to make changes to your package, you must delete this
   directory. Otherwise, Python will continue to use the unchanged cache file
   instead of your updated source code file.

**TECHNICAL
STUFF**

   The cached filename includes the version of Python for which it is meant, so it's
   BPPD_11_Packages.cpython-36.pyc in this case. The 36 in the filename
   means that this file is Python 3.6 specific. A .pyc file represents a compiled
   Python file, which is used to improve application speed.

4. **Type** dir(BPPD_11_Packages) **and click Run Cell.**

   You see a listing of the package contents, which includes the SayHello() and
   SayGoodbye() functions, as shown in Figure 11-3. (A discussion of the other
   entries appears in the "Viewing the Package Content" section, later in this
   chapter.)

5. **In a new cell, type** BPPD_11_Packages.SayHello("Josh")**.**

REMEMBER

   Notice that you must precede the attribute name, which is the SayHello()
   function in this case, with the package name, which is BPPD_11_Packages.
   The two elements are separated by a period. Every call to a package that you
   import follows the same pattern.

6. **Type** BPPD_11_Packages.SayGoodbye("Sally") **and click Run Cell.**

   The SayHello() and SayGoodbye() functions output the expected text, as
   shown in Figure 11-4.

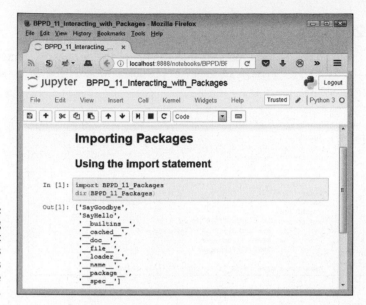

FIGURE 11-3:
A directory listing shows that Python imports both functions from the package.

FIGURE 11-4:
The SayHello() and SayGoodbye() functions output the expected text.

```
In [2]:  BPPD_11_Packages.SayHello("Josh")
         BPPD_11_Packages.SayGoodbye("Sally")

         Hello   Josh
         Goodbye  Sally
```

Using the from. . .import statement

The from. . .import statement has the advantage of importing only the attributes you need from a package. This difference means that the package uses less memory and other system resources than using the import statement does. In addition, the from. . .import statement makes the package a little easier to use because some commands, such as dir(), show less information, or only the information that you actually need. The point is that you get only what you want and not anything else. The following steps demonstrate using the from. . .import statement. However, before you can import BPPD_11_Packages selectively, you must remove it from the environment, which is the first part of the following process.

1. Type the following code into Notebook:

```
import sys
del sys.modules["BPPD_11_Packages"]
del BPPD_11_Packages
dir(BPPD_11_Packages)
```

2. **Click Run Cell.**

You see the error message shown in Figure 11-5. Listing the content of the BPPD_11_Packages package isn't possible anymore because it's no longer loaded.

```
In [3]: import sys
        del sys.modules["BPPD_11_Packages"]
        del BPPD_11_Packages
        dir(BPPD_11_Packages)

------------------------------------------------------------
------------

NameError                                 Traceback (most recen
t call last)
<ipython-input-3-c87e6f10a47b> in <module>()
      2 del sys.modules["BPPD_11_Packages"]
      3 del BPPD_11_Packages
----> 4 dir(BPPD_11_Packages)

NameError: name 'BPPD_11_Packages' is not defined
```

FIGURE 11-5:
Removing a package from the environment requires two steps.

3. **In a new cell, type** from BPPD_11_Packages import SayHello **and press Enter.**

Python imports the SayHello( ) function that you create in the "Creating Code Groupings" section, earlier in the chapter. Only this specific function is now ready for use.

REMEMBER

You can still import the entire package, should you want to do so. The two techniques for accomplishing the task are to create a list of packages to import (the names can be separated by commas, such as from BPPD_11_Packages import SayHello, SayGoodbye) or to use the asterisk (*) in place of a specific attribute name. The asterisk acts as a wildcard character that imports everything.

4. **Type** dir(BPPD_11_Packages) **and click Run Cell.**

Python displays an error message, as shown previously in Figure 11-5. Python imports only the attributes that you specifically request. This means that the BPPD_11_Packages package isn't in memory — only the attributes that you requested are in memory.

5. **In a new cell, type** dir(SayHello) **and click Run Cell.**

You see a listing of attributes that are associated with the SayHello( ) function, as shown in Figure 11-6 (which is only a partial list). You don't need to know how these attributes work just now, but you'll use some of them later in the book.

FIGURE 11-6:
Use the dir()
function to obtain
information
about the specific
attributes you
import.

```
In [5]: dir(SayHello)
Out[5]: ['__annotations__',
         '__call__',
         '__class__',
         '__closure__',
         '__code__',
         '__defaults__',
         '__delattr__',
         '__dict__',
         '__dir__',
```

6. **In a new cell, type** SayHello("Angie") **and click Run Cell.**

The SayHello() function outputs the expected text, as shown in Figure 11-7.

FIGURE 11-7:
The SayHello()
function no
longer requires
the package
name.

```
In [6]: SayHello("Angie")
        Hello  Angie
```

REMEMBER

When you import attributes by using the from...import statement, you don't need to precede the attribute name with a package name. This feature makes the attribute easier to access.

WARNING

Using the from...import statement can also cause problems. If two attributes have the same name, you can import only one of them. The import statement prevents name collisions, which is important when you have a large number of attributes to import. In sum, you must exercise care when using the from...import statement.

7. **In a new cell, type** SayGoodbye("Harold") **and click Run Cell.**

You imported only the SayHello() function, so Python knows nothing about SayGoodbye() and displays an error message. The selective nature of the from...import statement can cause problems when you assume that an attribute is present when it really isn't.

Finding Packages on Disk

To use the code in a package, Python must be able to locate the package and load it into memory. The location information is stored as paths within Python. Whenever you request that Python import a package, Python looks at all the files in its list of paths to find it. The path information comes from three sources:

>> **Environment variables:** Chapter 3 tells you about Python environment variables, such as PYTHONPATH, that tell Python where to find packages on disk.

>> **Current directory:** Earlier in this chapter, you discover that you can change the current Python directory so that it can locate any packages used by your application.

>> **Default directories:** Even when you don't define any environment variables and the current directory doesn't yield any usable packages, Python can still find its own libraries in the set of default directories that are included as part of its own path information.

Knowing the current path information is helpful because the lack of a path can cause your application to fail. To obtain path information, type **for p in sys.path: print(p)** in a new cell and click Run Cell. You see a listing of the path information, as shown in Figure 11-8. Your listing may be different from the one shown in Figure 11-8, depending on your platform, the version of Python you have installed, and the Python features you have installed.

FIGURE 11-8:
The sys.path
attribute contains
a listing of the
individual paths
for your system.

Finding Packages on Disk

```
In [8]: for p in sys.path: print(p)

        C:\BP4D
        C:\Users\John\Anaconda3\python36.zip
        C:\Users\John\Anaconda3\DLLs
        C:\Users\John\Anaconda3\lib
        C:\Users\John\Anaconda3
```

The sys.path attribute is reliable but may not always contain every path that Python can see. If you don't see a needed path, you can always check in another place that Python looks for information. The following steps show how to perform this task:

1. **In a new cell, type** import os **and press Enter.**

2. **Type** os.environ['PYTHONPATH'].split(os.pathsep) **and click Run Cell.**

When you have a PYTHONPATH environment variable defined, you see a list of paths, as shown in Figure 11-9. However, if you don't have the environment variable defined, you see an error message instead.

FIGURE 11-9:
You must
request
information
about
environment
variables
separately.

```
In [9]: import os
        os.environ['PYTHONPATH'].split(os.pathsep)
Out[9]: ['C:\\BP4D']
```

Notice that both the sys.path and the os.environ['PYTHONPATH'] attributes contain the C:\BP4D\Chapter11 entry in this case. The sys.path attribute doesn't include the split() function, which is why the example uses a for loop with it. However, the os.environ['PYTHONPATH'] attribute does include the split() function, so you can use it to create a list of individual paths.

You must provide split() with a value to look for in splitting a list of items. The os.pathsep *constant* (a variable that has one, unchangeable, defined value) defines the path separator for the current platform so that you can use the same code on any platform that supports Python.

TIP

You can also add and remove items from sys.path. For example, if you want to add the current working directory to the list of packages, you type **sys.path.append(os.getcwd())** in the Notebook cell and click Run Cell. When you list the sys.path contents again, you see that the new entry is added to the end of the list. Likewise, when you want to remove an entry you type **sys.path.remove(os.getcwd())** in the Notebook cell and click Run Cell. The addition is present only during the current session.

Downloading Packages from Other Sources

Your copy of Python and the associated Jupyter Notebook component of Anaconda come with a wide assortment of packages that fulfill many common needs. In fact, for experimentation purposes, you seldom have to go beyond these packages because you already have so many of them installed on your system. Of course, someone is always thinking of some new way to do things, which requires new code and packages to store the code. In addition, some coding techniques are so esoteric that including the packages to support them with a default install would consume space that most people will never use. Consequently, you may have to install packages from online or other sources from time to time.

The two most common methods of obtaining new packages are to use the conda or pip (also known by the recursive acronym Pip Installs Packages) utilities. However, you may find packages that use other installation methods with varying degrees of success. You use conda and pip for different purposes. Many misconceptions exist about the two package managers, but it really comes down to conda providing general-purpose package management for a wide range of languages with special needs in the conda environment, and to pip providing services specifically for Python in any environment. You can read more about these differences at https://jakevdp.github.io/blog/2016/08/25/conda-myths-and-misconceptions/. When you need a Python-specific package, look to pip first.

For example, `pip` gives you access to the Python Package Index (PyPI) found at `https://pypi.python.org/pypi`. The following sections discuss these two methods.

Opening the Anaconda Prompt

Before you can do much in the way of managing packages, you must open the Anaconda Prompt. The Anaconda Prompt is just like any other command prompt or terminal window, but it provide special configuration features to make working with the various command-line utilities supplied with Anaconda easier. To open the prompt, locate its icon in the Anaconda3 folder on your machine. For example, when using a Windows system, you can open the Anaconda Prompt by choosing Start⇨All Programs⇨Anaconda3⇨Anaconda Prompt. The Anaconda Prompt may take a moment or two to appear onscreen because of its configuration requirements.

Working with conda packages

You can perform a wide range of tasks using `conda`, but some tasks are more common than others. The following sections describe how to perform five essential tasks using `conda`. You can obtain additional information about this utility at `https://conda.io/docs/commands.html`. Typing **conda --help** and pressing Enter also yields an overview of help information.

Viewing conda packages

You can view `conda` packages in two ways. The first is to create a list of available packages, while the second is to search for a specific package. Listing helps you discover whether a package is already installed. Searching helps you discover the details about the installed package.

You can perform searching and listing in a general way to locate everything installed on a particular system. In this case, you use the commands by themselves:

```
conda list
conda search
```

The output of these commands is lengthy and might scroll right off the end of the screen buffer (making it impossible to scroll back and view all of the results). For example, Figure 11-10 shows what happens when you use `conda list` by itself.

FIGURE 11-10: The conda list output is rather lengthy and may overrun the screen buffer.

Note that the output shows the package name, version, and associated version of Python. You can use this output to determine whether a package is installed on your system. However, sometimes you need more, which requires a search. For example, say that you want to know what you have installed from the scikit-learn package for the Windows 64-bit platform. In this case, you type **conda search --platform win-64 scikit-learn** and press Enter, which outputs the details shown in Figure 11-11.

FIGURE 11-11: Searches output a lot more information than lists.

TIP

A number of flags exist to greatly increase the amount of information you receive. For example, when you use the --json flag, you obtain details such as a complete list of dependencies for the package, whether the package is completely installed, and a URL containing the location of the packages online. You can learn more about conda searches at https://conda.io/docs/commands/conda-search.html.

Installing conda **packages**

The conda packages appear at https://anaconda.org/. To determine whether a particular package, such as SciPy, is available, type its name in the search field near the top and press Enter. Oddly enough, you're apt to find a whole long list of candidates, as shown in Figure 11-12.

USING CONDA INFO

Even though the conda info command is normally associated with environment information, you can also use it to work with packages. To discover the specifics of a particular package, you just add the package name, such as conda info numpy. Unfortunately, using this command often results in information overload, so you need to shorten it a little. One way to do this is to add a version number after the package name separated by an equals (=) sign, such as conda info numpy=1.13.1 for version 1.13.1 of the NumPy package.

In most cases, you don't receive any additional information using the --verbose switch with packages. However, using the --json switch can yield a little additional information, and this switch puts the information in a form that lets you easily manipulate the output using code, such as a script. The point is that you can use conda info to discover even more deep, dark secrets about your packages. You can learn more about conda info at https://conda.io/docs/commands/conda-info.html.

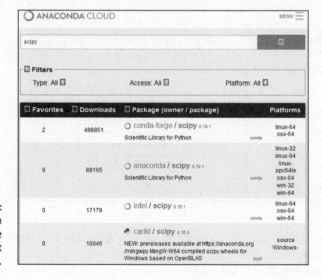

FIGURE 11-12: Choose a version of the package that you want to use.

To make any sense out of the long list of candidates, you must click the individual links, which takes you to a details page like the one shown in Figure 11-13. Note that you get links to all sorts of information about this particular copy of SciPy. However, the Installers section of the page is most important. You can download an installer or use conda to perform the task with the supplied command line, which is conda install -c anaconda scipy in this case.

FIGURE 11-13:
Locate the package version to install and use the condo command to install it.

Updating conda **packages**

The packages you use to develop applications can become outdated with time. The developers who maintain them might add new features or apply bug fixes. The problem with updates is that they can cause your application to work incorrectly, or sometimes not at all if you're depending on a broken behavior. However, it's generally a good idea to keep packages updated if for no other reason than to apply security-related bug fixes. Of course, you need to know that the package requires updating. To find outdated packages, you use the conda search --outdated command, followed by the name of the package you want to check.

TIP

If you want to check all of the packages, then you simply leave the package name off when performing your search. Unfortunately, at this point the output becomes so long that it's really tough to see anything (assuming the majority doesn't just scroll right off the screen buffer). Using the conda search --outdated --names-only command helps in this case by showing just the names of the packages that require updating.

After you know what you need to update, you can use the conda update command to perform the task. For example, you might want to update the NumPy package, which means typing **conda update numpy** and pressing Enter. Few packages are stand-alone, so conda will present a list of items that you need to update along with NumPy. Type **y** and press Enter to proceed. Figure 11-14 shows a typical sequence of events during the update process.

FIGURE 11-14:
You see a lot of
information
during the update
process.

WARNING

You do have the option of updating all packages at one time. Simply type **conda update --all** and press Enter to get started. However, you may find that interactions between packages make the update less successful than it could be if you performed the updates individually. In addition, the update can take a long time, so be sure to have plenty of coffee and a copy of *War and Peace* on hand. You can learn more about conda updates at https://conda.io/docs/commands/conda-update.html.

Removing conda packages

At some point, you might decide that you no longer need a conda package. The only problem is that you don't know whether other packages depend on the package in question. Because package dependencies can become quite complex, and you want to be sure that your applications will continue to run, you need to check which other packages depend on this particular package. Unfortunately, the conda info command (described at https://conda.io/docs/commands/conda-info.html) tells you only about the package requirements — that is, what it depends on. Best practice is to keep packages installed after you've install them.

REMEMBER

However, assuming that you really must remove the package, you use the conda remove command described at https://conda.io/docs/commands/conda-remove.html. This command removes the package that you specify, along with any packages that depend on this package. In this case, best practice is to use the --dry-run command-line switch first to ensure that you really do want to remove the package. For example, you may decide that you want to remove NumPy. In this case, you type **conda remove --dry-run numpy** and press Enter. The command won't actually execute; conda simply shows what would happen if you actually did run the command, as shown in Figure 11-15.

FIGURE 11-15:
A single package
can have a
huge effect.

As you can see, a single package can support many other packages —some of which you might need. If you really must insist on removing the package, type the same command as before without the --dry-run command line switch.

WARNING

Never use the --force command-line switch. This command-line switch removes the package without removing the dependent packages, which will end up destroying your Python installation. If you must remove a package, remove all the dependent packages as well to keep your installation in great shape.

Installing packages by using pip

Oddly enough, working with pip is much like working with conda. They both need to perform essentially the same tasks, so if you know how to use one, you know how to use the other. The reference at https://pip.pypa.io/en/stable/reference/ shows that pip does support essentially the same commands (with a few wording differences). For example, if you want to find a list of outdated packages, you type **pip list --outdated** and press Enter. Here is a list of the common commands that pip supports:

>> check: Verify that the installed packages have compatible dependencies.

>> download: Download the specified packages for later installation.

>> freeze: Output installed packages in requirements format.

>> help: Display a help screen listing an overview of the commands.

>> install: Install the specified packages.

>> list: List the installed packages.

>> `search`: Search online at PyPI for packages.

>> `show`: Show information about the installed packages.

>> `uninstall`: Uninstall the specified packages.

Viewing the Package Content

Python gives you several different ways to view package content. The method that most developers use is to work with the `dir()` function, which tells you about the attributes that the package provides.

Look at Figure 11-3, earlier in the chapter. In addition to the `SayGoodbye()` and `SayHello()` function entries discussed previously, the list has other entries. These attributes are automatically generated by Python for you. These attributes perform the following tasks or contain the following information:

>> `__builtins__`: Contains a listing of all the built-in attributes that are accessible from the package. Python adds these attributes automatically for you.

>> `__cached__`: Tells you the name and location of the cached file that is associated with the package. The location information (path) is relative to the current Python directory.

>> `__doc__`: Outputs help information for the package, assuming that you've actually filled it in. For example, if you type **os._doc_** and press Enter, Python will output the help information associated with the os library.

>> `__file__`: Tells you the name and location of the package. The location information (path) is relative to the current Python directory.

>> `__initializing__`: Determines whether the package is in the process of initializing itself. Normally this attribute returns a value of `False`. This attribute is useful when you need to wait until one package is done loading before you import another package that depends on it.

>> `__loader__`: Outputs the loader information for this package. The *loader* is a piece of software that gets the package and puts it into memory so that Python can use it. This is one attribute you rarely (if ever) use.

>> `__name__`: Tells you just the name of the package.

>> `__package__`: This attribute is used internally by the import system to make it easier to load and manage packages. You don't need to worry about this particular attribute.

It may surprise you to find that you can drill down even further into the attributes. Type **dir(BPPD_11_Packages.SayHello)** and press Enter. You see the entries shown in Figure 11-16.

Viewing the Package Content

```
In [12]: import BPPD_11_Packages
         dir(BPPD_11_Packages.SayHello)

Out[12]: ['__annotations__',
          '__call__',
          '__class__',
          '__closure__',
          '__code__',
          '__defaults__',
          '__delattr__',
          '__dict__',
          '__dir__',
          '__doc__',
          '__eq__',
          '__format__',
```

FIGURE 11-16:
Drill down as far as needed to understand the packages that you use in Python.

Some of these entries, such as __name__, also appeared in the package listing. However, you might be curious about some of the other entries. For example, you might want to know what __sizeof__ is all about. One way to get additional information is to type **help("__sizeof__")** and press Enter. You see some scanty (but useful) help information, as shown in Figure 11-17.

FIGURE 11-17:
Try getting some help information about the attribute you want to know about.

```
In [13]: help("__sizeof__")

         Help on built-in function __sizeof__:

         __sizeof__(...)
             __sizeof__() -> int
             size of object in memory, in bytes
```

Python isn't going to blow up if you try the attribute. Even if the Notebook does experience problems, you can always restart the kernel (or simply restart the environment as a whole). So, another way to check out a package is to simply try the attributes. For example, if you type **BPPD_11_Packages.SayHello.__sizeof__()** and press Enter, you see the size of the SayHello() function in bytes, as shown in Figure 11-18.

FIGURE 11-18:
Using the attributes will help you get a better feel for how they work.

```
In [14]: BPPD_11_Packages.SayHello.__sizeof__()
Out[14]: 112
```

Unlike many other programming languages, Python also makes the source code for its native language libraries available. For example, when you look into the \Python36\Lib directory, you see a listing of .py files that you can open in Notebook with no problem at all. Try uploading the os.py library that you use for various tasks in this chapter by using the Upload button on the Notebook dashboard. Make sure to click Upload next to the file after you've opened it; then click the resulting link, and you see the content shown in Figure 11-19. Note that .py files open in a simpler editor and don't display cells as the notebook files do that you've been using throughout the book.

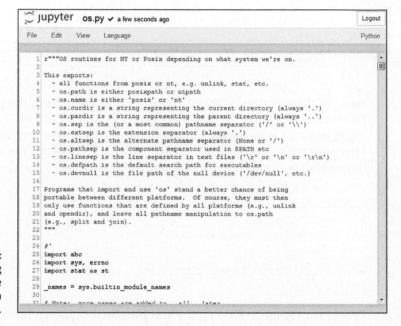

FIGURE 11-19:
Directly viewing
package code
can help in
understanding it.

Viewing the content directly can help you discover new programming techniques and better understand how the library works. The more time you spend working with Python, the better you'll become at using it to build interesting applications.

WARNING

Make sure that you just look at the library code and don't accidentally change it. If you accidentally change the code, your applications can stop working. Worse yet, you can introduce subtle bugs into your application that will appear only on your system and nowhere else. Always exercise care when working with library code.

Viewing Package Documentation

You can use the doc() function whenever needed to get quick help. However, you have a better way to study the packages and libraries located in the Python path — the Python Package Documentation. This feature often appears as Package Docs in the Python folder on your system. It's also referred to as Pydoc. Whatever you call it, the Python Package Documentation makes life a lot easier for developers. The following sections describe how to work with this feature.

Opening the Pydoc application

Pydoc is just another Python application. It actually appears in the \Python36\Lib directory of your system as pydoc.py. As with any other .py file, you can open this one with Notebook and study how it works. You can start it by using the Python 3.6 Module Docs shortcut that appears in the Python 3.6 folder on your system or by using a command at the Anaconda Prompt (see the "Opening the Anaconda Prompt" section, earlier in this chapter, for details).

TIP

You can use Pydoc in both graphical and textual mode. When opening an Anaconda Prompt, you can provide a keyword, such as JSON, and Pydoc displays textual help. Using the -k command-line switch, followed by a keyword such as if, lets you display a list of places where specific keywords appear. To actually start the server, you type **Pydoc -b** and press Enter. If you need to use a specific port for your browser, add the -p command-line switch with a port number.

The graphical mode of the Pydoc application creates a localized server that works with your browser to display information about the Python packages and libraries. So when you start this application, you see a command (terminal) window open.

REMEMBER

As with any server, your system may prompt you for permissions. For example, you may see a warning from your firewall telling you that Pydoc is attempting to access the local system. You need to give Pydoc permission to work with the system so that you can see the information it provides. Any virus detection that you have installed may need permission to let Pydoc continue as well. Some platforms, such as Windows, may require an elevation in privileges to run Pydoc.

Normally, the server automatically opens a new browser window for you, as shown in Figure 11-20. This window contains links to the various packages that are contained on your system, including any custom packages you create and include in the Python path. To see information about any package, you can simply click its link.

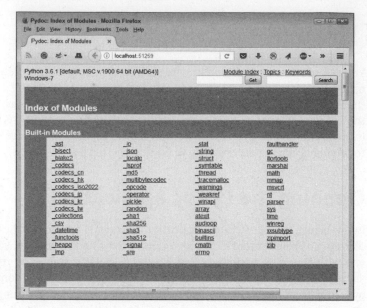

FIGURE 11-20:
Your browser
displays a
number of links
that appear
as part of the
Index page.

The Anaconda Prompt provides you with two commands to control the server. You simply type the letter associated with the command and press Enter to activate it. Here are the two commands:

>> b: Starts a new copy of the default browser with the index page loaded.

>> q: Stops the server.

REMEMBER

When you're done browsing the help information, make sure that you stop the server by typing q and pressing Enter at the command prompt. Stopping the server frees any resources it uses and closes any holes you made in your firewall to accommodate Pydoc.

Using the quick-access links

Refer back to Figure 11-20. Near the top of the web page, you see three links. These links provide quick access to the site features. The browser always begins at the Module Index. If you need to return to this page, simply click the Module Index link.

The Topics link takes you to the page shown in Figure 11-21. This page contains links for essential Python topics. For example, if you want to know more about Boolean values, click the BOOLEAN link. The page you see next describes how Boolean values work in Python. At the bottom of the page are related links that lead to pages that contain additional helpful information.

FIGURE 11-21:
The Topics page tells you about essential Python topics, such as how Boolean values work.

The Keywords link takes you to the page shown in Figure 11-22. What you see is a list of the keywords that Python supports. For example, if you want to know more about creating `for` loops, you click the for link.

FIGURE 11-22:
The Keywords page contains a listing of keywords that Python supports.

Typing a search term

The pages also include two text boxes near the top. The first has a Get button next to it and the second has a Search button next to it. When you type a search term in the first text box and click Get, you see the documentation for that particular package or attribute. Figure 11-23 shows what you see when you type **print** and click Get.

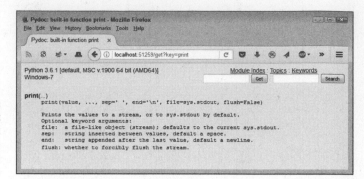

FIGURE 11-23:
Using Get obtains specific information about a search term.

When you type a search term in the second text box and click Search, you see all the topics that could relate to that search term. Figure 11-24 shows typical results when you type **print** and click Search. In this case, you click a link, such as calendar, to see additional information.

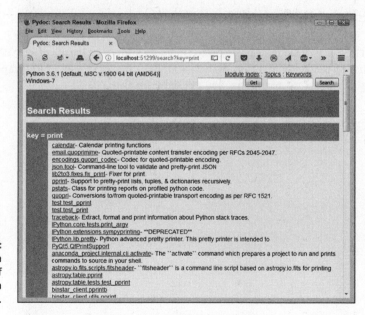

FIGURE 11-24:
Using Search obtains a list of topics about a search term.

Viewing the results

The results you get when you view a page depends on the topic. Some topics are brief, such as the one shown previously in Figure 11-23 for print. However, other topics are extensive. For example, if you were to click the calendar link in Figure 11-24, you would see a significant amount of information, as shown in Figure 11-25.

In this particular case, you see related package information, error information, functions, data, and all sorts of additional information about the calendar printing functions. The amount of information you see depends partly on the complexity of the topic and partly on the amount of information the developer provided with the package. For example, if you were to select BPPD_11_Packages from the Package Index page, you would see only a list of functions and no documentation at all.

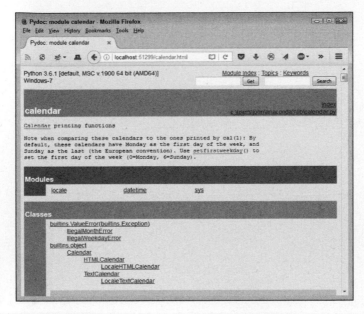

FIGURE 11-25:
Some pages contain extensive information.

Chapter **12**

Working with Strings

Your computer doesn't understand strings. It's a basic fact. Computers understand numbers, not letters. When you see a string on the computer screen, the computer actually sees a series of numbers. However, humans understand strings quite well, so applications need to be able to work with them. Fortunately, Python makes working with strings relatively easy. It translates the string you understand into the numbers the computer understands, and vice versa.

To make strings useful, you need to be able to manipulate them. Of course, that means taking strings apart and using just the pieces you need or searching the string for specific information. This chapter describes how you can build strings by using Python, dissect them as needed, and use just the parts you want after you find what's required. String manipulation is an important part of applications because humans depend on computers performing that sort of work for them (even though the computer has no idea of what a string is).

After you have the string you want, you need to present it to the user in an eye-pleasing manner. The computer doesn't really care how it presents the string, so often you get the information, but it lacks pizzazz. In fact, it may be downright difficult to read. Knowing how to format strings so that they look nice onscreen is important because users need to see information in a form they understand. By the time you complete this chapter, you know how to create, manipulate, and format strings so that the user sees precisely the right information. You can find the downloadable source code for the examples in this chapter in the BPPD_12_ Working_with_Strings.ipynb file, as described in the book's Introduction.

Understanding That Strings Are Different

Most aspiring developers (and even a few who have written code for a long time) really have a hard time understanding that computers truly do only understand 0s and 1s. Even larger numbers are made up of 0s and 1s. Comparisons take place with 0s and 1s. Data is moved by using 0s and 1s. In short, strings don't exist for the computer (and numbers just barely exist). Although grouping 0s and 1s to make numbers is relatively easy, strings are a lot harder because now you're talking about information that the computer must manipulate as numbers but present as characters.

REMEMBER

There are no strings in computer science. Strings are made up of characters, and individual characters are actually numeric values. When you work with strings in Python, what you're really doing is creating an assembly of characters that the computer sees as numeric values. That's why the following sections are so important. They help you understand why strings are so special. Understanding this material will save you a lot of headaches later.

Defining a character by using numbers

To create a character, you must first define a relationship between that character and a number. More important, everyone must agree that when a certain number appears in an application and is viewed as a character by that application, the number is translated into a specific character. One of the most common ways to perform this task is to use the American Standard Code for Information Interchange (ASCII). Python uses ASCII to translate the number 65 to the letter *A*. The chart at `http://www.asciitable.com/` shows the various numeric values and their character equivalents.

REMEMBER

Every character you use must have a different numeric value assigned to it. The letter *A* uses a value of 65. To create a lowercase *a*, you must assign a different number, which is 97. The computer views *A* and *a* as completely different characters, even though people view them as uppercase and lowercase versions of the same character.

The numeric values used in this chapter are in decimal. However, the computer still views them as 0s and 1s. For example, the letter *A* is really the value 01000001 and the letter *a* is really the value 01100001. When you see an *A* onscreen, the computer sees a binary value instead.

TECHNICAL STUFF

Having just one character set to deal with would be nice. However, not everyone could agree on a single set of numeric values to equate with specific characters. Part of the problem is that ASCII doesn't support characters used by other languages; also, it lacks the capability to translate special characters into an onscreen presentation. In fact, character sets abound. You can see a number of them at http://www.i18nguy.com/unicode/codepages.html. Click one of the character set entries to see how it assigns specific numeric values to each character. Most characters sets do use ASCII as a starting point.

Using characters to create strings

Python doesn't make you jump through hoops to create strings. However, the term *string* should actually give you a good idea of what happens. Think about beads or anything else you might string. You place one bead at a time onto the string. Eventually you end up with some type of ornamentation — perhaps a necklace or tree garland. The point is that these items are made up of individual beads.

The same concept used for necklaces made of beads holds true for strings in computers. When you see a sentence, you understand that the sentence is made up of individual characters that are strung together by the programming language you use. The language creates a structure that holds the individual characters together. So, the language, not the computer, knows that so many numbers in a row (each number being represented as a character) defines a string such as a sentence.

REMEMBER

You may wonder why it's important to even know how Python works with characters. The reason is that many of the functions and special features that Python provides work with individual characters, and you need to know that Python sees the individual characters. Even though you see a sentence, Python sees a specific number of characters.

Unlike most programming languages, strings can use either single quotes or double quotes. For example, "Hello There!" with double quotes is a string, as is 'Hello There!' with single quotes. Python also supports triple double and single quotes that let you create strings spanning multiple lines. The following steps help you create an example that demonstrates some of the string features that Python provides.

1. **Open a new notebook.**

   You can also use the downloadable source file, BPPD_12_Working_with_Strings.ipynb.

2. Type the following code into the notebook — pressing Enter after each line:

```
print('Hello There (Single Quote)!')
print("Hello There (Double Quote)!")
print("""This is a multiple line
string using triple double quotes.
You can also use triple single quotes.""")
```

Each of the three `print()` function calls demonstrates a different principle in working with strings. Equally acceptable is to enclose the string in either single or double quotes. When you use a triple quote (either single or double), the text can appear on multiple lines.

3. **Click Run Cell.**

Python outputs the expected text. Notice that the multiline text appears on three lines (see Figure 12-1), just as it does in the source code file, so this is a kind of formatting. You can use multiline formatting to ensure that the text breaks where you want it to onscreen.

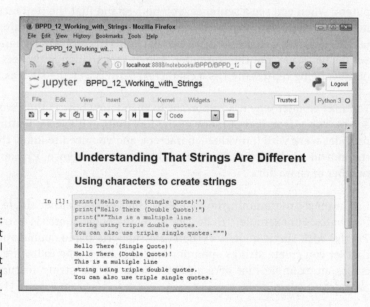

FIGURE 12-1:
Strings consist of individual characters that are linked together.

Creating Stings with Special Characters

Some strings include special characters. These characters are different from the alphanumeric and punctuation characters that you're used to using. In fact, they fall into these categories:

» **Control:** An application requires some means of determining that a particular character isn't meant to be displayed but rather to control the display. All the control movements are based on the *insertion pointer,* the line you see when you type text on the screen. For example, you don't see a tab character. The tab character provides a space between two elements, and the size of that space is controlled by a tab stop. Likewise, when you want to go to the next line, you use a carriage return (which returns the insertion pointer to the beginning of the line) and linefeed (which places the insertion pointer on the next line) combination.

» **Accented:** Characters that have accents, such as the acute ('), grave (` `), circumflex (^), umlaut or diaeresis (¨), tilde (~), or ring (°), represent special spoken sounds, in most cases. You must use special characters to create alphabetical characters with these accents included.

» **Drawing:** You can create rudimentary art with some characters. You can see examples of the box-drawing characters at `http://jrgraphix.net/r/ Unicode/2500–257F`. Some people actually create art by using ASCII characters as well (`http://www.asciiworld.com/`).

» **Typographical:** A number of typographical characters, such as the pilcrow (¶),are used when displaying certain kinds of text onscreen, especially when the application acts as an editor.

» **Other:** Depending on the character set you use, the selection of characters is nearly endless. You can find a character for just about any need. The point is that you need some means of telling Python how to present these special characters.

A common need when working with strings, even strings from simple console applications, is control characters. With this in mind, Python provides escape sequences that you use to define control characters directly (and a special escape sequence for other characters).

REMEMBER

An *escape sequence* literally escapes the common meaning of a letter, such as *a,* and gives it a new meaning (such as the ASCII bell or beep). The combination of the backslash (\) and a letter (such as *a*) is commonly viewed as a single letter by developers — an *escape character* or *escape code.* Table 12-1 provides an overview of these escape sequences.

TABLE 12-1 **Python Escape Sequences**

Escape Sequence	Meaning
\newline	Ignored
\\	Backslash (\)
\'	Single quote (')
\"	Double quote (")
\a	ASCII Bell (BEL)
\b	ASCII Backspace (BS)
\f	ASCII Formfeed (FF)
\n	ASCII Linefeed (LF)
\r	ASCII Carriage Return (CR)
\t	ASCII Horizontal Tab (TAB)
\u*hhhh*	Unicode character (a specific kind of character set with broad appeal across the world) with a hexadecimal value that replaces *hhhh*
\v	ASCII Vertical Tab (VT)
ooo	ASCII character with octal numeric value that replaces *ooo*
\x*hh*	ASCII character with hexadecimal value that replaces *hh*

The best way to see how the escape sequences work is to try them. The following steps help you create an example that tests various escape sequences so that you can see them in action.

1. **Type the following code into the notebook — pressing Enter after each line:**

```
print("Part of this text\r\nis on the next line.")
print("This is an A with a grave accent: \xC0.")
print("This is a drawing character: \u2562.")
print("This is a pilcrow: \266.")
print("This is a division sign: \xF7.")
```

The example code uses various techniques to achieve the same end — to create a special character. Of course, you use control characters directly, as shown in the first line. Many special letters are accessible by using a hexadecimal number that has two digits (as in the second and fifth lines). However, some require that you rely on Unicode numbers (which always require four digits), as shown in the third line. Octal values use three digits and have no special character associated with them, as shown in the fourth line.

2. **Click Run Cell.**

    Python outputs the expected text and special characters, as shown in Figure 12-2.

Creating Stings with Special Characters

```
In [2]:  print("Part of this text\r\nis on the next line.")
         print("This is an A with a grave accent: \xC0.")
         print("This is a drawing character: \u2562.")
         print("This is a pilcrow: \266.")
         print("This is a division sign: \xF7.")

         Part of this text
         is on the next line.
         This is an A with a grave accent: À.
         This is a drawing character: ╢.
         This is a pilcrow: ¶.
         This is a division sign: ÷.
```

WARNING

Notebook uses a standard character set across platforms, so you should see the same special characters no matter which platform you test. However, when creating your application, make sure to test it on various platforms to see how the application will react. A character set on one platform may use different numbers for special characters than another platform does. In addition, user selection of character sets could have an impact on how special characters displayed by your application appear. Always make sure that you test special character usage completely.

Selecting Individual Characters

Earlier in the chapter, you discover that strings are made up of individual characters. They are, in fact, just like beads on a necklace — with each bead being an individual element of the whole string.

Python makes it possible to access individual characters in a string. This is an important feature because you can use it to create new strings that contain only part of the original. In addition, you can combine strings to create new results. The secret to this feature is the square bracket. You place a square bracket with a number in it after the name of the variable. Here's an example:

```
MyString = "Hello World"
print(MyString[0])
```

REMEMBER

In this case, the output of the code is the letter *H*. Python strings are zero-based, which means they start with the number *o* and proceed from there. For example, if you were to type `print(MyString[1])`, the output would be the letter *e*.

You can also obtain a range of characters from a string. Simply provide the beginning and ending letter count separated by a colon in the square brackets. For example, `print(MyString[6:11])` would output the word World. The output would begin with letter 7 and end with letter 12 (remember that the index is zero based). The following steps demonstrate some basic tasks that you can perform by using Python's character-selection technique.

1. **Type the following code into the notebook — pressing Enter after each line.**

```
String1 = "Hello World"
String2 = "Python is Fun!"
print(String1[0])
print(String1[0:5])
print(String1[:5])
print(String1[6:])
String3 = String1[:6] + String2[:6]
print(String3)
print(String2[:7]*5)
```

The example begins by creating two strings. It then demonstrates various methods for using the index on the first string. Notice that you can leave out the beginning or ending number in a range if you want to work with the remainder of that string.

The next step is to combine two substrings. In this case, the code combines the beginning of String1 with the beginning of String2 to create String3.

REMEMBER

The use of the + sign to combine two strings is called *concatenation*. This sign is one of the handier operators to remember when you're working with strings in an application.

The final step is to use a Python feature called *repetition*. You use repetition to make a number of copies of a string or substring.

2. **Click Run Cell.**

Python outputs a series of substrings and string combinations, as shown in Figure 12-3.

```
In [3]: String1 = "Hello World"
        String2 = "Python is Fun!"
        print(String1[0])
        print(String1[0:5])
        print(String1[:5])
        print(String1[6:])
        String3 = String1[:6] + String2[:6]
        print(String3)
        print(String2[:7]*5)

        H
        Hello
        Hello
        World
        Hello Python
        Python Python Python Python Python
```

FIGURE 12-3:
You can select individual pieces of a string.

Slicing and Dicing Strings

Working with ranges of characters provides some degree of flexibility, but it doesn't provide you with the capability to actually manipulate the string content or discover anything about it. For example, you might want to change the characters to uppercase or determine whether the string contains all letters. Fortunately, Python has functions that help you perform tasks of this sort. Here are the most commonly used functions:

» capitalize(): Capitalizes the first letter of a string.

» center(*width*, *fillchar*=" "): Centers a string so that it fits within the number of spaces specified by *width*. If you supply a character for *fillchar*, the function uses that character. Otherwise, center() uses spaces to create a string of the desired width.

» expandtabs(*tabsize*=8): Expands tabs in a string by replacing the tab with the number of spaces specified by *tabsize*. The function defaults to 8 spaces per tab when *tabsize* isn't provided.

» isalnum(): Returns True when the string has at least one character and all characters are alphanumeric (letters or numbers).

» isalpha(): Returns True when the string has at least one character and all characters are alphabetic (letters only).

» isdecimal(): Returns True when a Unicode string contains only decimal characters.

» isdigit(): Returns True when a string contains only digits (numbers and not letters).

» islower(): Returns True when a string has at least one alphabetic character and all alphabetic characters are in lowercase.

>> `isnumeric()`: Returns True when a Unicode string contains only numeric characters.

>> `isspace()`: Returns True when a string contains only whitespace characters (which includes spaces, tabs, carriage returns, linefeeds, form feeds, and vertical tabs, but not the backspace).

>> `istitle()`: Returns True when a string is cased for use as a title, such as *Hello World*. However, the function requires that even little words have the title case. For example, *Follow a Star* returns False, even though it's properly cased, but *Follow A Star* returns True.

>> `isupper()`: Returns True when a string has at least one alphabetic character and all alphabetic characters are in uppercase.

>> `join(seq)`: Creates a string in which the base string is separated in turn by each character in *seq* in a repetitive fashion. For example, if you start with MyString = "Hello" and type print(MyString.join("!*!")), the output is !Hello*Hello!.

>> `len(string)`: Obtains the length of *string*.

>> `ljust(width, fillchar=" ")`: Left justifies a string so that it fits within the number of spaces specified by *width*. If you supply a character for *fillchar*, the function uses that character. Otherwise, `ljust()` uses spaces to create a string of the desired width.

>> `lower()`: Converts all uppercase letters in a string to lowercase letters.

>> `lstrip()`: Removes all leading whitespace characters in a string.

>> `max(str)`: Returns the character that has the maximum numeric value in *str*. For example, *a* would have a larger numeric value than *A*.

>> `min(str)`: Returns the character that has the minimum numeric value in *str*. For example, *A* would have a smaller numeric value than *a*.

>> `rjust(width, fillchar=" ")`: Right justifies a string so that it fits within the number of spaces specified by *width*. If you supply a character for *fillchar*, the function uses that character. Otherwise, `rjust()` uses spaces to create a string of the desired width.

>> `rstrip()`: Removes all trailing whitespace characters in a string.

>> `split(str=" ", num=string.count(str))`: Splits a string into substrings using the delimiter specified by *str* (when supplied). The default is to use a space as a delimiter. Consequently, if your string contains *A Fine Day*, the output would be three substrings consisting of *A*, *Fine*, and *Day*. You use *num* to define the number of substrings to return. The default is to return every substring that the function can produce.

>> `splitlines(`*num*`=string.count('\n'))`: Splits a string that contains newline (\n) characters into individual strings. Each break occurs at the newline character. The output has the newline characters removed. You can use *num* to specify the number of strings to return.

>> `strip()`: Removes all leading and trailing whitespace characters in a string.

>> `swapcase()`: Inverts the case for each alphabetic character in a string.

>> `title()`: Returns a string in which the initial letter in each word is in uppercase and all remaining letters in the word are in lowercase.

>> `upper()`: Converts all lowercase letters in a string to uppercase letters.

>> `zfill (`*width*`)`: Returns a string that is left-padded with zeros so that the resulting string is the size of *width*. This function is designed for use with strings containing numeric values. It retains the original sign information (if any) supplied with the number.

Playing with these functions a bit can help you understand them better. The following steps create an example that demonstrates some of the tasks you can perform by using these functions.

1. **Type the following code into the notebook — pressing Enter after each line:**

```
MyString = "  Hello World  "
print(MyString.upper())
print(MyString.strip())
print(MyString.center(21, "*"))
print(MyString.strip().center(21, "*"))
print(MyString.isdigit())
print(MyString.istitle())
print(max(MyString))
print(MyString.split())
print(MyString.split()[0])
```

The code begins by creating `MyString`, which includes spaces before and after the text so that you can see how space-related functions work. The initial task is to convert all the characters to uppercase.

Removing extra space is a common task in application development. The `strip()` function performs this task well. The `center()` function lets you add padding to both the left and right side of a string so that it consumes a desired amount of space. When you combine the `strip()` and `center()` functions, the output is different from when you use the `center()` function alone.

REMEMBER

You can combine functions to produce a desired result. Python executes each of the functions one at a time from left to right. The order in which the functions appear will affect the output, and developers commonly make the mistake of putting the functions in the wrong order. If your output is different from what you expected, try changing the function order.

Some functions work on the string as an input rather than on the string instance. The `max()` function falls into this category. If you had typed `MyString.max()`, Python would have displayed an error. The bulleted list that appears earlier in this section shows which functions require this sort of string input.

When working with functions that produce a list as an output, you can access an individual member by providing an index to it. The example shows how to use `split()` to split the string into substrings. It then shows how to access just the first substring in the list. You find out more about working with lists in Chapter 13.

2. Click Run Cell.

Python outputs a number of modified strings, as shown in Figure 12-4.

```
Slicing and Dicing Strings

In [4]: MyString = "  Hello World  "
        print(MyString.upper())
        print(MyString.strip())
        print(MyString.center(21, "*"))
        print(MyString.strip().center(21, "*"))
        print(MyString.isdigit())
        print(MyString.istitle())
        print(max(MyString))
        print(MyString.split())
        print(MyString.split()[0])

           HELLO WORLD
        Hello World
        ***  Hello World  ***
        *****Hello World*****
        False
        True
        r
        ['Hello', 'World']
        Hello
```

FIGURE 12-4: Using functions makes string manipulation a lot more flexible.

Locating a Value in a String

Sometimes you need to locate specific information in a string. For example, you may want to know whether a string contains the word Hello in it. One of the essential purposes behind creating and maintaining data is to be able to search it later to locate specific bits of information. Strings are no different — they're most useful when you can find what you need quickly and without any problems. Python provides a number of functions for searching strings. Here are the most commonly used functions:

» count(*str*, *beg*= 0, *end*=len(*string*)): Counts how many times *str* occurs in a string. You can limit the search by specifying a beginning index using *beg* or an ending index using *end*.

» endswith(*suffix*, *beg*=0, *end*=len(*string*)): Returns True when a string ends with the characters specified by *suffix*. You can limit the check by specifying a beginning index using *beg* or an ending index using *end*.

» find(*str*, *beg*=0, *end*=len(*string*)): Determines whether *str* occurs in a string and outputs the index of the location. You can limit the search by specifying a beginning index using *beg* or a ending index using *end*.

» index(*str*, *beg*=0, *end*=len(*string*)): Provides the same functionality as find( ), but raises an exception when *str* isn't found.

» replace(*old*, *new* [, *max*]): Replaces all occurrences of the character sequence specified by *old* in a string with the character sequence specified by *new*. You can limit the number of replacements by specifying a value for *max*.

» rfind(*str*, *beg*=0, *end*=len(*string*)): Provides the same functionality as find( ), but searches backward from the end of the string instead of the beginning.

» rindex(*str*, *beg*=0, *end*=len(*string*)): Provides the same functionality as index( ), but searches backward from the end of the string instead of the beginning.

» startswith(*prefix*, *beg*=0, *end*=len(string)): Returns True when a string begins with the characters specified by *prefix*. You can limit the check by specifying a beginning index using *beg* or an ending index using *end*.

Finding the data that you need is an essential programming task — one that is required no matter what kind of application you create. The following steps help you create an example that demonstrates the use of search functionality within strings.

1. Type the following code into the window — pressing Enter after each line:

```
SearchMe = "The apple is red and the berry is blue!"
print(SearchMe.find("is"))
print(SearchMe.rfind("is"))
print(SearchMe.count("is"))
print(SearchMe.startswith("The"))
print(SearchMe.endswith("The"))
print(SearchMe.replace("apple", "car")
        .replace("berry", "truck"))
```

The example begins by creating SearchMe, a string with two instances of the word *is*. The two instances are important because they demonstrate how searches differ depending on where you start. When using find(), the example starts from the beginning of the string. By contrast, rfind() starts from the end of the string.

Of course, you won't always know how many times a certain set of characters appears in a string. The count() function lets you determine this value.

Depending on the kind of data you work with, sometimes the data is heavily formatted and you can use a particular pattern to your advantage. For example, you can determine whether a particular string (or substring) ends or begins with a specific sequence of characters. You could just as easily use this technique to look for a part number.

The final bit of code replaces *apple* with *car* and *berry* with *truck*. Notice the technique used to place the code on two lines. In some cases, your code will need to appear on multiple lines to make it more readable.

2. **Click Run Cell.**

Python displays the output shown in Figure 12-5. Notice especially that the searches returned different indexes based on where they started in the string. Using the correct function when performing searches is essential to ensure that you get the results you expected.

Locating a Value in a String

```
In [5]:  SearchMe = "The apple is red and the berry is blue!"
         print(SearchMe.find("is"))
         print(SearchMe.rfind("is"))
         print(SearchMe.count("is"))
         print(SearchMe.startswith("The"))
         print(SearchMe.endswith("The"))
         print(SearchMe.replace("apple", "car")
              .replace("berry", "truck"))

         10
         31
         2
         True
         False
         The car is red and the truck is blue!
```

FIGURE 12-5: Typing the wrong input type generates an error instead of an exception.

Formatting Strings

You can format strings in a number of ways using Python. The main emphasis of formatting is to present the string in a form that is both pleasing to the user and easy to understand. Formatting doesn't mean adding special fonts or effects in this case, but refers merely to the presentation of the data. For example, the user might want a fixed-point number rather than a decimal number as output.

You have quite a few ways to format strings and you see a number of them as the book progresses. However, the focus of most formatting is the `format()` function. You create a formatting specification as part of the string and then use the `format()` function to add data to that string. A format specification may be as simple as two curly brackets {} that specify a placeholder for data. You can number the placeholder to create special effects. For example, {0} would contain the first data element in a string. When the data elements are numbered, you can even repeat them so that the same data appears more than once in the string.

The formatting specification follows a colon. When you want to create just a formatting specification, the curly brackets contain just the colon and whatever formatting you want to use. For example, {:f} would create a fixed-point number as output. If you want to number the entries, the number that precedes the colon: {0:f} creates a fixed-point number output for data element one. The formatting specification follows this form, with the italicized elements serving as placeholders here:

```
[[fill]align][sign][#][0][width][,][.precision][type]
```

The specification at `https://docs.python.org/3/library/string.html` provides you with the in-depth details, but here's an overview of what the various entries mean:

» **fill:** Defines the fill character used when displaying data that is too small to fit within the assigned space.

» **align:** Specifies the alignment of data within the display space. You can use these alignments:

- **<:** Left aligned
- **>:** Right aligned
- **^:** Centered
- **=:** Justified

» **sign:** Determines the use of signs for the output:

- **+:** Positive numbers have a plus sign and negative numbers have a minus sign.
- **-:** Negative numbers have a minus sign.
- **<space>:** Positive numbers are preceded by a space and negative numbers have a minus sign.

» **#:** Specifies that the output should use the alternative display format for numbers. For example, hexadecimal numbers will have a 0x prefix added to them.

» **0:** Specifies that the output should be sign aware and padded with zeros as needed to provide consistent output.

» **width:** Determines the full width of the data field (even if the data won't fit in the space provided).

» **,:** Specifies that numeric data should have commas as a thousands separator.

» **.precision:** Determines the number of characters after the decimal point.

» **type:** Specifies the output type, even if the input type doesn't match. The types are split into three groups:

   • *String:* Use an s or nothing at all to specify a string.

   • *Integer:* The integer types are as follows: b (binary); c (character); d (decimal); o (octal); x (hexadecimal with lowercase letters); X (hexadecimal with uppercase letters); and n (locale-sensitive decimal that uses the appropriate characters for the thousands separator).

   • *Floating point:* The floating-point types are as follows: e (exponent using a lowercase e as a separator); E (exponent using an uppercase E as a separator); f (lowercase fixed point); F (uppercase fixed point); g (lowercase general format); G (uppercase general format); n (local-sensitive general format that uses the appropriate characters for the decimal and thousands separators); and % (percentage).

The formatting specification elements must appear in the correct order or Python won't know what to do with them. If you specify the alignment before the fill character, Python displays an error message rather than performing the required formatting. The following steps help you see how the formatting specification works and demonstrate the order you need to follow in using the various formatting specification criteria.

1. Type the following code into the notebook — pressing Enter after each line:

```
Formatted = "{:d}"
print(Formatted.format(7000))
Formatted = "{:,d}"
print(Formatted.format(7000))
Formatted = "{:^15,d}"
print(Formatted.format(7000))
```

```
Formatted = "{:*^15,d}"
print(Formatted.format(7000))
Formatted = "{:*^15.2f}"
print(Formatted.format(7000))
Formatted = "{:*>15X}"
print(Formatted.format(7000))
Formatted = "{:*<#15x}"
print(Formatted.format(7000))
Formatted = "A {0} {1} and a {0} {2}."
print(Formatted.format("blue", "car", "truck"))
```

The example starts simply with a field formatted as a decimal value. It then adds a thousands separator to the output. The next step is to make the field wider than needed to hold the data and to center the data within the field. Finally, the field has an asterisk added to pad the output.

Of course, the example contains other data types. The next step is to display the same data in fixed-point format. The example also shows the output in both uppercase and lowercase hexadecimal format. The uppercase output is right aligned and the lowercase output is left aligned.

Finally, the example shows how you can use numbered fields to your advantage. In this case, it creates an interesting string output that repeats one of the input values.

2. **Click Run Cell.**

Python outputs data in various forms, as shown in Figure 12-6.

FIGURE 12-6:
Use formatting to present data in precisely the form you want.

Chapter **13**

Managing Lists

A lot of people lose sight of the fact that most programming techniques are based on the real world. Part of the reason is that programmers often use terms that other people don't to describe these real-world objects. For example, most people would call a place to store something a box or a cupboard — but programmers insist on using the term *variable.* Lists are different. Everyone makes lists and uses them in various ways to perform an abundance of tasks. In fact, you're probably surrounded by lists of various sorts where you're sitting right now as you read this book. So, this chapter is about something you already use quite a lot. The only difference is that you need to think of lists in the same way Python does.

You may read that lists are hard to work with. The reason that some people find working with lists difficult is that they're not used to actually thinking about the lists they create. When you create a list, you simply write items down in whatever order makes sense to you. Sometimes you rewrite the list when you're done to put it in a specific order. In other cases, you use your finger as a guide when going down the list to make looking through it easier. The point is that everything you normally do with lists is also doable within Python. The difference is that you must now actually think about what you're doing in order to make Python understand what you want done.

Lists are incredibly important in Python. This chapter introduces you to the concepts used to create, manage, search, and print lists (among other tasks). When you complete the chapter, you can use lists to make your Python applications more robust, faster, and more flexible. In fact, you'll wonder how you ever got along without using lists in the past. The important thing to keep in mind is that you have already used lists most of your life. There really isn't any difference now except that you must now think about the actions that you normally take for granted when managing your own lists. You can find the downloadable source code for the examples this chapter in the `BPPD_13_Managing_Lists.ipynb` file, as described in the book's Introduction.

Organizing Information in an Application

People create lists to organize information and make it easier to access and change. You use lists in Python for the same reason. In many situations, you really do need some sort of organizational aid to hold data. For example, you might want to create a single place to look for days of the week or months of the year. The names of these items would appear in a list, much as they would if you needed to commit them to paper in the real world. The following sections describe lists and how they work in more detail.

Defining organization using lists

The Python specification defines a list as a kind of sequence. *Sequences* simply provide some means of allowing multiple data items to exist together in a single storage unit, but as separate entities. Think about one of those large mail holders you see in apartment buildings. A single mail holder contains a number of small mailboxes, each of which can contain mail. Python supports other kinds of sequences as well (Chapter 14 discusses a number of these sequences):

>> Tuples

>> Dictionaries

>> Stacks

>> Queues

>> Deques

REMEMBER

Of all the sequences, lists are the easiest to understand and are the most directly related to a real-world object. Working with lists helps you become better able to work with other kinds of sequences that provide greater functionality and improved flexibility. The point is that the data is stored in a list much as you would write it on a piece of paper — one item comes after another, as shown in Figure 13-1. The list has a beginning, a middle, and an end. As shown in the figure, the items are numbered. (Even if you might not normally number them in real life, Python always numbers the items for you.)

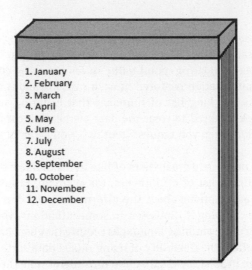

FIGURE 13-1:
A list is simply a
sequence of
items, much as
you would write
on a notepad.

1. January
2. February
3. March
4. April
5. May
6. June
7. July
8. August
9. September
10. October
11. November
12. December

Understanding how computers view lists

The computer doesn't view lists in the same way that you do. It doesn't have an internal notepad and use a pen to write on it. A computer has memory. The computer stores each item in a list in a separate memory location, as shown in Figure 13-2. The memory is contiguous, so as you add new items, they're added to the next location in memory.

In many respects, the computer uses something like a mailbox to hold your list. The list as a whole is the mail holder. As you add items, the computer places it in the next mailbox within the mail holder.

FIGURE 13-2:
Each item added
to a list takes
the next position
in memory.

| January | February | March | ... | October | November | December |

REMEMBER

Just as the mailboxes are numbered in a mail holder, the memory slots used for a list are numbered. The numbers begin with 0, not with 1 as you might expect. Each mailbox receives the next number in line. A mail holder with the months of the year would contain 12 mailboxes. The mailboxes would be numbered from 0 to 11 (not 1 to 12, as you might think). Getting the numbering scheme down as quickly as possible is essential because even experienced developers get into trouble by using 1 and not 0 as a starting point at times.

Depending on what sort of information you place in each mailbox, the mailboxes need not be of the same size. Python lets you store a string in one mailbox, an integer in another, and a floating-point value in another. The computer doesn't know what kind of information is stored in each mailbox and it doesn't care. All the computer sees is one long list of numbers that could be anything. Python performs all the work required to treat the data elements according to the right type and to ensure that when you request item five, you actually get item five.

TIP

In general, it's good practice to create lists of like items to make the data easier to manage. When creating a list of all integers, for example, rather than of mixed data, you can make assumptions about the information and don't have to spend nearly as much time checking it. However, in some situations, you might need to mix data. Many other programming languages require that lists have just one type of data, but Python offers the flexibility of using mixed data sorts. Just remember that using mixed data in a list means that you must determine the data type when retrieving the information in order to work with the data correctly. Treating a string as an integer would cause problems in your application.

Creating Lists

As in real life, before you can do anything with a list, you must create it. As previously stated, Python lists can mix types. However, restricting a list to a single type when you can is always the best practice. The following steps demonstrate how to create Python lists.

1. **Open a new notebook.**

   You can also use the downloadable source file, BPPD_13_Managing_Lists. ipynb.

2. **Type** List1 = ["One", 1, "Two", True] **and press Enter.**

   Python creates a list named List1 for you. This list contains two string values (One and Two), an integer value (1), and a Boolean value (True). Of course, you can't actually see anything because Python processes the command without saying anything.

REMEMBER

Notice that each data type that you type is a different color. When you use the default color scheme, Python displays strings in green, numbers in black, and Boolean values in orange. The color of an entry is a cue that tells you whether you have typed the entry correctly, which helps reduce errors when creating a list.

3. Type print(List1) **and click Run Cell.**

You see the content of the list as a whole, as shown in Figure 13-3. Notice that the string entries appear in single quotes, even though you typed them using double quotes. Strings can appear in either single quotes or double quotes in Python.

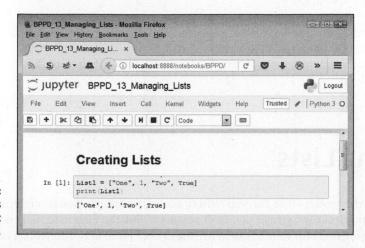

FIGURE 13-3:
Python displays the content of List1.

4. Type dir(List1) **and click Run Cell.**

Python displays a list of actions that you can perform using lists, as shown (partially) in Figure 13-4. Notice that the output is actually a list. So, you're using a list to determine what you can do with another list.

```
In [2]: dir(List1)

Out[2]: ['__add__',
         '__class__',
         '__contains__',
         '__delattr__',
         '__delitem__',
         '__dir__',
         '__doc__',
         '__eq__',
         '__format__',
         '__ge__',
```

FIGURE 13-4:
Python provides a listing of the actions you can perform using a list.

REMEMBER

As you start working with objects of greater complexity, you need to remember that the dir() command always shows what tasks you can perform using that object. The actions that appear without underscores are the main actions that you can perform using a list. These actions are the following:

- append
- clear

- copy
- count
- extend
- index
- insert
- pop
- remove
- reverse
- sort

Accessing Lists

After you create a list, you want to access the information it contains. An object isn't particularly useful if you can't at least access the information it contains. The previous section shows how to use the print() and dir() functions to interact with a list, but other ways exist to perform the task, as described in the following steps.

1. **Type** List1 = ["One", 1, "Two", True] **and click Run Cell.**

   Python creates a list named List1 for you.

2. **Type** List1[1] **and click Run Cell.**

   You see the value 1 as output, as shown in Figure 13-5. The use of a number within a set of square brackets is called an *index*. Python always uses zero-based indexes, so asking for the element at index 1 means getting the second element in the list.

FIGURE 13-5:
Make sure to use
the correct index
number.

Accessing Lists

```
In [3]: List1[1]
Out[3]: 1
```

3. **Type** List1[1:3] **and click Run Cell.**

   You see a range of values that includes two elements, as shown in Figure 13-6. When typing a range, the end of the range is always one greater than the number of elements returned. In this case, that means that you get elements 1 and 2, not elements 1 through 3 as you might expect.

FIGURE 13-6:
Ranges return
multiple values.

```
In [4]:  List1[1:3]
Out[4]:  [1, 'Two']
```

4. **Type** List1[1:] **and click Run Cell.**

   You see all the elements, starting from element 1 to the end of the list, as shown in Figure 13-7. A range can have a blank ending number, which simply means to print the rest of the list.

FIGURE 13-7:
Leaving the
ending number of
a range blank
prints the rest
of the list.

```
In [5]:  List1[1:]
Out[5]:  [1, 'Two', True]
```

5. **Type** List1[:3] **and click Run Cell.**

   Python displays the elements from 0 through 2. Leaving the start of a range blank means that you want to start with element 0, as shown in Figure 13-8.

FIGURE 13-8:
Leaving the
beginning
number of a
range blank
prints from
element 0.

```
In [6]:  List1[:3]
Out[6]:  ['One', 1, 'Two']
```

TECHNICAL
STUFF

Even though doing so is really confusing, you can use negative indexes with Python. Instead of working from the left, Python will work from the right and backward. For example, if you have List1 = ["One", 1, "Two", True] and type List1[-2], you get Two as output. Likewise, typing List[-3] results in an output of 1. The rightmost element is element -1 in this case.

Looping through Lists

To automate the processing of list elements, you need some way to loop through the list. The easiest way to perform this task is to rely on a for statement, as described in the following steps.

1. **Type the following code into the window — pressing Enter after each line:**

```
List1 = [0, 1, 2, 3, 4, 5]
for Item in List1:
    print(Item)
```

The example begins by creating a list consisting of numeric values. It then uses a for loop to obtain each element in turn and print it onscreen.

2. **Click Run Cell.**

Python shows the individual values in the list, one on each line, as shown in Figure 13-9.

Looping through Lists

```
In [7]: List1 = [0, 1, 2, 3, 4, 5]
        for Item in List1:
            print(Item)

0
1
2
3
4
5
```

FIGURE 13-9:
A loop makes it easy to obtain a copy of each item and process it as needed.

Modifying Lists

You can modify the content of a list as needed. Modifying a list means to change a particular entry, add a new entry, or remove an existing entry. To perform these tasks, you must sometimes read an entry. The concept of modification is found within the acronym CRUD, which stands for Create, Read, Update, and Delete. Here are the list functions associated with CRUD:

» append(): Adds a new entry to the end of the list.

» clear(): Removes all entries from the list.

» copy(): Creates a copy of the current list and places it in a new list.

» extend(): Adds items from an existing list and into the current list.

» insert(): Adds a new entry to the position specified in the list.

» pop(): Removes an entry from the end of the list.

» remove(): Removes an entry from the specified position in the list.

The following steps show how to perform modification tasks with lists. This is a hands-on exercise. As the book progresses, you see these same functions used within application code. The purpose of this exercise is to help you gain a feel for how lists work.

1. **Type** List2 = [ ] **and press Enter.**

   Python creates a list named List2 for you.

   Notice that the square brackets are empty. List2 doesn't contain any entries. You can create empty lists that you fill with information later. In fact, this is precisely how many lists start because you usually don't know what information they will contain until the user interacts with the list.

2. **Type** len(List2) **and click Run Cell.**

   The len( ) function outputs 0, as shown in Figure 13-10. When creating an application, you can check for an empty list by using the len( ) function. If a list is empty, you can't perform tasks such as removing elements from it because there is nothing to remove.

FIGURE 13-10:
Check for empty
lists as needed in
your application.

Modifying Lists

```
In [8]:  List2 = []
         len(List2)
Out[8]:  0
```

3. **Type** List2.append(1) **and press Enter.**

4. **Type** len(List2) **and click Run Cell.**

   The len( ) function now reports a length of 1.

5. **Type** List2[0] **and click Run Cell.**

   You see the value stored in element 0 of List2, as shown in Figure 13-11.

FIGURE 13-11:
Appending an
element changes
the list length
and stores the
value at the end
of the list.

```
In [9]:   List2.append(1)
          len(List2)
Out[9]:   1

In [10]:  List2[0]
Out[10]:  1
```

6. **Type** List2.insert(0, 2) **and press Enter.**

The insert( ) function requires two arguments. The first argument is the index of the insertion, which is element 0 in this case. The second argument is the object you want inserted at that point, which is 2 in this case.

7. **Type** List2 **and click Run Cell.**

Python has added another element to List2. However, using the insert( ) function lets you add the new element before the first element, as shown in Figure 13-12.

FIGURE 13-12:
Inserting provides flexibility in deciding where to add an element.

```
In [11]:  List2.insert(0, 2)
          List2
Out[11]:  [2, 1]
```

8. **Type** List3 = List2.copy() **and press Enter.**

The new list, List3, is a precise copy of List2. Copying is often used to create a temporary version of an existing list so that a user can make temporary modifications to it rather than to the original list. When the user is done, the application can either delete the temporary list or copy it to the original list.

9. **Type** List2.extend(List3) **and press Enter.**

Python copies all the elements in List3 to the end of List2. Extending is commonly used to consolidate two lists.

10. **Type** List2 **and click Run Cell.**

You see that the copy and extend processes have worked. List2 now contains the values 2, 1, 2, and 1, as shown in Figure 13-13.

FIGURE 13-13:
Copying and extending provide methods for moving a lot of data around quickly.

```
In [12]:  List3 = List2.copy()
          List2.extend(List3)
          List2
Out[12]:  [2, 1, 2, 1]
```

11. **Type** List2.pop() **and click Run Cell.**

Python displays a value of 1, as shown in Figure 13-14. The 1 was stored at the end of the list, and pop( ) always removes values from the end.

FIGURE 13-14:
Use pop() to
remove elements
from the end
of a list.

```
In [13]:  List2.pop()
Out[13]:  1
```

12. **Type** List2.remove(1) **and click Run Cell.**

This time, Python removes the item at element 1. Unlike the pop() function, the remove() function doesn't display the value of the item it removed.

13. **Type** List2.clear() **and press Enter.**

Using clear() means that the list shouldn't contain any elements now.

14. **Type** len(List2) **and click Run Cell.**

You see that the output is 0. List2 is definitely empty. At this point, you've tried all the modification methods that Python provides for lists. Work with List2 some more using these various functions until you feel comfortable making changes to the list.

USING OPERATORS WITH LISTS

Lists can also rely on operators to perform certain tasks. For example, if you want to create a list that contains four copies of the word *Hello*, you could use MyList = ["Hello"] * 4 to fill it. A list allows repetition as needed. The multiplication operator (*) tells Python how many times to repeat a given item. You need to remember that every repeated element is separate, so what MyList contains is ['Hello', 'Hello', 'Hello', 'Hello'].

You can also use concatenation to fill a list. For example, using MyList = ["Hello"] + ["World"] + ["!"] * 4 creates six elements in MyList. The first element is Hello, followed by World and ending with four elements with one exclamation mark (!) in each element.

The membership operator (in) also works with lists. This chapter uses a straightforward and easy-to-understand method of searching lists (the recommended approach). However, you can use the membership operator to make things shorter and simpler by using "Hello" in MyList. Assuming that you have your list filled with ['Hello', 'World', '!', '!', '!', '!'], the output of this statement is True.

Searching Lists

Modifying a list isn't very easy when you don't know what the list contains. The ability to search a list is essential if you want to make maintenance tasks easier. The following steps help you create an application that demonstrates the ability to search a list for specific values.

1. Type the following code into the notebook — pressing Enter after each line:

```
Colors = ["Red", "Orange", "Yellow", "Green", "Blue"]
ColorSelect = ""
while str.upper(ColorSelect) != "QUIT":
    ColorSelect = input("Please type a color name: ")
    if (Colors.count(ColorSelect) >= 1):
        print("The color exists in the list!")
    elif (str.upper(ColorSelect) != "QUIT"):
        print("The list doesn't contain the color.")
```

The example begins by creating a list named Colors that contains color names. It also creates a variable named ColorSelect to hold the name of the color that the user wants to find. The application then enters a loop where the user is asked for a color name that is placed in ColorSelect. As long as this variable doesn't contain the word QUIT, the application continues a loop that requests input.

Whenever the user inputs a color name, the application asks the list to count the number of occurrences of that color. When the value is equal to or greater than one, the list does contain the color and an appropriate message appears onscreen. On the other hand, when the list doesn't contain the requested color, an alternative message appears onscreen.

TIP

Notice how this example uses an elif clause to check whether ColorSelect contains the word QUIT. This technique of including an elif clause ensures that the application doesn't output a message when the user wants to quit the application. You need to use similar techniques when you create your applications to avoid potential user confusion or even data loss (when the application performs a task the user didn't actually request).

2. Click Run Cell.

Python asks you to type a color name.

3. Type Blue and press Enter.

You see a message telling you that the color does exist in the list, as shown in Figure 13-15.

Searching Lists

```
In [*]:  Colors = ["Red", "Orange", "Yellow", "Green", "Blue"]
         ColorSelect = ""
         while str.upper(ColorSelect) != "QUIT":
             ColorSelect = input("Please type a color name: ")
             if (Colors.count(ColorSelect) >= 1):
                 print("The color exists in the list!")
             elif (str.upper(ColorSelect) != "QUIT"):
                 print "The list doesn't contain the color."

         Please type a color name: Blue
         The color exists in the list!
```

4. **Type** Purple **and press Enter.**

   You see a message telling you that the color doesn't exist, as shown in Figure 13-16.

Searching Lists

```
In [*]:  Colors = ["Red", "Orange", "Yellow", "Green", "Blue"]
         ColorSelect = ""
         while str.upper(ColorSelect) != "QUIT":
             ColorSelect = input("Please type a color name: ")
             if (Colors.count(ColorSelect) >= 1):
                 print("The color exists in the list!")
             elif (str.upper(ColorSelect) != "QUIT"):
                 print "The list doesn't contain the color."

         Please type a color name: Blue
         The color exists in the list!
         Please type a color name: Purple
         The list doesn't contain the color.
```

5. **Type** Quit **and press Enter.**

   The application ends. Notice that the application displays neither a success nor a failure message.

Sorting Lists

The computer can locate information in a list no matter what order it appears in. It's a fact, though, that longer lists are easier to search when you put them in sorted order. However, the main reason to put a list in sorted order is to make it easier for the human user to actually see the information the list contains. People work better with sorted information. This example begins with an unsorted list. It then sorts the list and outputs it to the display. The following steps demonstrate how to perform this task.

1. **Type the following code into the notebook — pressing Enter after each line:**

```
Colors = ["Red", "Orange", "Yellow", "Green", "Blue"]
for Item in Colors:
    print(Item, end=" ")
print()
Colors.sort()
for Item in Colors:
    print(Item, end=" ")
print()
```

The example begins by creating an array of colors. The colors are currently in unsorted order. The example then prints the colors in the order in which they appear. Notice the use of the end=" " argument for the print() function to ensure that all color entries remain on one line (making them easier to compare).

Sorting the list is as easy as calling the sort() function. After the example calls the sort() function, it prints the list again so that you can see the result.

2. **Click Run Cell.**

Python outputs both the unsorted and sorted lists, as shown in Figure 13-17.

Sorting Lists

```
In [20]: Colors = ["Red", "Orange", "Yellow", "Green", "Blue"]
         for Item in Colors:
             print(Item, end=" ")
         print()
         Colors.sort()
         for Item in Colors:
             print(Item, end=" ")
         print()

         Red Orange Yellow Green Blue
         Blue Green Orange Red Yellow
```

FIGURE 13-17:
Sorting a list is as easy as calling the sort() function.

You may need to sort items in reverse order at times. To accomplish this task, you use the reverse() function. The function must appear on a separate line. So the previous example would look like this if you wanted to sort the colors in reverse order:

TIP

```
Colors = ["Red", "Orange", "Yellow", "Green", "Blue"]
for Item in Colors:
    print(Item, end=" ")
print()
Colors.sort()
```

```
Colors.reverse()
for Item in Colors:
    print(Item, end=" ")
print()
```

Printing Lists

Python provides myriad ways to output information. In fact, the number of ways would amaze you. This chapter has shown just a few of the most basic methods for outputting lists so far, using the most basic methods. Real-world printing can become more complex, so you need to know a few additional printing techniques to get you started. Using these techniques is actually a lot easier if you play with them as you go along.

1. **Type the following code into the notebook — pressing Enter after each line:**

```
Colors = ["Red", "Orange", "Yellow", "Green", "Blue"]
print(*Colors, sep='\n')
```

This example begins by using the same list of colors in the previous section. In that section, you use a for loop to print the individual items. This example takes another approach. It uses the splat (*) operator, also called the positional expansion operator (and an assortment of other interesting terms), to unpack the list and send each element to the print() method one item at a time. The sep argument tells how to separate each of the printed outputs, relying on a newline character in this case.

2. **Click Run Cell.**

Python outputs the list one item at a time, as shown in Figure 13-18.

FIGURE 13-18:
Using the splat operator can make your code significantly smaller.

Printing Lists

```
In [22]: Colors = ["Red", "Orange", "Yellow", "Green", "Blue"]
         print(*Colors, sep='\n')
         Red
         Orange
         Yellow
         Green
         Blue
```

3. **Type the following code into the notebook and click Run Cell.**

```
for Item in Colors: print(Item.rjust(8), sep='/n')
```

Code doesn't have to appear on multiple lines. This example takes two lines of code and places it on just a single line. However, it also demonstrates the use of the `rjust()` method, which right justifies the string, as shown in Figure 13-19. Numerous methods of this sort are described at `https://docs.python.org/2/library/string.html`. Even though they continue to work, Python may stop using them at any time.

```
In [23]: for Item in Colors: print(Item.rjust(8), sep='/n')
              Red
           Orange
           Yellow
            Green
             Blue
```

4. **Type the following code into the notebook and click Run Cell.**

```
print('\n'.join(Colors))
```

Python provides more than one way to perform any task. In this case, the code uses the `join()` method to join the newline character with each member of `Colors`. The output is the same as that shown previously in Figure 13-18, even though the approach is different. The point is to use the approach that best suits a particular need.

5. **Type the following code into the notebook and click Run Cell.**

```
print('First: {0}\nSecond: {1}'.format(*Colors))
```

In this case, the output is formatted in a specific way with accompanying text, and the result doesn't include every member of `Colors`. The `{0}` and `{1}` entries represent placeholders for the values supplied from `*Colors`. Figure 13-20 shows the output. You can read more about this approach (the topic is immense) at `https://docs.python.org/3/tutorial/inputoutput.html`.

```
In [25]: print 'First: {0}\nSecond: {1}'.format(*Colors)
         First: Red
         Second: Orange
```

This section touches on only some of the common techniques used to format output in Python. There are lots more. You see many of these approaches demonstrated in the chapters that follow. The essential goal is to use a technique that's easy to read, works well with all anticipated inputs, and doesn't paint you into a corner when you're creating additional output later.

Working with the Counter Object

Sometimes you have a data source and you simply need to know how often things happen (such as the appearance of a certain item in the list). When you have a short list, you can simply count the items. However, when you have a really long list, getting an accurate count is nearly impossible. For example, consider what it would take if you had a really long novel like *War and Peace* in a list and wanted to know the frequency of the words the novel used. The task would be impossible without a computer.

The Counter object lets you count items quickly. In addition, it's incredibly easy to use. This book shows the Counter object in use a number of times, but this chapter shows how to use it specifically with lists. The example in this section creates a list with repetitive elements and then counts how many times those elements actually appear.

1. **Type the following code into the notebook — pressing Enter after each line:**

```
from collections import Counter
MyList = [1, 2, 3, 4, 1, 2, 3, 1, 2, 1, 5]
ListCount = Counter(MyList)
print(ListCount)
for ThisItem in ListCount.items():
    print("Item: ", ThisItem[0],
          " Appears: ", ThisItem[1])
print("The value 1 appears {0} times."
      .format(ListCount.get(1)))
```

To use the Counter object, you must import it from collections. Of course, if you work with other collection types in your application, you can import the entire collections package by typing **import collections** instead.

The example begins by creating a list, MyList, with repetitive numeric elements. You can easily see that some elements appear more than once. The example places the list into a new Counter object, ListCount. You can create Counter objects in all sorts of ways, but this is the most convenient method when working with a list.

REMEMBER

The Counter object and the list aren't actually connected in any way. When the list content changes, you must re-create the Counter object because it won't automatically see the change. An alternative to re-creating the counter is to call the clear() method first and then call the update() method to fill the Counter object with the new data.

The application prints ListCount in various ways. The first output is the Counter as it appears without any manipulation. The second output prints the individual unique elements in MyList along with the number of times each element appears. To obtain both the element and the number of times it appears, you must use the items() function as shown. Finally, the example demonstrates how to obtain an individual count from the list by using the get() function.

2. **Click Run Cell.**

Python outputs the results of using the Counter object, as shown in Figure 13-21.

FIGURE 13-21:
The Counter is helpful in obtaining statistics about longer lists.

Working with the Counter Object

```
In [26]:  from collections import Counter
          MyList = [1, 2, 3, 4, 1, 2, 3, 1, 2, 1, 5]
          ListCount = Counter(MyList)
          print(ListCount)
          for ThisItem in ListCount.items():
              print("Item: ", ThisItem[0],
                    " Appears: ", ThisItem[1])
          print("The value 1 appears {0} times."
                .format(ListCount.get(1)))

          Counter({1: 4, 2: 3, 3: 2, 4: 1, 5: 1})
          Item:  1  Appears:  4
          Item:  2  Appears:  3
          Item:  3  Appears:  2
          Item:  4  Appears:  1
          Item:  5  Appears:  1
          The value 1 appears 4 times.
```

Notice that the information is actually stored in the Counter as a key and value pair. Chapter 14 discusses this topic in greater detail. All you really need to know for now is that the element found in MyList becomes a key in ListCount that identifies the unique element name. The value contains the number of times that that element appears within MyList.

Chapter **14**

Collecting All Sorts of Data

People collect all sorts of things. The CDs stacked near your entertainment center, the plates that are part of a series, baseball cards, and even the pens from every restaurant you've ever visited are all collections. The collections you encounter when you write applications are the same as the collections in the real world. A *collection* is simply a grouping of like items in one place and usually organized into some easily understood form.

REMEMBER

This chapter is about collections of various sorts. The central idea behind every collection is to create an environment in which the collection is properly managed and lets you easily locate precisely what you want at any given time. A set of bookshelves works great for storing books, DVDs, and other sorts of flat items. However, you probably put your pen collection in a holder or even a display case. The difference in storage locations doesn't change the fact that both house collections. The same is true with computer collections. Yes, differences exist between a stack and a queue, but the main idea is to provide the means to manage data properly and make it easy to access when needed. You can find the download-able source code for the examples this chapter in the BPPD_14_Collecting_All_Sorts_of_Data.ipynb file, as described in the book's Introduction.

Understanding Collections

In Chapter 13, you're introduced to sequences. A *sequence* is a succession of values that are bound together in a container. The simplest sequence is a string, which is a succession of characters. Next comes the list described in Chapter 13, which is a succession of objects. Even though a string and a list are both sequences, they have significant differences. For example, when working with a string, you can set all the characters to lowercase — something you can't do with a list. On the other hand, lists let you append new items, which is something a string doesn't support directly (concatenations actually create a new string). Collections are simply another kind of sequence, albeit a more complex sequence than you find in either a string or list.

REMEMBER

No matter which sequence you use, they all support two functions: index() and count(). The index() function always returns the position of a specified item in the sequence. For example, you can return the position of a character in a string or the position of an object in a list. The count() function returns the number of times a specific item appears in the list. Again, the kind of specific item depends upon the kind of sequence.

You can use collections to create database-like structures using Python. Each collection type has a different purpose, and you use the various types in specific ways. The important idea to remember is that collections are simply another kind of sequence. As with every other kind of sequence, collections always support the index() and count() functions as part of their base functionality.

Python is designed to be extensible. However, it does rely on a base set of collections that you can use to create most application types. This chapter describes the most common collections:

» **Tuple:** A tuple is a collection used to create complex list-like sequences. An advantage of tuples is that you can nest the content of a tuple. This feature lets you create structures that can hold employee records or x-y coordinate pairs.

» **Dictionary:** As with the real dictionaries, you create key/value pairs when using the dictionary collection (think of a word and its associated definition). A dictionary provides incredibly fast search times and makes ordering data significantly easier.

» **Stack:** Most programming languages support stacks directly. However, Python doesn't support the stack, although there's a work-around for that. A stack is a last in/first out (LIFO) sequence. Think of a pile of pancakes: You can add new pancakes to the top and also take them off of the top. A stack is an important collection that you can simulate in Python by using a list, which is precisely what this chapter does.

>> **queue:** A queue is a first in/first out (FIFO) collection. You use it to track items that need to be processed in some way. Think of a queue as a line at the bank. You go into the line, wait your turn, and are eventually called to talk with a teller.

>> **deque:** A double-ended queue (deque) is a queue-like structure that lets you add or remove items from either end, but not from the middle. You can use a deque as a queue or a stack or any other kind of collection to which you're adding and from which you're removing items in an orderly manner (in contrast to lists, tuples, and dictionaries, which allow randomized access and management).

Working with Tuples

As previously mentioned, a tuple is a collection used to create complex lists, in which you can embed one tuple within another. This embedding lets you create hierarchies with tuples. A hierarchy could be something as simple as the directory listing of your hard drive or an organizational chart for your company. The idea is that you can create complex data structures by using a tuple.

REMEMBER

Tuples are immutable, which means you can't change them. You can create a new tuple with the same name and modify it in some way, but you can't modify an existing tuple. Lists are mutable, which means that you can change them. So, a tuple can seem at first to be at a disadvantage, but immutability has all sorts of advantages, such as being more secure as well as faster. In addition, immutable objects are easier to use with multiple processors.

The two biggest differences between a tuple and a list are that a tuple is immutable and allows you to embed one tuple inside another. The following steps demonstrate how you can interact with a tuple in Python.

1. **Open a new notebook.**

You can also use the downloadable source file, BPPD_14_Collecting_All_Sorts_of_Data.ipynb.

2. **Type** MyTuple = ("Red", " Blue", " Green ") **and press Enter.**

Python creates a tuple containing three strings.

3. **Type** MyTuple **and click Run Cell.**

You see the content of MyTuple, which is three strings, as shown in Figure 14-1. Notice that the entries use single quotes, even though you used double quotes to create the tuple. In addition, notice that a tuple uses parentheses rather than square brackets, as lists do.

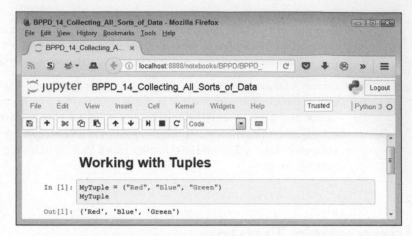

FIGURE 14-1:
Tuples use
parentheses, not
square brackets.

FIGURE 14-1:
Tuples use
parentheses, not
square brackets.

4. **Type** print(dir(MyTuple)) **and click Run Cell.**

    Python presents a list of functions that you can use with tuples, as shown
    (partially) in Figure 14-2. Notice that the list of functions appears significantly
    smaller than the list of functions provided with lists in Chapter 13. The count( )
    and index( ) functions are present.

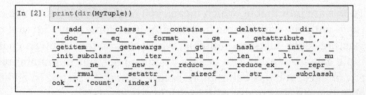

FIGURE 14-2:
Fewer functions
seem to be
available for use
with tuples.

REMEMBER

However, appearances can be deceiving. For example, you can add new items
by using the __add__( ) function. When working with Python objects, look at
all the entries before you make a decision as to functionality.

TIP

Also notice that the output differs when using the print( ) function with the
dir( ) function. Compare the dir( )-only output shown in the upcoming
Figure 14-4 with the combination output shown previously in Figure 14-2. The
output shown in Figure 14-2 looks more like the output that you see with other
IDEs, such as IDLE. The output you get is affected by the methods you use, but
the IDE also makes a difference, so in some situations, you must use a
different approach based on the IDE you prefer. Many people find that the
Notebook listing of one method per line is much easier to read and use, but
the combination method is certainly more compact.

5. **Type** MyTuple = MyTuple.__add__(("Purple",)) **and press Enter.**

    This code adds a new tuple to MyTuple and places the result in a new copy of
    MyTuple. The old copy of MyTuple is destroyed after the call.

REMEMBER

The __add__() function accepts only tuples as input. This means that you must enclose the addition in parentheses. In addition, when creating a tuple with a single entry, you must add a comma after the entry, as shown in the example. This is an odd Python rule that you need to keep in mind or you'll see an error message similar to this one:

```
TypeError: can only concatenate tuple (not "str") to
    tuple
```

6. **Type MyTuple and click Run Cell.**

   The addition to MyTuple appears at the end of the list, as shown in Figure 14-3. Notice that it appears at the same level as the other entries.

FIGURE 14-3:
This new copy of MyTuple contains an additional entry.

```
In [3]:  MyTuple = MyTuple.__add__(("Purple",))
         MyTuple
Out[3]:  ('Red', 'Blue', 'Green', 'Purple')
```

7. **Type MyTuple = MyTuple.__add__((" Yellow", (" Orange", "Black"))) and press Enter.**

   This step adds three entries: Yellow, Orange, and Black. However, Orange and Black are added as a tuple within the main tuple, which creates a hierarchy. These two entries are actually treated as a single entry within the main tuple.

TIP

You can replace the __add__() function with the concatenation operator. For example, if you want to add Magenta to the front of the tuple list, you type MyTuple = ("Magenta",) + MyTuple.

8. **Type MyTuple[4] and click Run Cell.**

   Python displays a single member of MyTuple, Yellow. Tuples use indexes to access individual members, just as lists do. You can also specify a range when needed. Anything you can do with a list index you can also do with a tuple index.

9. **Type MyTuple[5] and press Enter.**

   You see a tuple that contains Orange and Black. Of course, you might not want to use both members in tuple form.

TIP

Tuples do contain hierarchies on a regular basis. You can detect when an index has returned another tuple, rather than a value, by testing for type. For example, in this case, you could detect that the sixth item (index 5) contains a tuple by typing type(MyTuple[5]) == tuple. The output would be True in this case.

10. Type MyTuple[5][0] **and press Enter.**

At this point, you see Orange as output. Figure 14-4 shows the results of the previous commands so that you can see the progression of index usage. The indexes always appear in order of their level in the hierarchy.

```
In [4]:  MyTuple = MyTuple.__add__(("Yellow", ("Orange", "Black")))
         MyTuple[4]

Out[4]:  'Yellow'

In [5]:  MyTuple[5]

Out[5]:  ('Orange', 'Black')

In [6]:  type(MyTuple[5]) == tuple

Out[6]:  True

In [7]:  MyTuple[5][0]

Out[7]:  'Orange'
```

FIGURE 14-4:
Use indexes to gain access to the individual tuple members.

TIP

Using a combination of indexes and the __add__() function (or the concatenation operator, +), you can create flexible applications that rely on tuples. For example, you can remove an element from a tuple by making it equal to a range of values. If you wanted to remove the tuple containing Orange and Black, you type MyTuple = MyTuple[0:5].

Working with Dictionaries

A Python dictionary works just the same as its real-world counterpart — you create a key and value pair. It's just like the word and definition in a dictionary. As with lists, dictionaries are mutable, which means that you can change them as needed. The main reason to use a dictionary is to make information lookup faster. The key is always short and unique so that the computer doesn't spend a lot of time looking for the information you need.

The following sections demonstrate how to create and use a dictionary. When you know how to work with dictionaries, you use that knowledge to make up for deficiencies in the Python language. Most languages include the concept of a switch statement, which is essentially a menu of choices from which one choice is selected. Python doesn't include this option, so you must normally rely on if . . . elif statements to perform the task. (Such statements work, but they aren't as clear as they could be.)

Creating and using a dictionary

Creating and using a `dictionary` is much like working with a `list`, except that you must now define a key and value pair. Here are the special rules for creating a key:

>> **The key must be unique.** When you enter a duplicate key, the information found in the second entry wins — the first entry is simply replaced with the second.

>> **The key must be immutable.** This rule means that you can use strings, numbers, or tuples for the key. You can't, however, use a list for a key.

You have no restrictions on the values you provide. A value can be any Python object, so you can use a `dictionary` to access an employee record or other complex data. The following steps help you understand how to use dictionaries better.

1. **Type** Colors = {" Sam": " Blue", " Amy": "Red", " Sarah": " Yellow"} **and press Enter.**

Python creates a `dictionary` containing three entries with people's favorite colors. Notice how you create the key and value pair. The key comes first, followed by a colon and then the value. Each entry is separated by a comma.

2. **Type** Colors **and click Run Cell.**

You see the key and value pairs, as shown in Figure 14-5. However, notice that the entries are sorted in key order. A dictionary automatically keeps the keys sorted to make access faster, which means that you get fast search times even when working with a large data set. The downside is that creating the `dictionary` takes longer than using something like a `list` because the computer is busy sorting the entries.

FIGURE 14-5:
A dictionary
places entries in
sorted order.

Working with Dictionaries

Creating and using a dictionary

```
In [8]:   Colors = {"Sam": "Blue", "Amy": "Red", "Sarah": "Yellow"}
          Colors

Out[8]:   {'Amy': 'Red', 'Sam': 'Blue', 'Sarah': 'Yellow'}
```

FIGURE 14-5:
A dictionary places entries in sorted order.

3. **Type** Colors[" Sarah"] **and click Run Cell.**

You see the color associated with Sarah, Yellow, as shown in Figure 14-6. Using a string as a key, rather than using a numeric index, makes the code easier to read and makes it self-documenting to an extent. By making your code more readable, dictionaries save you considerable time in the long run (which is why they're so popular). However, the convenience of a `dictionary` comes at the cost of additional creation time and a higher use of resources, so you have trade-offs to consider.

FIGURE 14-6:
Dictionaries make value access easy and self-documenting.

```
In [9]:  Colors["Sarah"]
Out[9]:  'Yellow'
```

4. **Type** Colors.keys() **and click Run Cell.**

   The `dictionary` presents a list of the keys it contains, as shown in Figure 14-7. You can use these keys to automate access to the dictionary.

FIGURE 14-7:
You can ask a dictionary for a list of keys.

```
In [10]:  Colors.keys()
Out[10]:  dict_keys(['Sam', 'Amy', 'Sarah'])
```

5. **Type the following code pressing Enter after each line, and then click Run Cell.**

```python
for Item in Colors.keys():
    print("{0} likes the color {1}."
        .format(Item, Colors[Item]))
```

REMEMBER

The example code outputs a listing of each of the user names and the user's favorite color, as shown in Figure 14-8. Using dictionaries can make creating useful output a lot easier. The use of a meaningful key means that the key can easily be part of the output.

FIGURE 14-8:
You can create useful keys to output information with greater ease.

```
In [11]:  for Item in Colors.keys():
              print("{0} likes the color {1}."
                  .format(Item, Colors[Item]))

          Sam likes the color Blue.
          Amy likes the color Red.
          Sarah likes the color Yellow.
```

6. **Type** Colors[" Sarah"] ="Purple" **and press Enter.**

   The `dictionary` content is updated so that Sarah now likes Purple instead of Yellow.

7. **Type** Colors.update({" Harry": " Orange"}) **and press Enter.**

A new entry is added to the dictionary.

8. **Type the following code, pressing Enter after each line:**

```
for name, color in Colors.items():
    print("{0} likes the color {1}."
          .format(name, color))
```

Compare this code to the code in Step 5. This version obtains each of the items one at a time and places the key in name and the value in color. The output will always work the same from the item() method. You need two variables, one for the key and another value, presented in the order shown. The reason to consider this second form is that it might be easier to read in some cases. There doesn't seem to be much of a speed difference between the two versions.

9. **Click Run Cell.**

You see the updated output in Figure 14-9. Notice that Harry is added in sorted order. In addition, Sarah's entry is changed to the color Purple.

```
In [12]: Colors["Sarah"] = "Purple"
         Colors.update({"Harry": "Orange"})
         for name, color in Colors.items():
             print("{0} likes the color {1}."
                   .format(name, color)

         Sam likes the color Blue.
         Amy likes the color Red.
         Sarah likes the color Purple.
         Harry likes the color Orange.
```

FIGURE 14-9:
Dictionaries are
easy to modify.

10. **Type** del Colors[" Sam"] **and press Enter.**

Python removes Sam's entry from the dictionary.

11. **Repeat Steps 8 and 9.**

You verify that Sam's entry is actually gone.

12. **Type** len(Colors) **and click Run Cell.**

The output value of 3 verifies that the dictionary contains only three entries now, rather than 4.

13. **Type** Colors.clear() **and press Enter.**

14. **Type** len(Colors) **and click Run Cell.**

Python reports that Colors has 0 entries, so the dictionary is now empty.

Replacing the switch statement with a dictionary

Most programming languages provide some sort of switch statement. A switch statement provides for elegant menu type selections. The user has a number of options but is allowed to choose only one of them. The program takes some course of action based on the user selection. Here is some representative code (it won't execute) of a switch statement you might find in another language:

```
switch(n)
{
   case 0:
      print("You selected blue.");
      break;
   case 1:
      print("You selected yellow.");
      break;
   case 2:
      print("You selected green.");
      break;
}
```

The application normally presents a menu-type interface, obtains the number of the selection from the user, and then chooses the correct course of action from the switch statement. It's straightforward and much neater than using a series of if statements to accomplish the same task.

Unfortunately, Python doesn't come with a switch statement. The best you can hope to do is use an if...elif statement for the task. However, by using a dictionary, you can simulate the use of a switch statement. The following steps help you create an example that will demonstrate the required technique.

1. **Type the following code into the window — pressing Enter after each line:**

```
def PrintBlue():
    print("You chose blue!\r\n")
def PrintRed():
    print("You chose red!\r\n")
def PrintOrange():
    print("You chose orange!\r\n")
def PrintYellow():
    print("You chose yellow!\r\n")
```

Before the code can do anything for you, you must define the tasks. Each of these functions defines a task associated with selecting a color option onscreen. Only one of them gets called at any given time.

2. **Type the following code into the notebook — pressing Enter after each line:**

```
ColorSelect = {
    0: PrintBlue,
    1: PrintRed,
    2: PrintOrange,
    3: PrintYellow
}
```

This code is the `dictionary`. Each key is like the case part of the switch statement. The values specify what to do. In other words, this is the switch structure. The functions that you created earlier are the action part of the switch — the part that goes between the case statement and the break clause.

3. **Type the following code into the notebook — pressing Enter after each line:**

```
Selection = 0
while (Selection != 4):
    print("0. Blue")
    print("1. Red")
    print("2. Orange")
    print("3. Yellow")
    print("4. Quit")
    Selection = int(input("Select a color option: "))
    if (Selection >= 0) and (Selection < 4):
        ColorSelect[Selection]()
```

Finally, you see the user interface part of the example. The code begins by creating an input variable, `Selection`. It then goes into a loop until the user enters a value of 4.

During each loop, the application displays a list of options and then waits for user input. When the user does provide input, the application performs a range check on it. Any value between 0 and 3 selects one of the functions defined earlier using the `dictionary` as the switching mechanism.

4. **Click Run Cell.**

Python displays a menu like the one shown in Figure 14-10.

```
In [*]: def PrintBlue():
            print("You chose blue!\r\n")
        def PrintRed():
            print("You chose red!\r\n")
        def PrintOrange():
            print("You chose orange!\r\n")
        def PrintYellow():
            print("You chose yellow!\r\n")

        ColorSelect = {
            0: PrintBlue,
            1: PrintRed,
            2: PrintOrange,
            3: PrintYellow
        }

        Selection = 0
        while (Selection != 4):
            print("0. Blue")
            print("1. Red")
            print("2. Orange")
            print("3. Yellow")
            print("4. Quit")
            Selection = int(input("Select a color option: "))
            if (Selection >= 0) and (Selection < 4):
                ColorSelect[Selection]()
```

```
0. Blue
1. Red
2. Orange
3. Yellow
4. Quit

Select a color option:
```

FIGURE 14-10:
The application begins by displaying the menu.

5. **Type** 0 **and press Enter.**

The application tells you that you selected blue and then displays the menu again, as shown in Figure 14-11.

```
0. Blue
1. Red
2. Orange
3. Yellow
4. Quit
Select a color option: 0
You chose blue!

0. Blue
1. Red
2. Orange
3. Yellow
4. Quit

Select a color option:
```

FIGURE 14-11:
After displaying your selection, the application displays the menu again.

6. **Type** 4 **and press Enter.**

The application ends.

Creating Stacks Using Lists

A stack is a handy programming structure because you can use it to save an application execution environment (the state of variables and other attributes of the application environment at any given time) or as a means of determining an order of execution. Unfortunately, Python doesn't provide a stack as a collection. However, it does provide lists, and you can use a list as a perfectly acceptable stack. The following steps help you create an example of using a list as a stack.

1. **Type the following code into the notebook — pressing Enter after each line:**

```python
MyStack = []
StackSize = 3
def DisplayStack():
    print("Stack currently contains:")
    for Item in MyStack:
        print(Item)
def Push(Value):
    if len(MyStack) < StackSize:
        MyStack.append(Value)
    else:
        print("Stack is full!")
def Pop():
    if len(MyStack) > 0:
        MyStack.pop()
    else:
        print("Stack is empty.")
Push(1)
Push(2)
Push(3)
DisplayStack()
input("Press any key when ready...")
Push(4)
DisplayStack()
input("Press any key when ready...")
Pop()
DisplayStack()
input("Press any key when ready...")
Pop()
Pop()
Pop()
DisplayStack()
```

In this example, the application creates a `list` and a variable to determine the maximum stack size. Stacks normally have a specific size range. This is admittedly a really small stack, but it serves well for the example's needs.

REMEMBER

Stacks work by pushing a value onto the top of the stack and popping values back off the top of the stack. The `Push()` and `Pop()` functions perform these two tasks. The code adds `DisplayStack()` to make it easier to see the stack content as needed.

The remaining code *exercises the stack* (demonstrates its functionality) by pushing values onto it and then removing them. Four main exercise sections test stack functionality.

2. **Click Run Cell.**

   Python fills the stack with information and then displays it onscreen, as shown in Figure 14-12 (only part of the code appears in the screenshot). In this case, 3 is at the top of the stack because it's the last value added.

```
DisplayStack()
input("Press any key when ready...")
Push(4)
DisplayStack()
input("Press any key when ready...")
Pop()
DisplayStack()
input("Press any key when ready...")
Pop()
Pop()
Pop()
DisplayStack
```
```
Press any key when ready...
[                              ]

Stack currently contains:
1
2
3
```

FIGURE 14-12:
A stack pushes values one on top of the other.

TECHNICAL STUFF

Depending on the IDE you use, the `Press any key when ready` message can appear at the top or the bottom of the output area. In the case of Notebook, the message and associated entry field appear at the top after the first query (refer to Figure 14-12). The message will move to the bottom during the second and subsequent queries.

3. **Press Enter.**

   The application attempts to push another value onto the stack. However, the stack is full, so the task fails, as shown in Figure 14-13.

```
Stack currently contains:
1
2
3
Press any key when ready...
Stack is full!
Stack currently contains:
1
2
3
Press any key when ready...
```

FIGURE 14-13:
When the stack is full, it can't accept any more values.

4. **Press Enter.**

The application pops a value from the top of the stack. Remember that 3 is the top of the stack, so that's the value that is missing in Figure 14-14.

FIGURE 14-14:
Popping a value means removing it from the top of the stack.

```
Stack currently contains:
1
2
Press any key when ready...
```

5. **Press Enter.**

The application tries to pop more values from the stack than it contains, resulting in an error, as shown in Figure 14-15. Any stack implementation that you create must be able to detect both overflows (too many entries) and underflows (too few entries).

FIGURE 14-15:
Make sure that your stack implementation detects overflows and underflows.

```
Stack is empty.
Stack currently contains:
```

Working with queues

A queue works differently from a stack. Think of any line you've ever stood in: You go to the back of the line, and when you reach the front of the line you get to do whatever you stood in the line to do. A queue is often used for task scheduling and to maintain program flow — just as it is in the real world. The following steps help you create a queue-based application. This example also appears with the downloadable source code as QueueData.py.

1. **Type the following code into the notebook — pressing Enter after each line:**

```python
import queue
MyQueue = queue.Queue(3)
print(MyQueue.empty())
input("Press any key when ready...")
MyQueue.put(1)
MyQueue.put(2)
print(MyQueue.full())
input("Press any key when ready...")
MyQueue.put(3)
print(MyQueue.full())
input("Press any key when ready...")
print(MyQueue.get())
print(MyQueue.empty())
print(MyQueue.full())
input("Press any key when ready...")
print(MyQueue.get())
print(MyQueue.get())
```

To create a queue, you must import the queue package. This package actually contains a number of queue types, but this example uses only the standard FIFO queue.

REMEMBER

When a queue is empty, the empty() function returns True. Likewise, when a queue is full, the full() function returns True. By testing the state of empty() and full(), you can determine whether you need to perform additional work with the queue or whether you can add other information to it. These two functions help you manage a queue. You can't iterate through a queue by using a for loop as you have done with other collection types, so you must monitor empty() and full() instead.

The two functions used to work with data in a queue are put(), which adds new data, and get(), which removes data. A problem with queues is that if you try to put more items into the queue than it can hold, it simply waits until space is available to hold it. Unless you're using a *multithreaded application* (one that uses individual threads of execution to perform more than one task at one time), this state could end up freezing your application.

2. **Click Run Cell.**

Python tests the state of the queue. In this case, you see an output of True, which means that the queue is empty.

3. **Press Enter.**

The application adds two new values to the queue. In doing so, the queue is no longer empty, as shown in Figure 14-16.

Working with queues

```
In [*]:  import queue
         MyQueue = queue.Queue(3)
         print(MyQueue.empty())
         input("Press any key when ready...")
         MyQueue.put(1)
         MyQueue.put(2)
         print(MyQueue.full())
         input("Press any key when ready...")
         MyQueue.put(3)
         print(MyQueue.full())
         input("Press any key when ready...")
         print(MyQueue.get())
         print(MyQueue.empty())
         print(MyQueue.full())
         input("Press any key when ready...")
         print(MyQueue.get())
         print(MyQueue.get())
```

```
True
Press any key when ready...
False

Press any key when ready...
```

FIGURE 14-16:
When the application puts new entries in the queue, the queue no longer reports that it's empty.

4. **Press Enter.**

   The application adds another entry to the queue, which means that the queue is now full because it was set to a size of 3. This means that full() will return True because the queue is now full.

5. **Press Enter.**

   To free space in the queue, the application gets one of the entries. Whenever an application gets an entry, the get() function returns that entry. Given that 1 was the first value added to the queue, the print() function should return a value of 1, as shown in Figure 14-17. In addition, both empty() and full() should now return False.

```
True
Press any key when ready...
1
False
False

Press any key when ready...
```

FIGURE 14-17:
Monitoring is a key part of working with a queue.

6. **Press Enter.**

   The application gets the remaining two entries. You see 2 and 3 (in turn) as output.

Working with deques

A deque is simply a queue where you can remove and add items from either end. In many languages, a queue or stack starts out as a deque. Specialized code serves to limit deque functionality to what is needed to perform a particular task.

When working with a deque, you need to think of the deque as a sort of horizontal line. Certain individual functions work with the left and right ends of the deque so that you can add and remove items from either side. The following steps help you create an example that demonstrates deque usage. This example also appears with the downloadable source code as DequeData.py.

1. **Type the following code into Notebook — pressing Enter after each line.**

```
import collections
MyDeque = collections.deque("abcdef", 10)
print("Starting state:")
for Item in MyDeque:
    print(Item, end=" ")
print("\r\n\r\nAppending and extending right")
MyDeque.append("h")
MyDeque.extend("ij")
for Item in MyDeque:
    print(Item, end=" ")
print("\r\nMyDeque contains {0} items."
        .format(len(MyDeque)))
print("\r\nPopping right")
print("Popping {0}".format(MyDeque.pop()))
for Item in MyDeque:
    print(Item, end=" ")
print("\r\n\r\nAppending and extending left")
MyDeque.appendleft("a")
MyDeque.extendleft("bc")
for Item in MyDeque:
    print(Item, end=" ")
print("\r\nMyDeque contains {0} items."
        .format(len(MyDeque)))
print("\r\nPopping left")
print("Popping {0}".format(MyDeque.popleft()))
for Item in MyDeque:
    print(Item, end=" ")
print("\r\n\r\nRemoving")
MyDeque.remove("a")
for Item in MyDeque:
    print(Item, end=" ")
```

The implementation of deque is found in the collections package, so you need to import it into your code. When you create a deque, you can optionally specify a starting list of *iterable items* (items that can be accessed and processed as part of a loop structure) and a maximum size, as shown.

REMEMBER

A deque differentiates between adding one item and adding a group of items. You use append() or appendleft() when adding a single item. The extend() and extendleft() functions let you add multiple items. You use the pop() or popleft() functions to remove one item at a time. The act of popping values returns the value popped, so the example prints the value onscreen. The remove() function is unique in that it always works from the left side and always removes the first instance of the requested data.

Unlike some other collections, a deque is fully iterable. This means that you can obtain a list of items by using a for loop whenever necessary.

2. **Click Run Cell.**

Python outputs the information shown in Figure 14-18 (the screenshot shows only the output and none of the code).

WARNING

Following the output listing closely is important. Notice how the size of the deque changes over time. After the application pops the j, the deque still contains eight items. When the application appends and extends from the left, it adds three more items. However, the resulting deque contains only ten items. When you exceed the maximum size of a deque, the extra data simply falls off the other end.

```
Starting state:
a b c d e f

Appending and extending right
a b c d e f h i j
MyDeque contains 9 items.

Popping right
Popping j
a b c d e f h i

Appending and extending left
c b a a b c d e f h
MyDeque contains 10 items.

Popping left
Popping c
b a a b c d e f h

Removing
b a b c d e f h
```

FIGURE 14-18: A deque provides the double-ended functionality and other features you'd expect.

Chapter **15**

Creating and Using Classes

You've already worked with a number of classes in previous chapters. Many of the examples are easy to construct and use because they depend on the Python classes. Even though classes are briefly mentioned in previous chapters, those chapters largely ignore them simply because discussing them wasn't immediately important.

Classes make working with Python code more convenient by helping to make your applications easy to read, understand, and use. You use classes to create containers for your code and data, so they stay together in one piece. Outsiders see your class as a black box — data goes in and results come out.

REMEMBER

At some point, you need to start constructing classes of your own if you want to avoid the dangers of the spaghetti code that is found in older applications. *Spaghetti code* is much as the name implies — various lines of procedures are interwoven and spread out in such a way that it's hard to figure out where one piece of spaghetti begins and another ends. Trying to maintain spaghetti code is nearly impossible, and some organizations have thrown out applications because no one could figure them out.

Besides helping you understand classes as a packaging method that avoids spaghetti code, this chapter helps you create and use your own classes for the first time.

You gain insights into how Python classes work toward making your applications convenient to work with. This is an introductory sort of chapter, though, and you won't become so involved in classes that your head begins to spin around on its own. This chapter is about making class development simple and manageable. You can find the downloadable source code for the examples in this chapter in the `BPPD_15_Creating_and_Using_Classes.ipynb` file, as described in the book's Introduction.

Understanding the Class as a Packaging Method

A class is essentially a method for packaging code. The idea is to simplify code reuse, make applications more reliable, and reduce the potential for security breaches. Well-designed classes are black boxes that accept certain inputs and provide specific outputs based on those inputs. In short, a class shouldn't create any surprises for anyone and should have known (quantifiable) behaviors. How the class accomplishes its work is unimportant, and hiding the details of its inner workings is essential to good coding practice.

Before you move onto actual class theory, you need to know a few terms that are specific to classes. The following list defines terms that you need to know in order to use the material that follows later in the chapter. These terms are specific to Python. (Other languages may use different terms for the same techniques or define terms that Python uses in different ways.)

REMEMBER

» **Class:** Defines a blueprint for creating an object. Think of a builder who wants to create a building of some type. The builder uses a blueprint to ensure that the building will meet the required specifications. Likewise, Python uses classes as a blueprint for creating new objects.

WARNING

» **Class variable:** Provides a storage location used by all methods in an instance of the class. A class variable is defined within the class proper but outside of any of the class methods. Class variables aren't used very often because they're a potential security risk — every instance of the class has access to the same information. In addition to being a security risk, class variables are also visible as part of the class rather than a particular method of a class, so they pose the potential problem of class contamination.

Global variables have always been considered a bad idea in programming, doubly so in Python, because every instance can see the same information. In addition, data hiding really doesn't work in Python. Every variable is always visible. The article at http://www.geeksforgeeks.org/object-oriented-programming-in-python-set-2-data-hiding-and-object-printing/ describes this issue in greater detail, but the most important thing to remember in Python is that it lacks the data hiding found in other languages to promote true object orientation.

» **Data member:** Defines either a class variable or an instance variable used to hold data associated with a class and its objects.

» **Function overloading:** Creates more than one version of a function, which results in different behaviors. The essential task of the function may be the same, but the inputs are different and potentially the outputs as well. Function overloading is used to provide flexibility so that a function can work with applications in various ways or perform a task with different variable types.

» **Inheritance:** Uses a parent class to create child classes that have the same characteristics. The child classes usually have extended functionality or provide more specific behaviors than the parent class does.

REMEMBER

» **Instance:** Defines an object created from the specification provided by a class. Python can create as many instances of a class to perform the work required by an application. Each instance is unique.

» **Instance variable:** Provides a storage location used by a single method of an instance of a class. The variable is defined within a method. Instance variables are considered safer than class variables because only one method of the class can access them. Data is passed between methods by using arguments, which allows for controlled checks of incoming data and better control over data management.

REMEMBER

» **Instantiation:** Performs the act of creating an instance of a class. The resulting object is a unique class instance.

» **Method:** Defines the term used for functions that are part of a class. Even though function and method essentially define the same element, method is considered more specific because only classes can have methods.

» **Object:** Defines a unique instance of a class. The object contains all the methods and properties of the original class. However, the data for each object differs. The storage locations are unique, even if the data is the same.

» **Operator overloading:** Creates more than one version of a function that is associated with an operator such as: +, –, /, or *, which results in different behaviors. The essential task of the operator may be the same, but the way in which the operator interacts with the data differs. Operator overloading is used to provide flexibility so that an operator can work with applications in various ways.

Considering the Parts of a Class

A class has a specific construction. Each part of a class performs a particular task that gives the class useful characteristics. Of course, the class begins with a container that is used to hold the entire class together, so that's the part that the first section that follows discusses. The remaining sections describe the other parts of a class and help you understand how they contribute to the class as a whole.

Creating the class definition

A class need not be particularly complex. In fact, you can create just the container and one class element and call it a class. Of course, the resulting class won't do much, but you can *instantiate it* (tell Python to build an object by using your class as a blueprint) and work with it as you would any other class. The following steps help you understand the basics behind a class by creating the simplest class possible.

1. **Open a new notebook.**

   You can also use the downloadable source file, BPPD_15_Creating_and_Using_Classes.ipynb.

2. **Type the following code (pressing Enter after each line and pressing Enter twice after the last line):**

   ```
   class MyClass:
       MyVar = 0
   ```

   The first line defines the class container, which consists of the keyword class and the class name, which is MyClass. Every class you create must begin precisely this way. You must always include class followed by the class name.

   The second line is the class suite. All the elements that comprise the class are called the *class suite*. In this case, you see a class variable named MyVar, which is set to a value of 0. Every instance of the class will have the same variable and start at the same value.

3. **Type MyInstance = MyClass() and press Enter.**

   You have just created an instance of MyClass named MyInstance. Of course, you'll want to verify that you really have created such an instance. Step 4 accomplishes that task.

4. **Type** MyInstance.MyVar **and click Run Cell.**

The output of 0, as shown in Figure 15-1, demonstrates that MyInstance does indeed have a class variable named MyVar.

FIGURE 15-1:
The instance contains the required variable.

5. **Type** MyInstance.__class__ **and click Run Cell.**

Python displays the class used to create this instance, as shown in Figure 15-2. The output tells you that this class is part of the __main__ package, which means that you typed it directly into the application code and not as part of another package.

FIGURE 15-2:
The class name is also correct, so you know that this instance is created by using MyClass.

Considering the built-in class attributes

When you create a class, you can easily think that all you get is the class. However, Python adds built-in functionality to your class. For example, in the preceding section, you type __class__ and press Enter. The __class__ attribute is built in; you didn't create it. It helps to know that Python provides this functionality so that you don't have to add it. The functionality is needed often enough that every class should have it, so Python supplies it. The following steps help you work with the built-in class attributes. They assume that you followed the steps in the pre-ceding section, "Creating the class definition."

1. **Type** print(dir(MyInstance)) **and click Run Cell.**

   A list of attributes appears, as shown in Figure 15-3. These attributes provide specific functionality for your class. They're also common to every other class you create, so you can count on always having this functionality in the classes you create.

FIGURE 15-3:
Use the dir( )
function to
determine which
built-in attributes
are present.

```
Considering the built-in class attributes
In [3]: print(dir(MyInstance))

['MyVar', '__class__', '__delattr__', '__dict__', '__dir__', '__doc
__', '__eq__', '__format__', '__ge__', '__getattribute__', '__gt__',
'__hash__', '__init__', '__init_subclass__', '__le__', '__lt__', '__
module__', '__ne__', '__new__', '__reduce__', '__reduce_ex__', '__re
pr__', '__setattr__', '__sizeof__', '__str__', '__subclasshook__', '
__weakref__']
```

2. **Type** help('__class__') **and press Enter.**

   Python displays information on the __class__ attribute, as partially shown in Figure 15-4. You can use the same technique for learning more about any attribute that Python adds to your class.

```
In [4]: help('__class__')

Help on class module in module builtins:

__class__ = class module(object)
 |  module(name[, doc])
 |
 |  Create a module object.
 |  The name must be a string; the optional doc argument can have an
 y type.
 |
 |  Methods defined here:
 |
 |  __delattr__(self, name, /)
 |      Implement delattr(self, name).
 |
 |  __dir__(...)
 |      __dir__() -> list
 |      specialized dir() implementation
 |
 |  __getattribute__(self, name, /)
 |      Return getattr(self, name).
```

FIGURE 15-4:
Python provides
help for each of
the attributes
it adds to
your class.

Working with methods

Methods are simply another kind of function that reside in classes. You create and work with methods in precisely the same way that you do functions, except that methods are always associated with a class (you don't see freestanding methods as you do functions). You can create two kinds of methods: those associated with the class itself and those associated with an instance of a class. It's important to differentiate between the two. The following sections provide the details needed to work with both.

Creating class methods

A *class method* is one that you execute directly from the class without creating an instance of the class. Sometimes you need to create methods that execute from the class, such as the functions you used with the str class to modify strings. As an example, the multiple exception example in the "Nested exception handling" section of Chapter 10 uses the str.upper() function. The following steps demonstrate how to create and use a class method.

1. **Type the following code (pressing Enter after each line and pressing Enter twice after the last line):**

```
class MyClass:
    def SayHello():
        print("Hello there!")
```

The example class contains a single defined attribute, SayHello(). This method doesn't accept any arguments and doesn't return any values. It simply prints a message as output. However, the method works just fine for demonstration purposes.

2. **Type** MyClass.SayHello() **and click Run Cell.**

The example outputs the expected string, as shown in Figure 15-5. Notice that you didn't need to create an instance of the class — the method is available immediately for use.

FIGURE 15-5:
The class method outputs a simple message.

> Working with methods
>
> Creating class methods
>
> In [5]: `class MyClass:`
> `    def SayHello():`
> `        print("Hello there!")`
>
> `MyClass.SayHello()`
>
> `Hello there!`

REMEMBER

A class method can work only with class data. It doesn't know about any data associated with an instance of the class. You can pass it data as an argument, and the method can return information as needed, but it can't access the instance data. As a consequence, you need to exercise care when creating class methods to ensure that they're essentially self-contained.

Creating instance methods

An *instance method* is one that is part of the individual instances. You use instance methods to manipulate the data that the class manages. As a consequence, you can't use instance methods until you instantiate an object from the class.

REMEMBER

All instance methods accept a single argument as a minimum, self. The self argument points at the particular instance that the application is using to manipulate data. Without the self argument, the method wouldn't know which instance data to use. However, self isn't considered an accessible argument — the value for self is supplied by Python, and you can't change it as part of calling the method. The following steps demonstrate how to create and use instance methods in Python.

1. **Type the following code (pressing Enter after each line and pressing Enter twice after the last line):**

```
class MyClass:
    def SayHello(self):
        print("Hello there!")
```

The example class contains a single defined attribute, SayHello( ). This method doesn't accept any special arguments and doesn't return any values. It simply prints a message as output. However, the method works just fine for demonstration purposes.

2. **Type** MyInstance = MyClass() **and press Enter.**

Python creates an instance of MyClass named MyInstance.

3. **Type** MyInstance.SayHello() **and click Run Cell.**

You see the message shown in Figure 15-6.

FIGURE 15-6:
The instance message is called as part of an object and outputs this simple message.

```
Creating instance methods

In [6]: class MyClass:
            def SayHello(self):
                print("Hello there!")

        MyInstance = MyClass()
        MyInstance.SayHello()

        Hello there!
```

Working with constructors

A *constructor* is a special kind of method that Python calls when it instantiates an object by using the definitions found in your class. Python relies on the constructor to perform tasks such as *initializing* (assigning values to) any instance variables that the object will need when it starts. Constructors can also verify that there are enough resources for the object and perform any other start-up task you can think of.

The name of a constructor is always the same, `__init__()`. The constructor can accept arguments when necessary to create the object. When you create a class without a constructor, Python automatically creates a default constructor for you that doesn't do anything. Every class must have a constructor, even if it simply relies on the default constructor. The following steps demonstrate how to create a constructor:

1. **Type the following code (pressing Enter after each line and pressing Enter twice after the last line):**

```
class MyClass:
    Greeting = ""
    def __init__(self, Name="there"):
        self.Greeting = Name + "!"
    def SayHello(self):
        print("Hello {0}".format(self.Greeting))
```

This example provides your first example of function overloading. In this case, there are two versions of `__init__()`. The first doesn't require any special input because it uses the default value for the Name of "there". The second requires a name as an input. It sets Greeting to the value of this name, plus an exclamation mark. The SayHello() method is essentially the same as previous examples in this chapter.

Python doesn't support true function overloading. Many strict adherents to strict Object-Oriented Programming (OOP) principles consider default values to be something different from function overloading. However, the use of default values obtains the same result, and it's the only option that Python offers. In true function overloading, you see multiple copies of the same function, each of which could process the input differently.

2. **Type** MyInstance = MyClass() **and press Enter.**

Python creates an instance of MyClass named MyInstance.

3. **Type** MyInstance.SayHello() **and click Run Cell.**

You see the message shown in Figure 15-7. Notice that this message provides the default, generic greeting.

4. **Type** MyInstance2 = MyClass("Amy") **and press Enter.**

Python creates an instance of MyClass named MyInstance2. The instance MyInstance is completely different from the instance MyInstance2.

FIGURE 15-7:
The first version
of the constructor
provides a default
value for
the name.

```
Working with constructors

In [7]:  class MyClass:
             Greeting = ""
             def __init__(self, Name="there"):
                 self.Greeting = Name + "!"
             def SayHello(self):
                 print("Hello {0}".format(self.Greeting))

         MyInstance = MyClass()
         MyInstance.SayHello()

         Hello there!
```

FIGURE 15-7:
The first version of the constructor provides a default value for the name.

5. **Type** MyInstance2.SayHello() **and press Enter.**

   Python displays the message for MyInstance2, not the message for MyInstance.

6. **Type** MyInstance.Greeting ="Harry!" **and press Enter.**

   This step changes the greeting for MyInstance without changing the greeting for MyInstance2.

7. **Type** MyInstance.SayHello() **and click Run Cell.**

   You see the messages shown in Figure 15-8. Notice that this message provides a specific greeting for each of the instances. In addition, each instance is separate, and you were able to change the message for the first instance without affecting the second instance.

FIGURE 15-8:
Supplying the constructor with a name provides a customized output.

```
In [8]:  MyInstance2 = MyClass("Amy")
         MyInstance2.SayHello()
         MyInstance.Greeting = "Harry!"
         MyInstance.SayHello()

         Hello Amy!
         Hello Harry!
```

Working with variables

As mentioned earlier in the book, variables are storage containers that hold data. When working with classes, you need to consider how the data is stored and managed. A class can include both class variables and instance variables. The class variables are defined as part of the class itself, while instance variables are defined as part of methods. The following sections show how to use both variable types.

Creating class variables

Class variables provide global access to data that your class manipulates in some way. In most cases, you initialize global variables by using the constructor to ensure that they contain a known good value. The following steps demonstrate how class variables work.

1. **Type the following code (pressing Enter after each line and pressing Enter twice after the last line):**

```
class MyClass:
    Greeting = ""
    def SayHello(self):
        print("Hello {0}".format(self.Greeting))
```

This is a version of the code found in the "Working with constructors" section, earlier in this chapter, but this version doesn't include the constructor. Normally you do include a constructor to ensure that the class variable is initialized properly. However, this series of steps shows how class variables can go wrong.

2. **Type** MyClass.Greeting = " Zelda" **and press Enter.**

This statement sets the value of Greeting to something other than the value that you used when you created the class. Of course, anyone could make this change. The big question is whether the change will take.

3. **Type** MyClass.Greeting **and click Run Cell.**

You see that the value of Greeting has changed, as shown in Figure 15-9.

4. **Type** MyInstance = MyClass() **and press Enter.**

Python creates an instance of MyClass named MyInstance.

5. **Type** MyInstance.SayHello() **and click Run Cell.**

You see the message shown in Figure 15-10. The change that you made to Greeting has carried over to the instance of the class. It's true that the use of a class variable hasn't really caused a problem in this example, but you can imagine what would happen in a real application if someone wanted to cause problems.

REMEMBER

This is just a simple example of how class variables can go wrong. The two concepts you should take away from this example are as follows:

- Avoid class variables when you can because they're inherently unsafe.

- Always initialize class variables to a known good value in the constructor code.

```
In [10]: MyInstance = MyClass()
         MyInstance.SayHello()

         Hello Zelda
```

Creating instance variables

Instance variables are always defined as part of a method. The input arguments to a method are considered instance variables because they exist only when the method exists. Using instance variables is usually safer than using class variables because it's easier to maintain control over them and to ensure that the caller is providing the correct input. The following steps show an example of using instance variables.

1. **Type the following code (pressing Enter after each line and pressing Enter twice after the last line):**

```
class MyClass:
    def DoAdd(self, Value1=0, Value2=0):
        Sum = Value1 + Value2
        print("The sum of {0} plus {1} is {2}."
              .format(Value1, Value2, Sum))
```

In this case, you have three instance variables. The input arguments, Value1 and Value2, have default values of 0, so DoAdd() can't fail simply because the user forgot to provide values. Of course, the user could always supply something other than numbers, so you should provide the appropriate checks as part of your code. The third instance variable is Sum, which is equal to Value1 + Value2. The code simply adds the two numbers together and displays the result.

2. **Type MyInstance = MyClass() and press Enter.**

Python creates an instance of MyClass named MyInstance.

3. **Type MyInstance.DoAdd(1, 4) and click Run Cell.**

You see the message shown in Figure 15-11. In this case, you see the sum of adding 1 and 4.

FIGURE 15-11:
The output is simply the sum of two numbers.

```
Creating instance variables

In [11]:  class MyClass:
              def DoAdd(self, Value1=0, Value2=0):
                  Sum = Value1 + Value2
                  print("The sum of {0} plus {1} is {2}."
                      .format(Value1, Value2, Sum))

          MyInstance = MyClass()
          MyInstance.DoAdd(1, 4)

          The sum of 1 plus 4 is 5.
```

Using methods with variable argument lists

Sometimes you create methods that can take a variable number of arguments. Handling this sort of situation is something Python does well. Here are the two kinds of variable arguments that you can create:

>> *args: Provides a list of unnamed arguments.

>> **kwargs: Provides a list of named arguments.

REMEMBER

The actual names of the arguments don't matter, but Python developers use *args and **kwargs as a convention so that other Python developers know that they're a variable list of arguments. Notice that the first variable argument has just one asterisk (*) associated with it, which means the arguments are unnamed. The second variable has two asterisks, which means that the arguments are named. The following steps demonstrate how to use both approaches to writing an application.

1. **Type the following code into the window — pressing Enter after each line:**

```
class MyClass:
    def PrintList1(*args):
        for Count, Item in enumerate(args):
            print("{0}. {1}".format(Count, Item))
    def PrintList2(**kwargs):
        for Name, Value in kwargs.items():
            print("{0} likes {1}".format(Name, Value))
MyClass.PrintList1("Red", "Blue", "Green")
MyClass.PrintList2(George="Red", Sue="Blue",
                   Zarah="Green")
```

For the purposes of this example, you're seeing the arguments implemented as part of a class method. However, you can use them just as easily with an instance method.

Look carefully at PrintList1() and you see a new method of using a for loop to iterate through a list. In this case, the enumerate() function outputs both a count (the loop count) and the string that was passed to the function.

TIP

The `PrintList2()` function accepts a dictionary input. Just as with `PrintList1()`, this list can be any length. However, you must process the `items()` found in the dictionary to obtain the individual values.

2. **Click Run Cell.**

   You see the output shown in Figure 15-12. The individual lists can be of any length. In fact, in this situation, playing with the code to see what you can do with it is a good idea. For example, try mixing numbers and strings with the first list to see what happens. Try adding Boolean values as well. The point is that using this technique makes your methods incredibly flexible if all you want is a list of values as input.

Using methods with variable argument lists

```
In [12]: class MyClass:
             def PrintList1(*args):
                 for Count, Item in enumerate(args):
                     print("{0}. {1}".format(Count, Item))
             def PrintList2(**kwargs):
                 for Name, Value in kwargs.items():
                     print("{0} likes {1}".format(Name, Value))
         MyClass.PrintList1("Red", "Blue", "Green")
         MyClass.PrintList2(George="Red", Sue="Blue",
                            Zarah="Green")

         0. Red
         1. Blue
         2. Green
         George likes Red
         Sue likes Blue
         Zarah likes Green
```

FIGURE 15-12: The code can process any number of entries in the list.

Overloading operators

In some situations, you want to be able to do something special as the result of using a standard operator such as add (+). In fact, sometimes Python doesn't provide a default behavior for operators because it has no default to implement. No matter what the reason might be, overloading operators makes it possible to assign new functionality to existing operators so that they do what you want, rather than what Python intended. The following steps demonstrate how to overload an operator and use it as part of an application.

1. **Type the following code into the Notebook — pressing Enter after each line:**

```
class MyClass:
    def __init__(self, *args):
        self.Input = args
    def __add__(self, Other):
        Output = MyClass()
```

```
        Output.Input = self.Input + Other.Input
        return Output
    def __str__(self):
        Output = ""
        for Item in self.Input:
            Output += Item
            Output += " "
        return Output
Value1 = MyClass("Red", "Green", "Blue")
Value2 = MyClass("Yellow", "Purple", "Cyan")
Value3 = Value1 + Value2
print("{0} + {1} = {2}"
        .format(Value1, Value2, Value3))
```

The example demonstrates a few different techniques. The constructor, __init__(), demonstrates a method for creating an instance variable attached to the self object. You can use this approach to create as many variables as needed to support the instance.

When you create your own classes, no + operator is defined until you define one, in most cases. The only exception is when you inherit from an existing class that already has the + operator defined (see the "Extending Classes to Make New Classes" section, later in this chapter, for details). To add two MyClass entries together, you must define the __add__() method, which equates to the + operator.

The code used for the __add__() method may look a little odd, too, but you need to think about it one line at a time. The code begins by creating a new object, Output, from MyClass. Nothing is added to Output at this point — it's a blank object. The two objects that you want to add, self.Input and Other. Input, are actually tuples. (See "Working with Tuples," in Chapter 14, for more details about tuples.) The code places the sum of these two objects into Output.Input. The __add__() method then returns the new combined object to the caller.

Of course, you may want to know why you can't simply add the two inputs together as you would a number. The answer is that you'd end up with a tuple as an output, rather than a MyClass as an output. The type of the output would be changed, and that would also change any use of the resulting object.

To print MyClass properly, you also need to define a __str__() method. This method converts a MyClass object into a string. In this case, the output is a *space-delimited string* (in which each of the items in the string is separated from the other items by a space) containing each of the values found in self.Input.

Of course, the class that you create can output any string that fully represents the object.

The main procedure creates two test objects, Value1 and Value2. It adds them together and places the result in Value3. The result is printed onscreen.

2. **Click Run Cell.**

Figure 15-13 shows the result of adding the two objects together, converting them to strings, and then printing the result. It's a lot of code for such a simple output statement, but the result definitely demonstrates that you can create classes that are self-contained and fully functional.

Overloading operators

```
In [13]: class MyClass:
             def __init__(self, *args):
                 self.Input = args
             def __add__(self, Other):
                 Output = MyClass()
                 Output.Input = self.Input + Other.Input
                 return Output
             def __str__(self):
                 Output = ""
                 for Item in self.Input:
                     Output += Item
                     Output += " "
                 return Output
         Value1 = MyClass("Red", "Green", "Blue")
         Value2 = MyClass("Yellow", "Purple", "Cyan")
         Value3 = Value1 + Value2
         print("{0} + {1} = {2}"
               .format(Value1, Value2, Value3))

         Red Green Blue  + Yellow Purple Cyan  = Red Green Blue Yellow Purple
         Cyan
```

FIGURE 15-13:
The result of adding two MyClass objects is a third object of the same type.

Creating a Class

All the previous material in this chapter has helped prepare you for creating an interesting class of your own. In this case, you create a class that you place into an external package and eventually access within an application. The following sections describe how to create and save this class.

Defining the MyClass class

Listing 15-1 shows the code that you need to create the class. You can also find this code in the BPPD_15_MyClass.ipynb file found in the downloadable source, as described in the Introduction.

LISTING 15-1: **Creating an External Class**

```
class MyClass:
    def __init__(self, Name="Sam", Age=32):
        self.Name = Name
        self.Age = Age
    def GetName(self):
        return self.Name
    def SetName(self, Name):
        self.Name = Name
    def GetAge(self):
        return self.Age
    def SetAge(self, Age):
        self.Age = Age
    def __str__(self):
        return "{0} is aged {1}.".format(self.Name,
                                         self.Age)
```

In this case, the class begins by creating an object with two instance variables: Name and Age. If the user fails to provide these values, they default to Sam and 32.

REMEMBER

This example provides you with a new class feature. Most developers call this feature an *accessor*. Essentially, it provides access to an underlying value. There are two types of accessors: getters and setters. Both GetName() and GetAge() are *getters*. They provide read-only access to the underlying value. The SetName() and SetAge() methods are *setters*, which provide write-only access to the underlying value. Using a combination of methods like this allows you to check inputs for correct type and range, as well as verify that the caller has permission to view the information.

As with just about every other class you create, you need to define the __str__() method if you want the user to be able to print the object. In this case, the class provides formatted output that lists both of the instance variables.

Saving a class to disk

You could keep your class right in the same file as your test code, but that wouldn't reflect the real world very well. To use this class in a real-world way for the rest of the chapter, you must follow these steps:

1. **Create a new notebook called** BPPD_15_MyClass.ipynb.

2. **Click Run Cell.**

   Python will execute the code without error when you have typed the code correctly.

3. **Choose File ➪ Save and Checkpoint.**

   Notebook saves the file.

4. **Choose File ➪ Download As ➪ Python (.py).**

   Notebook outputs the code as a Python file.

5. **Import the resulting file into your Notebook.**

   The "Importing a notebook" section of Chapter 4 describes how to perform this task.

Using the Class in an Application

Most of the time, you use external classes when working with Python. It isn't very often that a class exists within the confines of the application file because the application would become large and unmanageable. In addition, reusing the class code in another application would be difficult. The following steps help you use the MyClass class that you created in the previous section.

1. **Type the following code into the notebook for this chapter — pressing Enter after each line:**

```
import BPPD_15_MyClass
SamsRecord = BPPD_15_MyClass.MyClass()
AmysRecord = BPPD_15_MyClass.MyClass("Amy", 44)
print(SamsRecord.GetAge())
SamsRecord.SetAge(33)
print(AmysRecord.GetName())
AmysRecord.SetName("Aimee")
print(SamsRecord)
print(AmysRecord)
```

REMEMBER

The example code begins by importing the BPPD_15_MyClass package. The package name is the name of the file used to store the external code, not the name of the class. A single package can contain multiple classes, so always think of the package as being the actual file that is used to hold one or more classes that you need to use with your application.

After the package is imported, the application creates two MyClass objects. Notice that you use the package name first, followed by the class name. The first object, SamsRecord, uses the default settings. The second object, AmysRecord, relies on custom settings.

Sam has become a year old. After the application verifies that the age does need to be updated, it updates Sam's age.

Somehow, HR spelled Aimee's name wrong. It turns out that *Amy* is an incorrect spelling. Again, after the application verifies that the name is wrong, it makes a correction to AmysRecord. The final step is to print both records in their entirety.

2. **Click Run Cell.**

The application displays a series of messages as it puts MyClass through its paces, as shown in Figure 15-14. At this point, you know all the essentials of creating great classes.

FIGURE 15-14:
The output shows that the class is fully functional.

Using the Class in an Application

```
In [14]:   import BPPD_15_MyClass
           SamsRecord = BPPD_15_MyClass.MyClass()
           AmysRecord = BPPD_15_MyClass.MyClass("Amy", 44)
           print(SamsRecord.GetAge())
           SamsRecord.SetAge(33)
           print(AmysRecord.GetName())
           AmysRecord.SetName("Aimee")
           print(SamsRecord)
           print(AmysRecord)

           32
           Amy
           Sam is aged 33.
           Aimee is aged 44.
```

Extending Classes to Make New Classes

As you might imagine, creating a fully functional, *production-grade class* (one that is used in a real-world application actually running on a system that is accessed by users) is time consuming because real classes perform a lot of tasks. Fortunately, Python supports a feature called *inheritance.* By using inheritance, you can obtain the features you want from a parent class when creating a child class. Overriding the features that you don't need and adding new features lets you create new classes relatively fast and with a lot less effort on your part. In addition, because the parent code is already tested, you don't have to put quite as much effort into ensuring that your new class works as expected. The following sections show how to build and use classes that inherit from each other.

Building the child class

Parent classes are normally supersets of something. For example, you might create a parent class named Car and then create child classes of various car types around it. In this case, you build a parent class named Animal and use it to define a child class named Chicken. Of course, you can easily add other child classes after you have Animal in place, such as a Gorilla class. However, for this example, you build just the one parent and one child class, as shown in Listing 15-2. To use this class with the remainder of the chapter, you need to save it to disk by using the technique found in the "Saving a class to disk" section, earlier in this chapter. However, give your file the name BPPD_15_Animals.ipynb.

LISTING 15-2: **Building a Parent and Child Class**

```
class Animal:
    def __init__(self, Name="", Age=0, Type=""):
        self.Name = Name
        self.Age = Age
        self.Type = Type
    def GetName(self):
        return self.Name
    def SetName(self, Name):
        self.Name = Name
    def GetAge(self):
        return self.Age
    def SetAge(self, Age):
        self.Age = Age
    def GetType(self):
        return self.Type
    def SetType(self, Type):
        self.Type = Type
    def __str__(self):
        return "{0} is a {1} aged {2}".format(self.Name,
                                              self.Type,
                                              self.Age)
class Chicken(Animal):
    def __init__(self, Name="", Age=0):
        self.Name = Name
        self.Age = Age
        self.Type = "Chicken"
    def SetType(self, Type):
        print("Sorry, {0} will always be a {1}"
              .format(self.Name, self.Type))
    def MakeSound(self):
        print("{0} says Cluck, Cluck, Cluck!".format(self.Name))
```

The Animal class tracks three characteristics: Name, Age, and Type. A production application would probably track more characteristics, but these characteristics do everything needed for this example. The code also includes the required accessors for each of the characteristics. The __str__() method completes the picture by printing a simple message stating the animal characteristics.

The Chicken class inherits from the Animal class. Notice the use of Animal in parentheses after the Chicken class name. This addition tells Python that Chicken is a kind of Animal, something that will inherit the characteristics of Animal.

Notice that the Chicken constructor accepts only Name and Age. The user doesn't have to supply a Type value because you already know that it's a chicken. This new constructor overrides the Animal constructor. The three attributes are still in place, but Type is supplied directly in the Chicken constructor.

Someone might try something funny, such as setting her chicken up as a gorilla. With this in mind, the Chicken class also overrides the SetType() setter. If someone tries to change the Chicken type, that user gets a message rather than the attempted change. Normally, you handle this sort of problem by using an exception, but the message works better for this example by making the coding technique clearer.

Finally, the Chicken class adds a new feature, MakeSound(). Whenever someone wants to hear the sound a chicken makes, he can call MakeSound() to at least see it printed on the screen.

Testing the class in an application

Testing the Chicken class also tests the Animal class to some extent. Some functionality is different, but some classes aren't really meant to be used. The Animal class is simply a parent for specific kinds of animals, such as Chicken. The following steps demonstrate the Chicken class so that you can see how inheritance works.

1. **Type the following code into the notebook for this chapter — pressing Enter after each line:**

```
import BPPD_15_Animals
MyChicken = BPPD_15_Animals.Chicken("Sally", 2)
print(MyChicken)
MyChicken.SetAge(MyChicken.GetAge() + 1)
```

```
print(MyChicken)
MyChicken.SetType("Gorilla")
print(MyChicken)
MyChicken.MakeSound()
```

The first step is to import the Animals package. Remember that you always import the filename, not the class. The Animals.py file actually contains two classes in this case: Animal and Chicken.

The example creates a chicken, MyChicken, named Sally, who is age 2. It then starts to work with MyChicken in various ways. For example, Sally has a birthday, so the code updates Sally's age by 1. Notice how the code combines the use of a setter, SetAge(), with a getter, GetAge(), to perform the task. After each change, the code displays the resulting object values for you. The final step is to let Sally say a few words.

2. **Click Run Cell.**

You see each of the steps used to work with MyChicken, as shown in Figure 15-15. As you can see, using inheritance can greatly simplify the task of creating new classes when enough of the classes have commonality so that you can create a parent class that contains some amount of the code.

Extending Classes to Make New Classes

Testing the class in an application

```
In [15]: import BPPD_15_Animals
         MyChicken = BPPD_15_Animals.Chicken("Sally", 2)
         print(MyChicken)
         MyChicken.SetAge(MyChicken.GetAge() + 1)
         print(MyChicken)
         MyChicken.SetType("Gorilla")
         print(MyChicken)
         MyChicken.MakeSound()

         Sally is a Chicken aged 2
         Sally is a Chicken aged 3
         Sorry, Sally will always be a Chicken
         Sally is a Chicken aged 3
         Sally says Cluck, Cluck, Cluck!
```

FIGURE 15-15:
Sally has a birthday and then says a few words.

4

Performing Advanced Tasks

Chapter **16**

Storing Data in Files

U ntil now, application development might seem to be all about presenting information onscreen. Actually, applications revolve around a need to work with data in some way. Data is the focus of all applications because it's the data that users are interested in. Be prepared for a huge disappointment the first time you present a treasured application to a user base and find that the only thing users worry about is whether the application will help them leave work on time after creating a presentation. The fact is, the best applications are invisible, but they present data in the most appropriate manner possible for a user's needs.

If data is the focus of applications, then storing the data in a permanent manner is equally important. For most developers, data storage revolves around a permanent media such as a hard drive, Solid State Drive (SSD), Universal Serial Bus (USB) flash drive, or some other methodology. (Even cloud-based solutions work fine, but you won't see them used in this book because they require different programming techniques that are beyond the book's scope.) The data in memory is temporary because it lasts only as long as the machine is running. A permanent storage device holds onto the data long after the machine is turned off so that it can be retrieved during the next session.

REMEMBER

In addition to permanent storage, this chapter also helps you understand the four basic operations that you can perform on files: Create, Read, Update, and Delete (CRUD). You see the CRUD acronym used quite often in database circles, but it applies equally well to any application. No matter how your application stores the data in a permanent location, it must be able to perform these four tasks in order to provide a complete solution to the user. Of course, CRUD operations must be performed in a secure, reliable, and controlled manner. This chapter also helps you set a few guidelines for how access must occur to ensure *data integrity* (a measure of how often data errors occur when performing CRUD operations). You can find the downloadable source code for the examples this chapter in the BPPD_16_ Storing_Data_in_Files.ipynb file, as described in the book's Introduction.

Understanding How Permanent Storage Works

You don't need to understand absolutely every detail about how permanent storage works in order to use it. For example, just how the drive spins (assuming that it spins at all) is unimportant. However, most platforms adhere to a basic set of principles when it comes to permanent storage. These principles have developed over a period of time, starting with mainframe systems in the earliest days of computing.

Data is generally stored in *files* (with pure data representing application state information), but you could also find it stored as *objects* (a method of storing serialized class instances). This chapter covers the use of files, not objects. You probably know about files already because almost every useful application out there relies on them. For example, when you open a document in your word processor, you're actually opening a data file containing the words that you or someone else has typed.

Files typically have an *extension* associated with them that defines the file type. The extension is generally standardized for any given application and is separated from the filename by a period, such as MyData.txt. In this case, .txt is the file extension, and you probably have an application on your machine for opening such files. In fact, you can likely choose from a number of applications to perform the task because the .txt file extension is relatively common.

Internally, files structure the data in some specific manner to make it easy to write and read data to and from the file. Any application you write must know about the file structure in order to interact with the data the file contains. The examples in this chapter use a simple file structure to make it easy to write the code required to access them, but file structures can become quite complex.

Files would be nearly impossible to find if you placed them all in the same location on the hard drive. Consequently, files are organized into *directories*. Many newer computer systems also use the term *folder* for this organizational feature of permanent storage. No matter what you call it, permanent storage relies on directories to help organize the data and make individual files significantly easier to find. To find a particular file so that you can open it and interact with the data it contains, you must know which directory holds the file.

Directories are arranged in hierarchies that begin at the uppermost level of the hard drive. For example, when working with the downloadable source code for this book, you find the code for the entire book in the BPPD directory within the user folder on your system. On my Windows system, that directory hierarchy is C:\Users\John\BPPD. However, my Mac and Linux systems have a different directory hierarchy to reach the same BPPD directory, and the directory hierarchy on your system will be different as well.

REMEMBER

Notice that I use a backslash (\) to separate the directory levels. Some platforms use the forward slash (/); others use the backslash. You can read about this issue on my blog at http://blog.johnmuellerbooks.com/2014/03/10/backslash-versus-forward-slash/. The book uses backslashes when appropriate and assumes that you'll make any required changes for your platform.

A final consideration for Python developers (at least for this book) is that the hierarchy of directories is called a *path*. You see the term *path* in a few places in this book because Python must be able to find any resources you want to use based on the path you provide. For example, C:\Users\John\BPPD is the complete path to the source code for this chapter on a Windows system. A path that traces the entire route that Python must search is called an *absolute path*. An incomplete path that traces the route to a resource using the current directory as a starting point is called a *relative path*.

TECHNICAL STUFF

To find a location using a relative path, you commonly use the current directory as the starting point. For example, BPPD__pycache__ would be the relative path to the Python cache. Note that it has no drive letter or beginning backslash. However, sometimes you must add to the starting point in specific ways to define a relative path. Most platforms define these special relative path character sets:

» \: The root directory of the current drive. The drive is relative, but the path begins at the root, the uppermost part, of that drive.

» .\: The current directory. You use this shorthand for the current directory when the current directory name isn't known. For example, you could also define the location of the Python cache as .__pycache__.

» ..\: The parent directory. You use this shorthand when the parent directory name isn't known.

» ..\..\: The parent of the parent directory. You can proceed up the hierarchy of directories as far as necessary to locate a particular starting point before you drill back down the hierarchy to a new location.

Creating Content for Permanent Storage

A file can contain structured or unstructured data. An example of *structured data* is a database in which each record has specific information in it. An employee database would include columns for name, address, employee ID, and so on. Each record would be an individual employee and each employee record would contain the name, address, and employee ID fields. An example of *unstructured data* is a word processing file whose text can contain any content in any order. There is no required order for the content of a paragraph, and sentences can contain any number of words. However, in both cases, the application must know how to perform CRUD operations with the file. This means that the content must be prepared in such a manner that the application can both write to and read from the file.

Even with word processing files, the text must follow a certain series of rules. Assume for a moment that the files are simple text. Even so, every paragraph must have some sort of delimiter telling the application to begin a new paragraph. The application reads the paragraph until it sees this delimiter, and then it begins a new paragraph. The more that the word processor offers in the way of features, the more structured the output becomes. For example, when the word processor offers a method of formatting the text, the formatting must appear as part of the output file.

REMEMBER

The cues that make content usable for permanent storage are often hidden from sight. All you see when you work with the file is the data itself. The formatting remains invisible for a number of reasons, such as these:

>> The cue is a control character, such as a carriage return or linefeed, that is normally invisible by default at the platform level.

>> The application relies on special character combinations, such as commas and double quotes, to delimit the data entries. These special character combinations are consumed by the application during reading.

>> Part of the reading process converts the character to another form, such as when a word processing file reads in content that is formatted. The formatting appears onscreen, but in the background the file contains special characters to denote the formatting.

>> The file is actually in an alternative format, such as eXtensible Markup Language (XML) (see http://www.w3schools.com/xml/default.ASP for information about XML). The alternative format is interpreted and presented onscreen in a manner the user can understand.

TECHNICAL STUFF

Other rules likely exist for formatting data. For example, Microsoft actually uses a .zip file to hold its latest word processing files (the .docx) file. The use of a compressed file catalog, such as .zip, makes storing a great deal of information in a small space possible. It's interesting to see how others store data because you can often find more efficient and secure means of data storage for your own applications.

Now that you have a better idea of what could happen as part of preparing content for disk storage, it's time to look at an example. In this case, the formatting strategy is quite simple. All this example does is accept input, format it for storage, and present the formatted version onscreen (rather than save it to disk just yet).

1. **Open a new notebook.**

   You can also use the downloadable source files BPPD_16_Storing_Data_in_ Files.ipynb, which contains the application code, and BPPD_16_FormattedData. ipynb, which contains the FormatData class code.

2. **Type the following code into the window — pressing Enter after each line:**

```python
class FormatData:
    def __init__(self, Name="", Age=0, Married=False):
        self.Name = Name
        self.Age = Age
        self.Married = Married

    def __str__(self):
        OutString = "'{0}', {1}, {2}".format(
            self.Name,
            self.Age,
            self.Married)
        return OutString
```

   This is a shortened class. Normally, you'd add accessors (getter and setter methods) and error-trapping code. (Remember that *getter methods* provide read-only access to class data and *setter methods* provide write-only access to class data.) However, the class works fine for the demonstration.

   The main feature to look at is the __str__() function. Notice that it formats the output data in a specific way. The string value, self.Name, is enclosed in single quotes. Each of the values is also separated by a comma. This is actually a form of a standard output format, comma-separated value (CSV), that is used on a wide range of platforms because it's easy to translate and is in plain text, so nothing special is needed to work with it.

3. **Save the code as** BPPD_16_FormattedData.ipynb.

To use this class with the remainder of the chapter, you need to save it to disk by using the technique found in the "Saving a class to disk" section of Chapter 15. You must also create the BPPD_16_FormattedData.py file to import the class into the application code.

4. **Open another new notebook.**

5. **Type the following code into the window — pressing Enter after each line:**

```
from BPPD_16_FormattedData import FormatData
NewData = [FormatData("George", 65, True),
           FormatData("Sally", 47, False),
           FormatData("Doug", 52, True)]
for Entry in NewData:
    print(Entry)
```

The code begins by importing just the FormatData class from BPPD_16_FormattedData. In this case, it doesn't matter because the BPPD_16_FormattedData module contains only a single class. However, you need to keep this technique in mind when you need only one class from a module.

Most of the time, you work with multiple records when you save data to disk. You might have multiple paragraphs in a word processed document or multiple records, as in this case. The example creates a list of records and places them in NewData. In this case, NewData represents the entire document. The representation will likely take other forms in a production application, but the idea is the same.

Any application that saves data goes through some sort of output loop. In this case, the loop simply prints the data onscreen. However, in the upcoming sections, you actually output the data to a file.

6. **Click Run Cell.**

You see the output shown in Figure 16-1. This is a representation of how the data would appear in the file. In this case, each record is separated by a carriage return and linefeed control character combination. That is, George, Sally, and Doug are all separate records in the file. Each *field* (data element) is separated by a comma. Text fields appear in quotes so that they aren't confused with other data types.

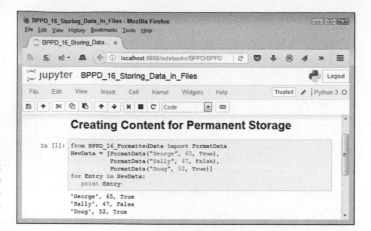

FIGURE 16-1:
The example
presents how the
data might look in
CSV format.

Creating a File

Any data that the user creates and wants to work with for more than one session must be put on some sort of permanent media. Creating a file and then placing the data into it is an essential part of working with Python. You can use the following steps to create code that will write data to the hard drive.

1. **Open the previously saved** BPPD_16_FormattedData.ipynb **file.**

   You see the code originally created in the "Creating Content for Permanent Storage" section, earlier in this chapter, appear onscreen. This example makes adds a new class to the original code so that the package can now save a file to disk.

2. **Type the following code into the notebook — pressing Enter after each line:**

```python
import csv

class FormatData2:
    def __init__(self, Name="", Age=0, Married=False):
        self.Name = Name
        self.Age = Age
        self.Married = Married

    def __str__(self):
        OutString = "'{0}', {1}, {2}".format(
            self.Name,
            self.Age,
            self.Married)
        return OutString
```

```
def SaveData(Filename = "", DataList = []):
    with open(Filename,
              "w", newline='\n') as csvfile:
        DataWriter = csv.writer(
            csvfile,
            delimiter='\n',
            quotechar=" ",
            quoting=csv.QUOTE_NONNUMERIC)
        DataWriter.writerow(DataList)
        csvfile.close()
        print("Data saved!")
```

The csv module contains everything needed to work with CSV files.

REMEMBER

Python actually supports a huge number of file types natively, and libraries that provide additional support are available. If you have a file type that you need to support using Python, you can usually find a third-party library to support it when Python doesn't support it natively. Unfortunately, no comprehensive list of supported files exists, so you need to search online to find how Python supports the file you need. The documentation divides the supported files by types and doesn't provide a comprehensive list. For example, you can find all the archive formats at https://docs.python.org/3/library/archiving.html and the miscellaneous file formats at https://docs.python.org/3/library/fileformats.html.

TIP

This example uses essentially the same text formatting code as you saw in the FormatData class, but now it adds the SaveData() method to put the formatted data on disk. Using a new class notifies everyone of the increased capability, so FormatData2 is the same class, but with more features.

Notice that the SaveData() method accepts two arguments as input: a filename used to store the data and a list of items to store. This is a class method rather than an instance method. Later in this procedure, you see how using a class method is an advantage. The DataList argument defaults to an empty list so that if the caller doesn't pass anything at all, the method won't throw an exception. Instead, it produces an empty output file. Of course, you can also add code to detect an empty list as an error, if desired.

REMEMBER

The with statement tells Python to perform a series of tasks with a specific resource — an open csvfile named Testfile.csv. The open() function accepts a number of inputs depending in how you use it. For this example, you open it in write mode (signified by the w). The newline attribute tells Python to treat the \n control character (linefeed) as a newline character.

In order to write output, you need a writer object. The DataWriter object is configured to use csvfile as the output file, to use /n as the record character, to quote records using a space, and to provide quoting only on nonnumeric values.

This setup will produce some interesting results later, but for now, just assume that this is what you need to make the output usable.

Actually writing the data takes less effort than you might think. A single call to `DataWriter.writerow()` with the `DataList` as input is all you need. Always close the file when you get done using it. This action *flushes the data* (makes sure that it gets written) to the hard drive. The code ends by telling you that the data has been saved.

3. **Save the code as** `BPPD_16_FormattedData.ipynb`.

   To use this class with the remainder of the chapter, you need to save it to disk using the technique found in the "Saving a class to disk" section of Chapter 15. You must also recreate the `BPPD_16_FormattedData.py` file to import the class into the application code. If you don't recreate the Python file, the client code won't be able to import `FormatData2`. Make sure that you delete the old version of `BPPD_16_FormattedData.py` from the code repository before you import the new one (or you can simply tell Notebook to overwrite the old copy).

4. **Type the following code into the application notebook — pressing Enter after each line:**

   ```
   from BPPD_16_FormattedData import FormatData2
   NewData = [FormatData2("George", 65, True),
              FormatData2("Sally", 47, False),
              FormatData2("Doug", 52, True)]
   FormatData2.SaveData("TestFile.csv", NewData)
   ```

   This example should look similar to the one you created in the "Creating Content for Permanent Storage" section, earlier in the chapter. You still create `NewData` as a list. However, instead of displaying the information onscreen, you send it to a file instead by calling `FormatData2.SaveData()`. This is one of those situations in which using an instance method would actually get in the way. To use an instance method, you would first need to create an instance of `FormatData` that wouldn't actually do anything for you.

5. **Restart the Kernel by choosing Kernel ▷ Restart or by clicking the Restart the Kernel button.**

   You must perform this step to unload the previous version of `BPPD_16_FormattedData`. Otherwise, even though the new copy of `BPPD_16_FormattedData.py` appears in the code directory, the example won't run.

6. **Click Run Cell.**

   The application runs, and you see a data saved message as output. Of course, that doesn't tell you anything about the data. In the source code file, you see a new file named `Testfile.csv`. Most platforms have a default application that opens such a file. With Windows, you can open it using Excel and WordPad (among other applications). Figure 16-2 shows the output in Excel, while Figure 16-3 shows it in WordPad. In both cases, the output looks surprisingly similar to the output shown in Figure 16-1.

FIGURE 16-2:
The application output as it appears in Excel.

FIGURE 16-3:
The application output as it appears in WordPad.

Reading File Content

At this point, the data is on the hard drive. Of course, it's nice and safe there, but it really isn't useful because you can't see it. To see the data, you must read it into memory and then do something with it. The following steps show how to read data from the hard drive and into memory so that you can display it onscreen.

1. **Open the previously saved** BPPD_16_FormattedData.ipynb **file.**

   The code originally created in the "Creating Content for Permanent Storage" section, earlier in this chapter, appears onscreen. This example adds a new class to the original code so that the package can now save a file to disk.

2. Type the following code into the notebook — pressing Enter after each line:

```python
import csv

class FormatData3:
    def __init__(self, Name="", Age=0, Married=False):
        self.Name = Name
        self.Age = Age
        self.Married = Married

    def __str__(self):
        OutString = "'{0}', {1}, {2}".format(
            self.Name,
            self.Age,
            self.Married)
        return OutString

    def SaveData(Filename = "", DataList = []):
        with open(Filename,
                  "w", newline='\n') as csvfile:
            DataWriter = csv.writer(
                csvfile,
                delimiter='\n',
                quotechar=" ",
                quoting=csv.QUOTE_NONNUMERIC)
            DataWriter.writerow(DataList)
            csvfile.close()
            print("Data saved!")

    def ReadData(Filename = ""):
        with open(Filename,
                  "r", newline='\n') as csvfile:
            DataReader = csv.reader(
                csvfile,
                delimiter="\n",
                quotechar=" ",
                quoting=csv.QUOTE_NONNUMERIC)
            Output = []
            for Item in DataReader:
                Output.append(Item[0])
            csvfile.close()
            print("Data read!")
            return Output
```

Opening a file for reading is much like opening it for writing. The big difference is that you need to specify r (for read) instead of w (for write) as part of the csv.reader() constructor. Otherwise, the arguments are precisely the same and work the same.

REMEMBER

It's important to remember that you're starting with a text file when working with a .csv file. Yes, it has delimiters, but it's still text. When reading the text into memory, you must rebuild the Python structure. In this case, Output is an empty list when it starts.

The file currently contains three records that are separated by the /n control character. Python reads each record in using a for loop. Notice the odd use of Item[0]. When Python reads the record, it sees the nonterminating entries (those that aren't last in the file) as actually being two list entries. The first entry contains data; the second is blank. You want only the first entry. These entries are appended to Output so that you end up with a complete list of the records that appear in the file.

As before, make sure that you close the file when you get done with it. The method prints a data read message when it finishes. It then returns Output (a list of records) to the caller.

3. **Save the code as** BPPD_16_FormattedData.ipynb.

To use this class with the remainder of the chapter, you need to save it to disk by using the technique found in the "Saving a class to disk" section of Chapter 15. You must also recreate the BPPD_16_FormattedData.py file to import the class into the application code. If you don't recreate the Python file, the client code won't be able to import FormatData3. Make sure that you delete the old version of BPPD_16_FormattedData.py from the code repository before you import the new one.

4. **Type the following code into the application notebook — pressing Enter after each line:**

```
from BPPD_16_FormattedData import FormatData3
NewData = FormatData3.ReadData("TestFile.csv")
for Entry in NewData:
    print(Entry)
```

The ReadCSV.py code begins by importing the FormatData class. It then creates a NewData object, a list, by calling FormatData.ReadData(). Notice that the use of a class method is the right choice in this case as well because it makes the code shorter and simpler. The application then uses a for loop to display the NewData content.

5. **Restart the kernel and then click Run Cell.**

You see the output shown in Figure 16-4. Notice that this output looks similar to the output in Figure 16-1, even though the data was written to disk and read back in. This is how applications that read and write data are supposed to work. The data should appear the same after you read it in as it did when you wrote it out to disk. Otherwise, the application is a failure because it has modified the data.

FIGURE 16-4:
The application
input after it has
been processed.

```
                Reading File Content

In [3]:   from BPPD_16_FormattedData import FormatData3
          NewData = FormatData3.ReadData("TestFile.csv")
          for Entry in NewData:
              print(Entry)

          Data read!
          'George', 65, True
          'Sally', 47, False
          'Doug', 52, True
```

Updating File Content

Some developers treat updating a file as something complex. It can be complex if you view it as a single task. However, updates actually consist of three activities:

1. Read the file content into memory.

2. Modify the in-memory presentation of the data.

3. Write the resulting content to permanent storage.

In most applications, you can further break down the second step of modifying the in-memory presentation of the data. An application can provide some or all of these features as part of the modification process:

» Provide an onscreen presentation of the data.

» Allow additions to the data list.

» Allow deletions from the data list.

» Make changes to existing data, which can actually be implemented by adding a new record with the changed data and deleting the old record.

So far in this chapter, you have performed all but one of the activities in these two lists. You've already read file content and written file content. In the modification list, you've added data to a list and presented the data onscreen. The only interesting activity that you haven't performed is deleting data from a list.

The modification of data is often performed as a two-part process of creating a new record that starts with the data from the old record and then deleting the old record after the new record is in place in the list.

REMEMBER

Don't get into a rut by thinking that you must perform every activity mentioned in this section for every application. A monitoring program wouldn't need to display the data onscreen. In fact, doing so might be harmful (or at least inconvenient). A data logger only creates new entries — it never deletes or modifies them. An email application usually allows the addition of new records and deletion of old records, but not modification of existing records. On the other hand, a word processor implements all the features mentioned. What you implement and how you implement it depends solely on the kind of application you create.

Separating the user interface from the activities that go on behind the user interface is important. To keep things simple, this example focuses on what needs to go on behind the user interface to make updates to the file you created in the "Creating a File" section, earlier in this chapter. The following steps demonstrate how to read, modify, and write a file in order to update it. The updates consist of an addition, a deletion, and a change. To allow you to run the application more than once, the updates are actually sent to another file.

1. Type the following code into the application notebook — pressing Enter after each line:

```
from BPPD_16_FormattedData import FormatData3
import os.path

if not os.path.isfile("Testfile.csv"):
    print("Please run the CreateFile.py example!")
    quit()

NewData = FormatData3.ReadData("TestFile.csv")
for Entry in NewData:
    print(Entry)

print("\r\nAdding a record for Harry.")
NewRecord = "'Harry', 23, False"
NewData.append(NewRecord)
for Entry in NewData:
    print(Entry)

print("\r\nRemoving Doug's record.")
Location = NewData.index("'Doug', 52, True")
Record = NewData[Location]
```

```
NewData.remove(Record)
for Entry in NewData:
    print(Entry)

print("\r\nModifying Sally's record.")
Location = NewData.index("'Sally', 47, False")
Record = NewData[Location]
Split = Record.split(",")
NewRecord = FormatData3(Split[0].replace("'", ""),
                        int(Split[1]),
                        bool(Split[2]))
NewRecord.Married = True
NewRecord.Age = 48
NewData.append(NewRecord.__str__())
NewData.remove(Record)
for Entry in NewData:
    print(Entry)

FormatData3.SaveData("ChangedFile.csv", NewData)
```

This example has quite a bit going on. First, it checks to ensure that the Testfile.csv file is actually present for processing. This is a check that you should always perform when you expect a file to be present. In this case, you aren't creating a new file, you're updating an existing file, so the file must be present. If the file isn't present, the application ends.

The next step is to read the data into NewData. This part of the process looks much like the data reading example earlier in the chapter.

REMEMBER

You have already seen code for using list functions in Chapter 13. This example uses those functions to perform practical work. The append() function adds a new record to NewData. However, notice that the data is added as a string, not as a FormatData object. The data is stored as strings on disk, so that's what you get when the data is read back in. You can either add the new data as a string or create a FormatData object and then use the __str__() method to output the data as a string.

The next step is to remove a record from NewData. To perform this task, you must first find the record. Of course, that's easy when working with just four records (remember that NewData now has a record for Harry in it). When working with a large number of records, you must first search for the record using the index() function. This act provides you with a number containing the location of the record, which you can then use to retrieve the actual record. After you have the actual record, you can remove it using the remove() function.

Modifying Sally's record looks daunting at first, but again, most of this code is part of dealing with the string storage on disk. When you obtain the record from NewData, what you receive is a single string with all three values in it. The split() function produces a list containing the three entries as strings, which still won't work for the application. In addition, Sally's name is enclosed in both double and single quotes.

The simplest way to manage the record is to create a FormatData object and to convert each of the strings into the proper form. This means removing the extra quotes from the name, converting the second value to an int, and converting the third value to a bool. The FormatData class doesn't provide accessors, so the application modifies both the Married and Age fields directly. Using accessors (getter methods that provide read-only access and setter methods that provide write-only access) is a better policy.

The application then appends the new record to and removes the existing record from NewData. Notice how the code uses NewRecord.__str__() to convert the new record from a FormatData object to the required string.

The final act is to save the changed record. Normally, you'd use the same file to save the data. However, the example saves the data to a different file in order to allow examination of both the old and new data.

2. **Click Run Cell.**

You see the output shown in Figure 16-5. Notice that the application lists the records after each change so that you can see the status of NewData. This is actually a useful troubleshooting technique for your own applications. Of course, you want to remove the display code before you release the application to production.

```
Data read!
'George', 65, True
'Sally', 47, False
'Doug', 52, True

Adding a record for Harry.
'George', 65, True
'Sally', 47, False
'Doug', 52, True
'Harry', 23, False

Removing Doug's record.
'George', 65, True
'Sally', 47, False
'Harry', 23, False

Modifying Sally's record.
'George', 65, True
'Harry', 23, False
'Sally', 48, True
Data saved!
```

FIGURE 16-5:
The application shows each of the modifications in turn.

3. **Open the** ChangedFile.csv **file using an appropriate application.**

You see output similar to that shown in Figure 16-6. This output is shown using WordPad, but the data won't change when you use other applications. So, even if your screen doesn't quite match Figure 16-6, you should still see the same data.

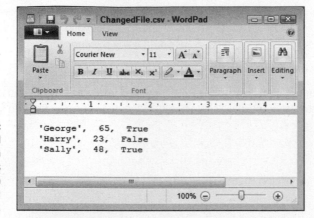

FIGURE 16-6:
The updated information appears as expected in Changed File.csv.

Deleting a File

The previous section of this chapter, "Updating File Content," explains how to add, delete, and update records in a file. However, at some point you may need to delete the file. The following steps describe how to delete files that you no longer need. This example also appears with the downloadable source code as DeleteCSV.py.

1. **Type the following code into the application notebook — pressing Enter after each line:**

```
import os
os.remove("ChangedFile.csv")
print("File Removed!")
```

WARNING

The task looks simple in this case, and it is. All you need to do to remove a file is call os.remove() with the appropriate filename and path (as needed, Python defaults to the current directory, so you don't need to specify a path if the file you want to remove is in the default directory). The ease with which you can perform this task is almost scary because it's too easy. Putting safeguards in place is always a good idea. You may want to remove other items, so here are other functions you should know about:

- `os.rmdir()`: Removes the specified directory. The directory must be empty or Python will display an exception message.

- `shutil.rmtree()`: Removes the specified directory, all subdirectories, and all files. This function is especially dangerous because it removes everything without checking (Python assumes that you know what you're doing). As a result, you can easily lose data using this function.

2. **Click Run Cell.**

   The application displays the `File Removed!` message. When you look in the directory that originally contained the `ChangedFile.csv` file, you see that the file is gone.

Chapter **17**

Sending an Email

This chapter helps you understand the process of sending an email using Python. More important, this chapter is generally about helping you understand what happens when you communicate outside the local PC. Even though this chapter is specifically about email, it also contains principles you can use when performing other tasks. For example, when working with an external service, you often need to create the same sort of packaging as you do for an email. So, the information you see in this chapter can help you understand all sorts of communication needs.

To make working with email as easy as possible, this chapter uses standard mail as a real-world equivalent of email. The comparison is apt. Email was actually modeled on real-world mail. Originally, the term email was used for any sort of electronic document transmission, and some forms of it required the sender and recipient to be online at the same time. As a result, you may find some confusing references online about the origins and development of email. This chapter views email as it exists today — as a storing and forwarding mechanism for exchanging documents of various types.

The examples in this chapter rely on the availability of a Simple Mail Transfer Protocol (SMTP) server. If that sounds like Greek to you, read the sidebar entitled "Considering the SMTP server" that appears later in the chapter. You can find the downloadable source code for the examples in this chapter in the BPPD_17_ Sending_an_Email.ipynb file, as described in the book's Introduction.

Understanding What Happens When You Send Email

Email has become so reliable and so mundane that most people don't understand what a miracle it is that it works at all. Actually, the same can be said of the real mail service. When you think about it, the likelihood of one particular letter leaving one location and ending up precisely where it should at the other end seems impossible — mind-boggling, even. However, both email and its real-world equivalent have several aspects in common that improve the likelihood that they'll actually work as intended. The following sections examine what happens when you write an email, click Send, and the recipient receives it on the other end. You might be surprised at what you discover.

CONSIDERING THE SIMPLE MAIL TRANSFER PROTOCOL

When you work with email, you see a lot of references to Simple Mail Transfer Protocol (SMTP). Of course, the term looks really technical, and what happens under the covers truly *is* technical, but all you really need to know is that it works. On the other hand, understanding SMTP a little more than as a "black box" that takes an email from the sender and spits it out at the other end to the recipient can be useful. Taking the term apart (in reverse order), you see these elements:

- **Protocol:** A standard set of rules. Email work by requiring rules that everyone agrees upon. Otherwise, email would become unreliable.

  Mail transfer: Documents are sent from one place to another, much the same as what the post office does with real mail. In email's case, the transfer process relies on short commands that your email application issues to the SMTP server. For example, the MAIL FROM command tells the SMTP server who is sending the email, while the RCPT TO command states where to send it.

- **Simple:** States that this activity goes on with the least amount of effort possible. The fewer parts to anything, the more reliable it becomes.

If you were to look at the rules for transferring the information, you would find they're anything but simple. For example, RFC1123 is a standard that specifies how Internet hosts are supposed to work (see http://www.faqs.org/rfcs/rfc1123.html for details). These rules are used by more than one Internet technology, which explains why most of them appear to work about the same (even though their resources and goals may be different).

Another, entirely different standard, RFC2821, describes how SMTP specifically implements the rules found in RFC1123 (see http://www.faqs.org/rfcs/rfc2821.html for details). The point is, a whole lot of rules are written in jargon that only a true geek could love (and even the geeks aren't sure). If you want a plain-English explanation of how email works, check out the article at http://computer.howstuffworks.com/e-mail-messaging/email.htm. Page 4 of this article (http://computer.howstuffworks.com/e-mail-messaging/email3.htm) describes the commands that SMTP uses to send information hither and thither across the Internet. In fact, if you want the shortest possible description of SMTP, page 4 is probably the right place to look.

Viewing email as you do a letter

The best way to view email is the same as how you view a letter. When you write a letter, you provide two pieces of paper as a minimum. The first contains the content of the letter, the second is an envelope. Assuming that the postal service is honest, the content is never examined by anyone other than the recipient. The same can be said of email. An email actually consists of these components:

>> **Message:** The content of the email, which is actually composed of two subparts:

   ● *Header:* The part of the email content that includes the subject, the list of recipients, and other features, such as the urgency of the email.

   ● *Body:* The part of the email content that contains the actual message. The message can be in plain text, formatted as HTML, and consisting of one or more documents, or it can be a combination of all these elements.

>> **Envelope:** A container for the message. The envelope provides sender and recipient information, just as the envelope for a physical piece of mail provides. However, an email doesn't include a stamp.

When working with email, you create a message using an email application. As part of the email application setup, you also define account information. When you click send:

1. The email application wraps up your message, with the header first, in an envelope that includes both your sender and the recipient's information.

2. The email application uses the account information to contact the SMTP server and send the message for you.

3. The SMTP server reads only the information found in the message envelope and redirects your email to the recipient.

4. The recipient email application logs on to the local server, picks up the email, and then displays only the message part for the user.

The process is a little more complex than this explanation, but this is essentially what happens. In fact, it's much the same as the process used when working with physical letters in that the essential steps are the same. With physical mail, the email application is replaced by you on one end and the recipient at the other. The SMTP server is replaced by the post office and the employees who work there (including the postal carriers). However, someone generates a message, the message is transferred to a recipient, and the recipient receives the message in both cases.

Defining the parts of the envelope

There is a difference in how the envelope for an email is configured and how it's actually handled. When you view the envelope for an email, it looks just like a letter in that it contains the address of the sender and the address of the recipient. It may not look physically like an envelope, but the same components are there. When you visualize a physical envelope, you see certain specifics, such as the sender's name, street address, city, state, and zip code. The same is true for the recipient. These elements define, in physical terms, where the postal carrier should deliver the letter or return the letter when it can't be delivered.

However, when the SMTP server processes the envelope for an email, it must look at the specifics of the address, which is where the analogy of a physical envelope used for mail starts to break down a little. An email address contains different information from a physical address. In summary, here is what the email address contains:

» **Host:** The host is akin to the city and state used by a physical mail envelope. A host address is the address used by the card that is physically connected to the Internet, and it handles all the traffic that the Internet consumes or provides for this particular machine. A PC can use Internet resources in a lot of ways, but the host address for all these uses is the same.

» **Port:** The port is akin to the street address used by a physical mail envelope. It specifies which specific part of the system should receive the message. For example, an SMTP server used for outgoing messages normally relies on port 25. However, the Point-of-Presence (POP3) server used for incoming email messages usually relies on port 110. Your browser typically uses port 80 to communicate with websites. However, secure websites (those that use https as a protocol, rather than http) rely on port 443 instead. You can see a list of typical ports at http://en.wikipedia.org/wiki/List_of_TCP_and_UDP_port_numbers.

» **Local hostname:** The local hostname is the human-readable form of the combination of the host and port. For example, the website http://www.myplace.com might resolve to an address of 55.225.163.40:80 (where the first four numbers are the host address and the number after the colon is the port).

Python takes care of these details behind the scenes for you, so normally you don't need to worry about them. However, it's nice to know that this information is available.

Now that you have a better idea of how the address is put together, it's time to look at it more carefully. The following sections describe the envelope of an email in more precise terms.

Host

A *host address* is the identifier for a connection to a server. Just as an address on an envelope isn't the actual location, neither is the host address the actual server. It merely specifies the location of the server.

REMEMBER

The connection used to access a combination of a host address and a port is called a *socket*. Just who came up with this odd name and why isn't important. What is important is that you can use the socket to find out all kinds of information that's useful in understanding how email works. The following steps help you see host-names and host addresses at work. More important, you begin to understand the whole idea of an email envelope and the addresses it contains.

1. Open a new notebook.

You can also use the downloadable source file, BPPD_17_Sending_an_Email. ipynb, which contains the application code.

2. Type import socket **and press Enter.**

Before you can work with sockets, you must import the socket library. This library contains all sorts of confusing attributes, so use it with caution. However, this library also contains some interesting functions that help you see how the Internet addresses work.

3. Type print(socket.gethostbyname("localhost")) **and press Enter.**

You see a host address as output. In this case, you should see 127.0.0.1 as output because localhost is a standard hostname. The address, 127.0.0.1, is associated with the host name, localhost.

4. Type print(socket.gethostbyaddr("127.0.0.1")) **and click Run Cell.**

Be prepared for a surprise. You get a tuple as output, as shown in Figure 17-1. However, instead of getting localhost as the name of the host, you get the name of your machine. You use localhost as a common name for the local machine, but when you specify the address, you get the machine name instead. In this case, Main is the name of my personal machine. The name you see on your screen will correspond to your machine.

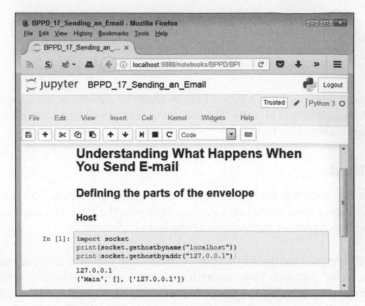

5. **Type** print(socket.gethostbyname("www.johnmuellerbooks.com")) **and click Run Cell.**

   You see the output shown in Figure 17-2. This is the address for my website. The point is that these addresses work wherever you are and whatever you're doing — just like those you place on a physical envelope. The physical mail uses addresses that are unique across the world, just as the Internet does.

FIGURE 17-2:
The addresses
that you use to
send email are
unique across the
Internet.

```
In [2]: print(socket.gethostbyname("www.johnmuellerbooks.com"))
        166.62.109.105
```

Port

A *port* is a specific entryway for a server location. The host address specifies the location, but the port defines where to get in. Even if you don't specify a port every time you use a host address, the port is implied. Access is always granted using a combination of the host address and the port. The following steps help illustrate how ports work with the host address to provide server access:

1. **Type** import socket **and press Enter.**

   Remember that a socket provides both host address and port information. You use the socket to create a connection that includes both items.

2. **Type** socket.getaddrinfo("localhost", 110) **and click Run Cell.**

The first value is the name of a host you want to obtain information about. The second value is the port on that host. In this case, you obtain the information about localhost port 110.

You see the output shown in Figure 17-3. The output consists of two tuples: one for the Internet Protocol version 6 (IPv6) output and one for the Internet Protocol version 4 (IPv4) address. Each of these tuples contains five entries, four of which you really don't need to worry about because you'll likely never need them. However, the last entry, ('127.0.0.1', 110), shows the address and port for localhost port 110.

FIGURE 17-3:
The localhost
host provides
both an IPv6 and
an IPv4 address.

```
              Port

In [3]:   import socket
          socket.getaddrinfo("localhost", 110)

Out[3]:   [(<AddressFamily.AF_INET6: 23>, 0, 0, '', ('::1', 110, 0, 0
          )),
           (<AddressFamily.AF_INET: 2>, 0, 0, '', ('127.0.0.1', 110))
          ]
```

3. **Type** socket.getaddrinfo("johnmuellerbooks.com", 80) **and press Enter.**

Figure 17-4 shows the output from this command. Notice that this Internet location provides only an IPv4 address, not an IPv6, address, for port 80. The socket.getaddrinfo() method provides a useful method for determining how you can access a particular location. Using IPv6 provides significant benefits over IPv4 (see http://www.networkcomputing.com/networking/six-benefits-of-ipv6/d/d-id/1232791 for details), but many Internet locations provide only IPv4 support now. (If you live in a larger city, you'll probably see both an IPv4 and an IPv6 address.)

FIGURE 17-4:
Most Internet
locations provide
only an IPv4
address.

```
In [4]:   socket.getaddrinfo("johnmuellerbooks.com", 80)

Out[4]:   [(<AddressFamily.AF_INET: 2>, 0, 0, '', ('166.62.109.105',
          80))]
```

4. **Type** socket.getservbyport(25) **and press Enter.**

You see the output shown in Figure 17-5. The socket.getservbyport() method provides the means to determine how a particular port is used. Port 25 is always dedicated to SMTP support on any server. So, when you access 127.0.0.1:25, you're asking for the SMTP server on localhost. In short, a port provides a specific kind of access in many situations.

```
In [5]:  socket.getservbyport(25)
Out[5]:  'smtp'
```

REMEMBER

Some people assume that the port information is always provided. However, this isn't always the case. Python will provide a default port when you don't supply one, but relying on the default port is a bad idea because you can't be certain which service will be accessed. In addition, some systems use nonstandard port assignments as a security feature. Always get into the habit of using the port number and ensuring that you have the right one for the task at hand.

Local hostname

A *hostname* is simply the human-readable form of the host address. Humans don't really understand 127.0.0.1 very well (and the IPv6 addresses make even less sense). However, humans do understand localhost just fine. There is a special server and setup to translate human-readable hostnames to host addresses, but you really don't need to worry about it for this book (or programming in general). When your application suddenly breaks for no apparent reason, it helps to know that one does exist, though.

The "Host" section, earlier in this chapter, introduces you to the hostname to a certain extent through the use of the socket.gethostbyaddr() method, whereby an address is translated into a hostname. You saw the process in reverse using the socket.gethostbyname() method. The following steps help you understand some nuances about working with the hostname:

1. **Type** import socket **and press Enter.**

2. **Type** socket.gethostname() **and click Run Cell.**

    You see the name of the local system, as shown in Figure 17-6. The name of your system will likely vary from mine, so your output will be different than that shown in Figure 17-6, but the idea is the same no matter which system you use.

FIGURE 17-6:
Sometimes you
need to know the
name of the local
system.

Local hostname

```
In [6]:  import socket
         socket.gethostname()
Out[6]:  'Main'
```

3. **Type** socket.gethostbyname(socket.gethostname()) **and click Run Cell.**

You see the IP address of the local system, as shown in Figure 17-7. Again, your setup is likely different from mine, so the output you see will differ. This is a method you can use in your applications to determine the address of the sender when needed. Because it doesn't rely on any hard-coded value, the method works on any system.

FIGURE 17-7:
Avoid using hard-coded values for the local system whenever possible.

```
In [7]:    socket.gethostbyname(socket.gethostname())
Out[7]:    '192.168.0.101'
```

Defining the parts of the letter

The "envelope" for an email address is what the SMTP server uses to route the email. However, the envelope doesn't include any content — that's the purpose of the letter. A lot of developers get the two elements confused because the letter contains sender and receiver information as well. This information appears in the letter just like the address information that appears in a business letter — it's for the benefit of the viewer. When you send a business letter, the postal delivery person doesn't open the envelope to see the address information inside. Only the information on the envelope matters.

TECHNICAL STUFF

It's because the information in the email letter is separate from its information in the envelope that nefarious individuals can spoof email addresses. The envelope potentially contains legitimate sender information, but the letter may not. (When you see the email in your email application, all that is present is the letter, not the envelope — the envelope has been stripped away by the email application.) For that matter, neither the sender nor the recipient information may be correct in the letter that you see onscreen in your email reader.

The letter part of an email is actually made of separate components, just as the envelope is. Here is a summary of the three components:

>> **Sender:** The sender information tells you who sent the message. It contains just the email address of the sender.

>> **Receiver:** The receiver information tells you who will receive the message. This is actually a list of recipient email addresses. Even if you want to send the message to only one person, you must supply the single email address in a list.

>> **Message:** Contains the information that you want the recipient to see. This information can include the following:

- **From:** The human-readable form of the sender.

- **To:** The human-readable form of the recipients.

- **CC:** Visible recipients who also received the message, even though they aren't the primary targets of the message.

- **Subject:** The purpose of the message.

- **Documents:** One or more documents, including the text message that appears with the email.

Emails can actually become quite complex and lengthy. Depending on the kind of email that is sent, a message could include all sorts of additional information. However, most emails contain these simple components, and this is all the information you need to send an email from your application. The following sections describe the process used to generate a letter and its components in more detail.

Defining the message

Sending an empty envelope to someone will work, but it isn't very exciting. In order to make your email message worthwhile, you need to define a message. Python supports a number of methods of creating messages. However, the easiest and most reliable way to create a message is to use the Multipurpose Internet Mail Extensions (MIME) functionality that Python provides (and no, a MIME is not a silent person with white gloves who acts out in public).

As with many email features, MIME is standardized, so it works the same no matter which platform you use. There are also numerous forms of MIME that are all part of the `email.mime` module described at `https://docs.python.org/3/library/email.mime.html`. Here are the forms that you need to consider most often when working with email:

>> **MIMEApplication:** Provides a method for sending and receiving application input and output

>> **MIMEAudio:** Contains an audio file

>> **MIMEImage:** Contains an image file

>> **MIMEMultipart:** Allows a single message to contain multiple subparts, such as including both text and graphics in a single message

>> **MIMEText:** Contains text data that can be in ASCII, HTML, or another standardized format

Although you can create any sort of an email message with Python, the easiest type to create is one that contains plain text. The lack of formatting in the content lets you focus on the technique used to create the message, rather than on the message content. The following steps help you understand how the message-creating process works, but you won't actually send the message anywhere.

1. **Type the following code (pressing Enter after each line):**

    ```
    from email.mime.text import MIMEText
    msg = MIMEText("Hello There")
    msg['Subject'] = "A Test Message"
    msg['From']='John Mueller <John@JohnMuellerBooks.com>'
    msg['To'] = 'John Mueller <John@JohnMuellerBooks.com>'
    ```

    REMEMBER

    This is a basic plain-text message. Before you can do anything, you must import the required class, which is MIMEText. If you were creating some other sort of message, you'd need to import other classes or import the email.mime module as a whole.

    The MIMEText() constructor requires message text as input. This is the body of your message, so it might be quite long. In this case, the message is relatively short — just a greeting.

    At this point, you assign values to standard attributes. The example shows the three common attributes that you always define: Subject, From, and To. The two address fields, From and To, contain both a human-readable name and the email address. All you have to include is the email address.

2. **Type msg.as_string() and click Run Cell.**

    You see the output shown in Figure 17-8. This is how the message actually looks. If you have ever looked under the covers at the messages produced by your email application, the text probably looks familiar.

    The Content-Type reflects the kind of message you created, which is a plain-text message. The charset tells what kind of characters are used in the message so that the recipient knows how to handle them. The MIME-Version specifies the version of MIME used to create the message so that the recipient knows whether it can handle the content. Finally, the Context-Transfer-Encoding determines how the message is converted into a bit stream before it is sent to the recipient.

FIGURE 17-8:
Python adds
some additional
information
required to make
your message
work.

> **Defining the parts of the letter**
>
> **Defining the message**
>
> ```
> In [8]:  from email.mime.text import MIMEText
>          msg = MIMEText("Hello There")
>          msg['Subject'] = "A Test Message"
>          msg['From']='John Mueller <John@JohnMuellerBooks.com>'
>          msg['To'] = 'John Mueller <John@JohnMuellerBooks.com>'
>
>          msg.as_string()
> ```
>
> ```
> Out[8]:  'Content-Type: text/plain; charset="us-ascii"\nMIME-Version:
>          1.0\nContent-Transfer-Encoding: 7bit\nSubject: A Test Message
>          \nFrom: John Mueller <John@JohnMuellerBooks.com>\nTo: John Mu
>          eller <John@JohnMuellerBooks.com>\n\nHello There'
> ```

Specifying the transmission

An earlier section ("Defining the parts of the envelope") describes how the envelope is used to transfer the message from one location to another. The process of sending the message entails defining a transmission method. Python actually creates the envelope for you and performs the transmission, but you must still define the particulars of the transmission. The following steps help you understand the simplest approach to transmitting a message using Python. These steps won't result in a successful transmission unless you modify them to match your setup. Read the "Considering the SMTP server" sidebar for additional information.

1. **Type the following code (pressing Enter after each line and pressing Enter twice after the last line):**

```
import smtplib
s = smtplib.SMTP('localhost')
```

The smtplib module contains everything needed to create the message envelope and send it. The first step in this process is to create a connection to the SMTP server, which you name as a string in the constructor. If the SMTP server that you provide doesn't exist, the application will fail at this point, saying that the host actively refused the connection.

2. **Type** s.sendmail('*SenderAddress*', ['*RecipientAddress*'], msg.as_string()) **and click Run Cell.**

WARNING

For this step to work, you must replace SenderAddress and RecipientAddress with real addresses. Don't include the human-readable form this time — the server requires only an address. If you don't include a real address, you'll definitely see an error message when you click Run Cell. You might also see an error if your email server is temporarily offline, there is a glitch in the network connection, or any of a number of other odd things occur. If you're sure that you typed everything correctly, try sending the message a second time before you panic. See the sidebar "Considering the SMTP server" for additional details.

This is the step that actually creates the envelope, packages the email message, and sends it off to the recipient. Notice that you specify the sender and recipient information separately from the message, which the SMTP server doesn't read.

Considering the message subtypes

The "Defining the message" section, earlier in this chapter, describes the major email message types, such as application and text. However, if email had to rely on just those types, transmitting coherent messages to anyone would be difficult. The problem is that the type of information isn't explicit enough. If you send someone a text message, you need to know what sort of text it is before you can process it, and guessing just isn't a good idea. A text message could be formatted as plain text, or it might actually be an HTML page. You wouldn't know from just seeing the type, so messages require a subtype. The type is text and the subtype is html when you send an HTML page to someone. The type and subtype are separated by a forward slash, so you'd see text/html if you looked at the message.

REMEMBER

Theoretically, the number of subtypes is unlimited as long as the platform has a handler defined for that subtype. However, the reality is that everyone needs to agree on the subtypes or there won't be a handler (unless you're talking about a custom application for which the two parties have agreed to a custom subtype in advance). With this in mind, you can find a listing of standard types and subtypes at `http://www.freeformatter.com/mime-types-list.html`. The nice thing about the table on this site is that it provides you with a common file extension associated with the subtype and a reference to obtain additional information about it.

Creating the Email Message

So far, you've seen how both the envelope and the message work. Now it's time to put them together and see how they actually work. The following sections show how to create two messages. The first message is a plain-text message and the second message uses HTML formatting. Both messages should work fine with most email readers — nothing fancy is involved.

Working with a text message

Text messages represent the most efficient and least resource-intensive method of sending communication. However, text messages also convey the least amount of information. Yes, you can use emoticons to help get the point across, but the lack of formatting can become a problem in some situations. The following steps describe how to create a simple text message using Python.

1. **Type the following code into the window — pressing Enter after each line:**

```
from email.mime.text import MIMEText
import smtplib
msg = MIMEText("Hello There!")
msg['Subject'] = 'A Test Message'
msg['From']='SenderAddress'
msg['To'] = 'RecipientAddress'
s = smtplib.SMTP('localhost')
s.sendmail('SenderAddress',
            ['RecipientAddress'],
            msg.as_string())
print("Message Sent!")
```

This example is a combination of everything you've seen so far in the chapter. However, this is the first time you've seen everything put together. Notice that you create the message first, and then the envelope (just as you would in real life).

WARNING

The example will display an error if you don't replace SenderAddress and RecipientAddress with real addresses. These entries are meant only as placeholders. As with the example in the previous section, you may also encounter errors when other situations occur, so always try to send the message at least twice if you see an error the first time. See the sidebar "Considering the SMTP server" for additional details.

2. **Click Run Cell.**

The application tells you that it has sent the message to the recipient.

CONSIDERING THE SMTP SERVER

If you tried the example in this chapter without modifying it, you're probably scratching your head right now trying to figure out what went wrong. It's unlikely that your system has an SMTP server connected to localhost. The reason for the examples to use localhost is to provide a placeholder that you replace later with the information for your particular setup.

In order to see the example actually work, you need an SMTP server as well as a real-world email account. Of course, you could install all the software required to create such an environment on your own system, and some developers who work extensively with email applications do just that. Most platforms come with an email package that you can install, or you can use a freely available substitute such as Sendmail, an open source product available for download at https://www.sendmail.com/sm/open_source/download/. The easiest way to see the example work is to use the same SMTP server that your email application uses. When you set up your email application, you either asked the email application to detect the SMTP server or you supplied the SMTP server on your own. The configuration settings for your email application should contain the required information. The exact location of this information varies widely by email application, so you need to look at the documentation for your particular product.

No matter what sort of SMTP server you eventually find, you need to have an account on that server in most cases to use the functionality it provides. Replace the information in the examples with the information for your SMTP server, such as smtp.myisp.com, along with your email address for both sender and receiver. Otherwise, the example won't work.

Working with an HTML message

An HTML message is basically a text message with special formatting. The following steps help you create an HTML email to send off.

1. **Type the following code into the window — pressing Enter after each line:**

```
from email.mime.text import MIMEText
import smtplib
msg = MIMEText(
    "<h1>A Heading</h1><p>Hello There!</p>","html")
msg['Subject'] = 'A Test HTML Message'
msg['From']='SenderAddress'
msg['To'] = 'RecipientAddress'
s = smtplib.SMTP('localhost')
s.sendmail('SenderAddress',
            ['RecipientAddress'],
            msg.as_string())
print("Message Sent!")
```

The example follows the same flow as the text message example in the previous section. However, notice that the message now contains HTML tags. You create an HTML body, not an entire page. This message will have an H1 header and a paragraph.

REMEMBER

The most important part of this example is the text that comes after the message. The "html" argument changes the subtype from text/plain to text/html, so the recipient knows to treat the message as HTML content. If you don't make this change, the recipient won't see the HTML output.

2. **Click Run Cell.**

The application tells you that it has sent the message to the recipient.

Seeing the Email Output

At this point, you have between one and three application-generated messages (depending on how you've gone through the chapter) waiting in your Inbox. To see the messages you created in earlier sections, your email application must receive the messages from the server — just as it would with any email. Figure 17-9 shows an example of the HTML version of the message when viewed in Output. (Your message will likely look different depending on your platform and email application.)

FIGURE 17-9:
The HTML output contains a header and a paragraph as expected.

If your email application offers the capability to look at the message source, you find that the message actually does contain the information you saw earlier in the chapter. Nothing is changed or different about it because after it leaves the application, the message isn't changed in any way during its trip.

REMEMBER

The point of creating your own application to send and receive email isn't convenience — using an off-the-shelf application serves that purpose much better. The point is flexibility. As you can see from this short chapter on the subject, you control every aspect of the message when you create your own application. Python hides much of the detail from view, so what you really need to worry about are the essentials of creating and transmitting the message using the correct arguments.

5

The Part of Tens

Chapter **18**

Ten Amazing Programming Resources

This book is a great start to your Python programming experience, but you'll want additional resources at some point. This chapter provides you with ten amazing programming resources that you can use to make your development experience better. By using these resources, you save both time and energy in creating your next dazzling Python application.

REMEMBER

Of course, this chapter is only the beginning of your Python resource experience. Reams of Python documentation are out there, along with mountains of Python code. One might be able to write an entire book (or two) devoted solely to the Python libraries. This chapter is designed to provide you with ideas of where to look for additional information that's targeted toward meeting your specific needs. Don't let this be the end of your search — consider this chapter the start of your search instead.

Working with the Python Documentation Online

An essential part of working with Python is knowing what is available in the base language and how to extend it to perform other tasks. The Python documentation at `https://docs.python.org/3/` (created for the 3.6.x version of the product at the time of this writing; it may be updated by the time you read this chapter) contains a lot more than just the reference to the language that you receive as part of a download. In fact, you see these topics discussed as part of the documentation:

>> New features in the current version of the language

>> Access to a full-fledged tutorial

>> Complete library reference

>> Complete language reference

>> How to install and configure Python

>> How to perform specific tasks in Python

>> Help with installing Python modules from other sources (as a means of extending Python)

>> Help with distributing Python modules you create so that others can use them

>> How to extend Python using C/C++ and then embed the new features you create

>> Complete reference for C/C++ developers who want to extend their applications using Python

>> Frequently Asked Questions (FAQ) pages

REMEMBER

All this information is provided in a form that is easy to access and use. In addition to the usual table-of-contents approach to finding information, you have access to a number of indexes. For example, if you aren't interested in anything but locating a particular module, class, or method, you can use the Global Module Index.

The `https://docs.python.org/3/` web page is also the place where you report problems with Python (the specific URL is `https://docs.python.org/3/bugs.html`). It's important to work through problems you're having with the product, but as with any other language, Python does have bugs in it. Locating and destroying the bugs will only make Python a better language.

TIP

You do have some flexibility in using the online documentation. Two drop-down list boxes appear in the upper-left corner for the documentation page. The first lets you choose your preferred language (as long as it's English, French, or Japanese, as of this writing). The second provides access to documentation for earlier versions of Python, including version 2.7.

Using the LearnPython.org Tutorial

Many tutorials are available for Python and many of them do a great job, but they're all lacking a special feature that you find when using the LearnPython.org tutorial at `http://www.learnpython.org/`: interactivity. Instead of just reading about a Python feature, you read it and then try it yourself using the interactive feature of the site.

You may have already worked through all the material in the simple tutorials in this book. However, you likely haven't worked through the advanced tutorials at LearnPython.org yet. These tutorials present the following topics:

>> **Generators:** Specialized functions that return iterators.

>> **List comprehensions:** A method to generate new lists based on existing lists.

>> **Multiple function arguments:** An extension of the methods described in the "Using methods with variable argument lists" in Chapter 15.

>> **Regular expressions:** Wildcard setups used to match patterns of characters, such as telephone numbers.

>> **Exception handling:** An extension of the methods described in Chapter 10.

>> **Sets:** Demonstrates a special kind of list that never contains duplicate entries.

>> **Serialization:** Shows how to use a data storage methodology called JavaScript Object Notation (JSON).

>> **Partial functions:** A technique for creating specialized versions of simple functions that derive from more complex functions. For example, if you have a `multiply()` function that requires two arguments, a partial function named `double()` might require only one argument that it always multiplies by 2.

>> **Code introspection:** Provides the ability to examine classes, functions, and keywords to determine their purpose and capabilities.

>> **Decorator:** A method for making simple modifications to callable objects.

Performing Web Programming by Using Python

This book discusses the ins and outs of basic programming, so it relies on desktop applications because of their simplicity. However, many developers specialize in creating online applications of various sorts using Python. The Web Programming in Python site at `https://wiki.python.org/moin/WebProgramming` helps you make the move from the desktop to online application development. It doesn't just cover one sort of online application — it covers almost all of them (an entire book free for the asking). The tutorials are divided into these three major (and many minor) areas:

>> Server

- Developing server-side frameworks for applications
- Creating a Common Gateway Interface (CGI) script
- Providing server applications
- Developing Content Management Systems (CMS)
- Designing data access methods through web services solutions

>> Client

- Interacting with browsers and browser-based technologies
- Creating browser-based clients
- Accessing data through various methodologies, including web services

>> Related

- Creating common solutions for Python-based online computing
- Interacting with DataBase Management Systems (DBMSs)
- Designing application templates
- Building Intranet solutions

Getting Additional Libraries

The Pythonware site (`http://www.pythonware.com/`) doesn't look all that interesting until you start clicking the links. It provides you with access to a number of third-party libraries that help you perform additional tasks using Python.

Although all the links provide you with useful resources, the "Downloads (`downloads.effbot.org`)" link is the one you should look at first. This download site provides you with access to

>> **aggdraw:** A library that helps you create anti-aliased drawings.

>> **celementtree:** An add-on to the elementtree library that makes working with XML data more efficient and faster.

>> **console:** An interface for Windows that makes it possible to create better console applications.

>> **effbot:** A collection of useful add-ons and utilities, including the EffNews RSS news reader.

>> **elementsoap:** A library that helps you create Simple Object Access Protocol (SOAP) connections to Web services providers.

>> **elementtidy:** An add-on to the elementtree library that helps you create nicer-looking and more functional XML tree displays than the standard ones in Python.

>> **elementtree:** A library that helps you interact with XML data more efficiently than standard Python allows.

>> **exemaker:** A utility that creates an executable program from your Python script so that you can execute the script just as you would any other application on your machine.

>> **ftpparse:** A library for working with FTP sites.

>> **grabscreen:** A library for performing screen captures.

>> **imaging:** Provides the source distribution to the Python Imaging Library (PIL) that lets you add image-processing capabilities to the Python interpreter. Having the source lets you customize PIL to meet specific needs.

>> **pil:** Binary installers for PIL, which make obtaining a good installation for your system easier. (There are other PIL-based libraries as well, such as pilfont — a library for adding enhanced font functionality to a PIL-based application.)

>> **pythondoc:** A utility for creating documentation from the comments in your Python code that works much like JavaDoc.

>> **squeeze:** A utility for converting your Python application contained in multiple files into a one- or two-file distribution that will execute as normal with the Python interpreter.

>> **tkinter3000:** A widget-building library for Python that includes a number of subproducts. *Widgets* are essentially bits of code that create controls, such as buttons, to use in GUI applications. There are a number of add-ons for the tkinter3000 library, such as wckgraph, which helps you add graphing support to an application.

Creating Applications Faster by Using an IDE

An Interactive Development Environment (IDE) helps you create applications in a specific language. The Integrated DeveLopment Environment (IDLE) editor that comes with Python works well for experimentation, but you may find it limited after a while. For example, IDLE doesn't provide the advanced debugging functionality that many developers favor. In addition, you may find that you want to create graphical applications, which is difficult using IDLE.

The limitations in IDLE are the reason this edition of this book uses Jupyter Notebook instead of IDLE, which the first edition used. However, you may find that Jupyter doesn't meet your needs, either. You can talk to 50 developers and get little consensus as to the best tool for any job, especially when discussing IDEs. Every developer has a favorite product and isn't easily swayed to try another. Developers invest many hours learning a particular IDE and extending it to meet specific requirements (when the IDE allows such tampering).

REMEMBER

An inability (at times) to change IDEs later is why it's important to try a number of different IDEs before you settle on one. (The most common reason for not wanting to change an IDE after you select one is that the project types are incompatible, which would mean having to re-create your projects every time you change editors, but there are many other reasons that you can find listed online.) The PythonEditors wiki at `https://wiki.python.org/moin/PythonEditors` provides an extensive list of IDEs that you can try. The table provides you with particulars about each editor so that you can eliminate some of the choices immediately.

Checking Your Syntax with Greater Ease

The IDLE editor provides some level of syntax highlighting, which is helpful in finding errors. For example, if you mistype a keyword, it doesn't change color to the color used for keywords on your system. Seeing that it hasn't changed makes it possible for you to know to correct the error immediately, instead of having to run the application and find out later that something has gone wrong (sometimes after hours of debugging).

Jupyter Notebook provides syntax highlighting as well, along with some advanced error checking not found in a standard IDE. However, for some developers, it, too, can come up short because you actually have to run the cell in order to see the error information. Some developers prefer interactive syntax checking, in which the IDE flags the error immediately, even before the developer leaves the errant line of code.

The python.vim utility (`http://www.vim.org/scripts/script.php?script_id=790`) provides enhanced syntax highlighting that makes finding errors in your Python script even easier. This utility runs as a script, which makes it fast and efficient to use on any platform. In addition, you can tweak the source code as needed to meet particular needs.

Using XML to Your Advantage

The eXtensible Markup Language (XML) is used for data storage of all types in most applications of any substance today. You probably have a number of XML files on your system and don't even know it because XML data appears under a number of file extensions. For example, many `.config` files, used to hold application settings, rely on XML. In short, it's not a matter of if you'll encounter XML when writing Python applications, but when.

XML has a number of advantages over other means of storing data. For example, it's platform independent. You can use XML on any system, and the same file is readable on any other system as long as that system knows the file format. The platform independence of XML is why it appears with so many other technologies, such as Web Services. In addition, XML is relatively easy to learn and because it's text, you can usually fix problems with it without too many problems.

REMEMBER

It's important to learn about XML itself, and you can do so using an easy tutorial such as the one found on the W3Schools site at `http://www.w3schools.com/xml/default.ASP`. Some developers rush ahead and later find that they can't understand the Python-specific materials that assume they already know how to write basic XML files. The W3Schools site is nice because it breaks up the learning process into chapters so that you can work with XML a little at a time, as follows:

» Taking a basic XML tutorial

» Validating your XML files

» Using XML with JavaScript (which may not seem important, but JavaScript is prominent in many online application scenarios)

» Gaining an overview of XML-related technologies

» Using advanced XML techniques

» Working with XML examples that make seeing XML in action easier

After you get the fundamentals down, you need a resource that shows how to use XML with Python. One of the better places to find this information is the Tutorials on XML Processing with Python site at `https://wiki.python.org/moin/Tutorials%20on%20XML%20processing%20with%20Python`. Between these two resources, you can quickly build a knowledge of XML that will have you building Python applications that use XML in no time.

Getting Past the Common Python Newbie Errors

Absolutely everyone makes coding mistakes — even that snobby fellow down the hall who has been programming for the last 30 years (he started in kindergarten). No one likes to make mistakes and some people don't like to own up to them, but everyone does make them. So you shouldn't feel too bad when you make a mistake. Simply fix it up and get on with your life.

REMEMBER

Of course, there is a difference between making a mistake and making an avoidable, common mistake. Yes, even the professionals sometimes make the avoidable common mistakes, but it's far less likely because they have seen the mistake in the past and have trained themselves to avoid it. You can gain an advantage over your competition by avoiding the newbie mistakes that everyone has to learn about sometime. To avoid these mistakes, check out this two-part series:

» Python: Common Newbie Mistakes, Part 1 (http://blog.amir.rachum.com/blog/2013/07/06/python-common-newbie-mistakes-part-1/)

» Python: Common Newbie Mistakes, Part 2 (http://blog.amir.rachum.com/blog/2013/07/09/python-common-newbie-mistakes-part-2/)

Many other resources are available for people who are just starting with Python, but these particular resources are succinct and easy to understand. You can read them in a relatively short time, make some notes about them for later use, and avoid those embarrassing errors that everyone tends to remember.

Understanding Unicode

Although this book tries to sidestep the thorny topic of Unicode, you'll eventually encounter it when you start writing serious applications. Unfortunately, Unicode is one of those topics that had a committee deciding what Unicode would look like, so we ended up with more than one poorly explained definition of Unicode and a multitude of standards to define it. In short, there is no one definition for Unicode.

You'll encounter a wealth of Unicode standards when you start working with more advanced Python applications, especially when you start working with multiple human languages (each of which seems to favor its own flavor of Unicode). Keeping in mind the need to discover just what Unicode is, here are some resources you should check out:

» The Absolute Minimum Every Software Developer Absolutely, Positively Must Know About Unicode and Character Sets (No Excuses!) (http://www.joelonsoftware.com/articles/Unicode.html)

» The Updated Guide to Unicode on Python (http://lucumr.pocoo.org/2013/7/2/the-updated-guide-to-unicode/)

» Python Encodings and Unicode (http://eric.themoritzfamily.com/python-encodings-and-unicode.html)

» Unicode Tutorials and Overviews (http://www.unicode.org/standard/tutorial-info.html)

» Explain it like I'm five: Python and Unicode? (http://www.reddit.com/r/Python/comments/1g62eh/explain_it_like_im_five_python_and_unicode/)

» Unicode Pain (http://nedbatchelder.com/text/unipain.html)

Making Your Python Application Fast

Nothing turns off a user faster than an application that performs poorly. When an application performs poorly, you can count on users not using it at all. In fact, poor performance is a significant source of application failure in enterprise environments. An organization can spend a ton of money to build an impressive application that does everything, but no one uses it because it runs too slowly or has other serious performance problems.

REMEMBER

Performance is actually a mix of reliability, security, and speed. In fact, you can read about the performance triangle on my blog at http://blog.johnmuellerbooks.com/2012/04/16/considering-the-performance-triangle/. Many developers focus on just the speed part of performance but end up not achieving their goal. It's important to look at every aspect of your application's use of resources and to ensure that you use the best coding techniques.

Numerous resources are available to help you understand performance as it applies to Python applications. However, one of the best resources out there is "A guide to analyzing Python performance," at http://zqpythonic.qiniucdn.com/data/20170602154836/index.html. The author takes the time to explain why something is a performance bottleneck, rather than simply tell you that it is. After you read this article, make sure to check out the PythonSpeed Performance Tips at https://wiki.python.org/moin/PythonSpeed/PerformanceTips as well.

Chapter **19**

Ten Ways to Make a Living with Python

You can literally write any application you want using any language you desire given enough time, patience, and effort. However, some undertakings would be so convoluted and time consuming as to make the effort a study in frustration. In short, most (possibly all) things are possible, but not everything is worth the effort. Using the right tool for the job is always a plus in a world that views time as something in short supply and not to be squandered.

Python excels at certain kinds of tasks, which means that it also lends itself to certain types of programming. The kind of programming you can perform determines the job you get and the way in which you make your living. For example, Python probably isn't a very good choice for writing device drivers, as C/C++ are, so you probably won't find yourself working for a hardware company. Likewise, Python can work with databases, but not at the same depth that comes natively to other languages such as Structured Query Language (SQL), so you won't find yourself working on a huge corporate database project. However, you may find yourself using Python in academic settings because Python does make a great learning language. (See my blog post on the topic at `http://blog.johnmuellerbooks.com/2014/07/14/python-as-a-learning-tool/`.)

The following sections describe some of the occupations that do use Python regularly so that you know what sorts of things you might do with your new-found knowledge. Of course, a single source can't list every kind of job. Consider this an overview of some of the more common uses for Python.

Working in QA

A lot of organizations have separate Quality Assurance (QA) departments that check applications to ensure that they work as advertised. Many different test script languages are on the market, but Python makes an excellent language in this regard because it's so incredibly flexible. In addition, you can use this single language in multiple environments — both on the client and on the server. The broad reach of Python means that you can learn a single language and use it for testing anywhere you need to test something, and in any environment.

REMEMBER

In this scenario, the developer usually knows another language, such as C++, and uses Python to test the applications written in C++. However, the QA person doesn't need to know another language in all cases. In some situations, blind test-ing may be used to confirm that an application behaves in a practical manner or as a means for checking the functionality of an external service provider. You need to check with the organization you want to work with as to the qualifications required for a job from a language perspective.

WHY YOU NEED TO KNOW MULTIPLE PROGRAMMING LANGUAGES

Most organizations see knowledge of multiple programming languages as a big plus (some see it as a requirement). Of course, when you're an employer, it's nice to get the best deal you can when hiring a new employee. Knowing a broader range of languages means that you can work in more positions and offer greater value to an organization. Rewriting applications in another language is time consuming, error prone, and expen-sive, so most companies look for people who can support an application in the existing language, rather than rebuild it from scratch.

From your perspective, knowing more languages means that you'll get more interesting jobs and will be less likely to get bored doing the same old thing every day. In addition, knowing multiple languages tends to reduce frustration. Most large applications today rely on components written in a number of computer languages. To understand the application and how it functions better, you need to know every language used to construct it.

Knowing multiple languages also makes it possible to learn new languages faster. After a while, you start to see patterns in how computer languages are put together, so you spend less time with the basics and can move right on to advanced topics. The faster you can learn new technologies, the greater your opportunities to work in exciting areas of computer science. In short, knowing more languages opens a lot of doors.

Becoming the IT Staff for a Smaller Organization

A smaller organization may have only one or two IT staff, which means that you have to perform a broad range of tasks quickly and efficiently. With Python, you can write utilities and in-house applications quite swiftly. Even though Python might not answer the needs of a large organization because it's interpreted (and potentially open to theft or fiddling by unskilled employees), using it in a smaller organization makes sense because you have greater access control and need to make changes fast. In addition, the ability to use Python in a significant number of environments reduces the need to use anything but Python to meet your needs.

TIP

Some developers are unaware that Python is available in some non-obvious products. For example, even though you can't use Python scripting with Internet Information Server (IIS) right out of the box, you can add Python scripting support to this product by using the steps found in the Microsoft Knowledge Base article at http://support.microsoft.com/kb/276494. If you aren't sure whether a particular application can use Python for scripting, make sure that you check it out online.

You can also get Python support in some products that you might think couldn't possibly support it. For example, you can use Python with Visual Studio (see https://www.visualstudio.com/vs/python/) to make use of Microsoft technologies with this language. The site at https://code.visualstudio.com/docs/languages/python provides some additional details about Python support.

Performing Specialty Scripting for Applications

A number of products can use Python for scripting purposes. For example, Maya (http://www.autodesk.com/products/autodesk-maya/overview) relies on Python for scripting purposes. By knowing which high-end products support Python, you can find a job working with that application in any business that uses it. Here are some examples of products that rely on Python for scripting needs:

>> 3ds Max

>> Abaqus

>> Blender

- » Cinema 4D
- » GIMP
- » Google App Engine
- » Houdini
- » Inkscape
- » Lightwave
- » Modo
- » MotionBuilder
- » Nuke
- » Paint Shop Pro
- » Scribus
- » Softimage

This is just the tip of the iceberg. You can also use Python with the GNU debugger to create more understandable output of complex structures, such as those found in C++ containers. Some video games also rely on Python as a scripting language. In short, you could build a career around creating application scripts using Python as the programming language.

Administering a Network

More than a few administrators use Python to perform tasks such as monitoring network health or creating utilities that automate tasks. Administrators are often short of time, so anything they can do to automate tasks is a plus. In fact, some network management software, such as Trigger (http://trigger.readthedocs. org/en/latest/), is actually written in Python. A lot of these tools are open source and free to download, so you can try them on your network. Also, some interesting articles discuss using Python for network administration, such as "Intro to Python & Automation for Network Engineers" at http://packetpushers.net/show-176-intro-to-python-automation-for-network-engineers/. The point is that knowing how to use Python on your network can ultimately decrease your workload and help you perform your tasks more easily. If you want to see some scripts that are written with network management in mind, check out 25 projects tagged "Network Management" at http://freecode.com/tags/network-management.

Teaching Programming Skills

Many teachers are looking for a faster, more consistent method of teaching computer technology. Raspberry Pi (http://www.raspberrypi.org/) is a single-board computer that makes obtaining the required equipment a lot less expensive for schools. The smallish device plugs into a television or computer monitor to provide full computing capabilities with an incredibly simple setup. Interestingly enough, Python plays a big role into making Raspberry Pi into a teaching platform for programming skills (http://www.piprogramming.org/main/?page_id=372).

TIP

In reality, teachers often use Python to extend native Raspberry Pi capabilities so that it can perform all sorts of interesting tasks (http://www.raspberrypi.org/tag/python/). The project entitled, Boris, the Twitter Dino-Bot (http://www.raspberrypi.org/boris-the-twitter-dino-bot/), is especially interesting. The point is that if you have a teaching goal in mind, combining Raspberry Pi with Python is a fantastic idea.

Helping People Decide on Location

A Geographic Information System (GIS) provides a means of viewing geographic information with business needs in mind. For example, you could use GIS to determine the best place to put a new business or to determine the optimum routes for shipping goods. However, GIS is used for more than simply deciding on locations — it also provides a means for communicating location information better than maps, reports, and other graphics, and a method of presenting physical locations to others. Also interesting is the fact that many GIS products use Python as their language of choice. In fact, a wealth of Python-specific information related to GIS is currently available, such as

>> The GIS and Python Software Laboratory (https://sgillies.net/2009/09/18/reintroducing-the-gis-and-python-software-laboratory.html and http://gispython.org/)

>> Python and GIS Resources (http://www.gislounge.com/python-and-gis-resources/)

>> GIS Programming and Automation (https://www.e-education.psu.edu/geog485/node/17)

Many GIS-specific products, such as ArcGIS (http://www.esri.com/software/arcgis), rely on Python to automate tasks. Entire communities develop around these software offerings, such as Python for ArcGIS (http://resources.arcgis.com/en/communities/python/). The point is that you can use your new programming skills in areas other than computing to earn an income.

Performing Data Mining

Everyone is collecting data about everyone and everything else. Trying to sift through the mountains of data collected is an impossible task without a lot of fine-tuned automation. The flexible nature of Python, combined with its terse language that makes changes extremely fast, makes it a favorite with people who perform data mining on a daily basis. In fact, you can find an online book on the topic, *A Programmer's Guide to Data Mining,* at http://guidetodatamining.com/. Python makes data mining tasks a lot easier. The purpose of data mining is to recognize trends, which means looking for patterns of various sorts. The use of artificial intelligence with Python makes such pattern recognition possible. A paper on the topic, "Data Mining: Discovering and Visualizing Patterns with Python" (http://refcardz.dzone.com/refcardz/data-mining-discovering-and), helps you understand how such analysis is possible. You can use Python to create just the right tool to locate a pattern that could net sales missed by your competitor.

REMEMBER

Of course, data mining is used for more than generating sales. For example, people use data mining to perform tasks such as locating new planets around stars or other types of analysis that increase our knowledge of the universe. Python figures into this sort of data mining as well. You can likely find books and other resources dedicated to any kind of data mining that you want to perform, with many of them mentioning Python as the language of choice.

Interacting with Embedded Systems

An embedded system exists for nearly every purpose on the planet. For example, if you own a programmable thermostat for your house, you're interacting with an embedded system. Raspberry Pi (mentioned earlier in the chapter) is an example of a more complex embedded system. Many embedded systems rely on Python as their programming language. In fact, a special form of Python, Embedded Python (https://wiki.python.org/moin/EmbeddedPython), is sometimes used for these devices. You can even find a YouTube presentation on using Python to build an embedded system at http://www.youtube.com/watch?v=WZoeqnsY9AY.

TIP

Interestingly enough, you might already be interacting with a Python-driven embedded system. For example, Python is the language of choice for many car security systems (http://www.pythoncarsecurity.com/). The remote start feature that you might have relies on Python to get the job done. Your home automation and security system (http://www.linuxjournal.com/article/8513) might also rely on Python.

Python is so popular for embedded systems because it doesn't require compilation. An embedded-system vendor can create an update for any embedded system and simply upload the Python file. The interpreter automatically uses this file without having to upload any new executables or jump through any of the types of hoops that other languages can require.

Carrying Out Scientific Tasks

Python seems to devote more time to scientific and numerical processing tasks than many of the computer languages out there. The number of Python's scientific and numeric processing packages is staggering (https://wiki.python.org/moin/NumericAndScientific). Scientists love Python because it's small, easy to learn, and yet quite precise in its treatment of data. You can produce results by using just a few lines of code. Yes, you could produce the same result using another language, but the other language might not include the prebuilt packages to perform the task, and it would most definitely require more lines of code even if it did.

REMEMBER

The two sciences that have dedicated Python packages are space sciences and life sciences. For example, there is actually a package for performing tasks related to solar physics. You can also find a package for working in genomic biology. If you're in a scientific field, the chances are good that your Python knowledge will significantly impact your ability to produce results quickly while your colleagues are still trying to figure out how to analyze the data.

Performing Real-Time Analysis of Data

Making decisions requires timely, reliable, and accurate data. Often, this data must come from a wide variety of sources, which then require a certain amount of analysis before becoming useful. A number of the people who report using Python do so in a management capacity. They use Python to probe those disparate sources of information, perform the required analysis, and then present the big picture to the manager who has asked for the information. Given that this task occurs regularly, trying to do it manually every time would be time consuming. In fact, it would simply be a waste of time. By the time the manager performed the required work, the need to make a decision might already have passed. Python makes it possible to perform tasks quickly enough for a decision to have maximum impact.

Previous sections have pointed out Python's data-mining, number-crunching, and graphics capabilities. A manager can combine all these qualities while using a language that isn't nearly as complex to learn as C++. In addition, any changes are easy to make, and the manager doesn't need to worry about learning programming skills such as compiling the application. A few changes to a line of code in an interpreted package usually serve to complete the task.

REMEMBER

As with other sorts of occupational leads in this chapter, thinking outside the box is important when getting a job. A lot of people need real-time analysis. Launching a rocket into space, controlling product flow, ensuring that packages get delivered on time, and all sorts of other occupations rely on timely, reliable, and accurate data. You might be able to create your own new job simply by employing Python to perform real-time data analysis.

Chapter **20**

Ten Tools That Enhance Your Python Experience

P ython, like most other programming languages, has strong third-party support in the form of various tools. A *tool* is any utility that enhances the natural capabilities of Python when building an application. So, a debugger is considered a tool because it's a utility, but a library isn't. Libraries are instead used to create better applications. (You can see some of them listed in Chapter 21.)

Even making the distinction between a tool and something that isn't a tool, such as a library, doesn't reduce the list by much. Python enjoys access to a wealth of general-purpose and special tools of all sorts. In fact, the site at https://wiki. python.org/moin/DevelopmentTools breaks these tools down into the following 13 categories:

>> AutomatedRefactoringTools

>> BugTracking

>> ConfigurationAndBuildTools

>> DistributionUtilities

>> DocumentationTools

>> IntegratedDevelopmentEnvironments

» PythonDebuggers

» PythonEditors

» PythonShells

» SkeletonBuilderTools

» TestSoftware

» UsefulModules

» VersionControl

Interestingly enough, the lists on the Python DevelopmentTools site might not even be complete. You can find Python tools listed in quite a few places online.

Given that a single chapter can't possibly cover all the tools out there, this chapter discusses a few of the more interesting tools — those that merit a little extra attention on your part. After you whet your appetite with this chapter, seeing what other sorts of tools you can find online is a good idea. You may find that the tool you thought you might have to create is already available, and in several different forms.

Tracking Bugs with Roundup Issue Tracker

You can use a number of bug-tracking sites with Python, such as the following: **Github** (https://github.com/); **Google Code** (https://code.google.com/); **BitBucket** (https://bitbucket.org/); and **Launchpad** (https://launchpad.net/). However, these public sites are generally not as convenient to use as your own specific, localized bug-tracking software. You can use a number of tracking systems on your local drive, but Roundup Issue Tracker (http://roundup.sourceforge.net/) is one of the better offerings. Roundup should work on any platform that supports Python, and it offers these basic features without any extra work:

» Bug tracking

» TODO list management

If you're willing to put a little more work into the installation, you can get additional features, and these additional features are what make the product special. However, to get them, you may need to install other products, such as a DataBase Management System (DBMS). The product instructions tell you what to install and which third-party products are compatible. After you make the additional installations, you get these upgraded features:

- » Customer help-desk support with the following features:
  - Wizard for the phone answerers
  - Network links
  - System and development issue trackers
- » Issue management for Internet Engineering Task Force (IETF) working groups
- » Sales lead tracking
- » Conference paper submission
- » Double-blind referee management
- » Blogging (extremely basic right now, but will become a stronger offering later)

Creating a Virtual Environment by Using VirtualEnv

Reasons abound to create virtual environments, but the main reason for to do so with Python is to provide a safe and known testing environment. By using the same testing environment each time, you help ensure that the application has a stable environment until you have completed enough of it to test in a production-like environment. VirtualEnv (https://pypi.python.org/pypi/virtualenv) provides the means to create a virtual Python environment that you can use for the early testing process or to diagnose issues that could occur because of the environment. It's important to remember that there are at least three standard levels of testing that you need to perform:

- » **Bug:** Checking for errors in your application
- » **Performance:** Validating that your application meets speed, reliability, and security requirements
- » **Usability:** Verifying that your application meets user needs and will react to user input in the way the user expects

REMEMBER

Because of the manner in which most Python applications are used (see Chapter 19 for some ideas), you generally don't need to run them in a virtual environment after the application has gone to a production site. Most Python applications require access to the outside world, and the isolation of a virtual environment would prevent that access.

NEVER TEST ON A PRODUCTION SERVER

A mistake that some developers make is to test their unreleased application on the production server where the user can easily get to it. Of the many reasons not to test your application on a production server, data loss has to be the most important. If you allow users to gain access to an unreleased version of your application that contains bugs that might corrupt the database or other data sources, the data could be lost or damaged permanently.

You also need to realize that you get only one chance to make a first impression. Many software projects fail because users don't use the end result. The application is complete, but no one uses it because of the perception that the application is flawed in some way. Users have only one goal in mind: to complete their tasks and then go home. When users see that an application is costing them time, they tend not to use it.

Unreleased applications can also have security holes that nefarious individuals will use to gain access to your network. It doesn't matter how well your security software works if you leave the door open for anyone to come in. After they have come in, getting rid of them is nearly impossible, and even if you do get rid of them, the damage to your data is already done. Recovery from security breaches is notoriously difficult — and sometimes impossible. In short, never test on your production server because the costs of doing so are simply too high.

Installing Your Application by Using PyInstaller

Users don't want to spend a lot of time installing your application, no matter how much it might help them in the end. Even if you can get the user to attempt an installation, less skilled users are likely to fail. In short, you need a surefire method of getting an application from your system to the user's system. Installers, such as PyInstaller (http://www.pyinstaller.org/), do just that. They make a nice package out of your application that the user can easily install.

Fortunately, PyInstaller works on all the platforms that Python supports, so you need just the one tool to meet every installation need you have. In addition, you can get platform-specific support when needed. For example, when working on a Windows platform, you can create code-signed executables. Mac developers will appreciate that PyInstaller provides support for bundles. In many cases, avoiding the platform-specific features is best unless you really do need them. When you use a platform-specific feature, the installation will succeed only on the target platform.

WARNING

A number of the installer tools that you find online are platform specific. For example, when you look at an installer that reportedly creates executables, you need to be careful that the executables aren't platform specific (or at least match the platform you want to use). It's important to get a product that will work everywhere it's needed so that you don't create an installation package that the user can't use. Having a language that works everywhere doesn't help when the installation package actually hinders installation.

Building Developer Documentation by Using pdoc

Two kinds of documentation are associated with applications: user and developer. User documentation shows how to use the application, while developer documentation shows how the application works. A library requires only one sort of documentation, developer, while a desktop application may require only user documentation. A service might actually require both kinds of documentation depending on who uses it and how the service is put together. The majority of your documentation is likely to affect developers, and pdoc (https://github.com/BurntSushi/pdoc) is a simple solution for creating it.

The pdoc utility relies on the documentation that you place in your code in the form of docstrings and comments. The output is in the form of a text file or an HTML document. You can also have pdoc run in a way that provides output through a web server so that people can see the documentation directly in a browser. This is actually a replacement for epydoc, which is no longer supported by its originator.

Developing Application Code by Using Komodo Edit

Several chapters in this book discuss the issue of Interactive Development Environments (IDEs), but none make a specific recommendation (except for the use of Jupyter Notebook throughout the book). The IDE you choose depends partly on your needs as a developer, your skill level, and the kinds of applications you want to create. Some IDEs are better than others when it comes to certain kinds of application development. One of the better general-purpose IDEs for novice developers is Komodo Edit (http://komodoide.com/komodo-edit/). You can obtain this IDE for free, and it includes a wealth of features that will make your coding experience much better than what you'll get from IDLE. Here are some of those features:

>> Support for multiple programming languages

>> Automatic completion of keywords

>> Indentation checking

>> Project support so that applications are partially coded before you even begin

>> Superior support

However, the feature that sets Komodo Edit apart from other IDEs is that it has an upgrade path. When you start to find that your needs are no longer met by Komodo Edit, you can upgrade to Komodo IDE (http://komodoide.com/), which includes a lot of professional-level support features, such as code profiling (a feature that checks application speed) and a database explorer (to make working with databases easier).

Debugging Your Application by Using pydbgr

A high-end IDE, such as Komodo IDE, comes with a complete debugger. Even Komodo Edit comes with a simple debugger. However, if you're using something smaller, less expensive, and less capable than a high-end IDE, you might not have a debugger at all. A *debugger* helps you locate errors in your application and fix them. The better your debugger, the less effort required to locate and fix the error. When your editor doesn't include a debugger, you need an external debugger such as pydbgr (https://code.google.com/p/pydbgr/).

REMEMBER

A reasonably good debugger includes a number of standard features, such as code colorization (the use of color to indicate things like keywords). However, it also includes a number of nonstandard features that set it apart. Here are some of the standard and nonstandard features that make pydbgr a good choice when your editor doesn't come with a debugger:

>> **Smarteval:** The eval command helps you see what will happen when you execute a line of code, before you actually execute it in the application. It helps you perform "what if" analysis to see what is going wrong with the application.

>> **Out-of-process debugging:** Normally you have to debug applications that reside on the same machine. In fact, the debugger is part of the application's process, which means that the debugger can actually interfere with the debugging process. Using out-of-process debugging means that the debugger doesn't affect the application and you don't even have to run the application on the same machine as the debugger.

>> **Thorough byte-code inspection:** Viewing how the code you write is turned into *byte code* (the code that the Python interpreter actually understands) can sometimes help you solve tough problems.

> » **Event filtering and tracing:** As your application runs in the debugger, it generates events that help the debugger understand what is going on. For example, moving to the next line of code generates an event, returning from a function call generates another event, and so on. This feature makes it possible to control just how the debugger traces through an application and which events it reacts to.

Entering an Interactive Environment by Using IPython

The Python shell works fine for many interactive tasks. However, if you have used this product, you may have already noted that the default shell has certain deficiencies. Of course, the biggest deficiency is that the Python shell is a pure text environment in which you must type commands to perform any given task. A more advanced shell, such as IPython (http://ipython.org/), can make the interactive environment friendlier by providing GUI features so that you don't have to remember the syntax for odd commands.

REMEMBER

IPython is actually more than just a simple shell. It provides an environment in which you can interact with Python in new ways, such as by displaying graphics that show the result of formulas you create using Python. In addition, IPython is designed as a kind of front end that can accommodate other languages. The IPython application actually sends commands to the real shell in the background, so you can use shells from other languages such as Julia and Haskell. (Don't worry if you've never heard of these languages.)

One of the more exciting features of IPython is the ability to work in parallel computing environments. Normally a shell is single threaded, which means that you can't perform any sort of parallel computing. In fact, you can't even create a multithreaded environment. This feature alone makes IPython worthy of a trial.

Testing Python Applications by Using PyUnit

At some point, you need to test your applications to ensure that they work as instructed. You can test them by entering in one command at a time and verifying the result, or you can automate the process. Obviously, the automated approach is better because you really do want to get home for dinner someday and manual testing is really, really slow (especially when you make mistakes, which are guaranteed to happen). Products such as PyUnit (`https://wiki.python.org/moin/PyUnit`) make unit testing (the testing of individual features) significantly easier.

The nice part of this product is that you actually create Python code to perform the testing. Your script is simply another, specialized, application that tests the main application for problems.

REMEMBER

You may be thinking that the scripts, rather than your professionally written application, could be bug ridden. The testing script is designed to be extremely simple, which will keep scripting errors small and quite noticeable. Of course, errors can (and sometimes do) happen, so yes, when you can't find a problem with your application, you do need to check the script.

Tidying Your Code by Using Isort

It may seem like an incredibly small thing, but code can get messy, especially if you don't place all your `import` statements at the top of the file in alphabetical order. In some situations, it becomes difficult, if not impossible, to figure out what's going on with your code when it isn't kept neat. The Isort utility (`http://timothycrosley.github.io/isort/`) performs the seemingly small task of sorting your `import` statements and ensuring that they all appear at the top of the source code file. This small step can have a significant effect on your ability to understand and modify the source code.

Just knowing which modules a particular module needs can be a help in locating potential problems. For example, if you somehow get an older version of a needed module on your system, knowing which modules the application needs can make the process of finding that module easier.

In addition, knowing which modules an application needs is important when it comes time to distribute your application to users. Knowing that the user has the correct modules available helps ensure that the application will run as anticipated.

Providing Version Control by Using Mercurial

The applications you created while working through this book aren't very complex. In fact, after you finish this book and move on to more advanced training applications, you're unlikely to need version control. However, after you start working in an organizational development environment in which you create real applications that users need to have available at all times, version control becomes essential. *Version control* is simply the act of keeping track of the changes that occur in an application between application releases to the production environment. When you say you're using MyApp 1.2, you're referring to version 1.2 of the MyApp application. Versioning lets everyone know which application release is being used when bug fixes and other kinds of support take place.

Numerous version control products are available for Python. One of the more interesting offerings is Mercurial (https://www.mercurial-scm.org/). You can get a version of Mercurial for almost any platform that Python will run on, so you don't have to worry about changing products when you change platforms. (If your platform doesn't offer a binary, executable, release, you can always build one from the source code provided on the download site.)

Unlike a lot of the other offerings out there, Mercurial is free. Even if you find that you need a more advanced product later, you can gain useful experience by working with Mercurial on a project or two.

REMEMBER

The act of storing each version of an application in a separate place so that changes can be undone or redone as needed is called *source code management* or SCM. For many people, source code management seems like a hard task. Because the Mercurial environment is quite forgiving, you can learn about SCM in a friendly environment. Being able to interact with any version of the source code for a particular application is essential when you need to go back and fix problems created by a new release.

The best part about Mercurial is that it provides a great online tutorial at https://www.mercurial-scm.org/wiki/Tutorial. Following along on your own machine is the best way to learn about SCM, but even just reading the material is helpful. Of course, the first tutorial is all about getting a good installation of Mercurial. The tutorials then lead you through the process of creating a repository (a place where application versions are stored) and using the repository as you create your application code. By the time you finish the tutorials, you should have a great idea of how source control should work and why versioning is an important part of application development.

IN THIS CHAPTER

» Securing your data by using cryptology

» Managing and displaying data

» Working with graphics

» Finding the information you need

» Allowing access to Java code

Chapter **21**

Ten (Plus) Libraries You Need to Know About

Python provides you with considerable power when it comes to creating average applications. However, most applications aren't average and require some sort of special processing to make them work. That's where libraries come into play. A good library will extend Python functionality so that it supports the special programming needs that you have. For example, you might need to plot statistics or interact with a scientific device. These sorts of tasks require the use of one or more libraries.

TIP

One of the best places to find a library listing online is the UsefulModules site at `https://wiki.python.org/moin/UsefulModules`. Of course, you have many other places to look for libraries as well. For example, the article entitled "7 Python Libraries you should know about" (`http://www.11eess.com/2013/03/7-python-libraries-you-should-know-about.html`) provides you with a relatively complete description of the seven libraries its title refers to. If you're working on a specific platform, such as Windows, you can find platform-specific sites, such as Unofficial Windows Binaries for Python Extension Packages (`http://www.1fd.uci.edu/~gohlke/pythonlibs/`). The point is that you can find lists of libraries everywhere.

The purpose of this chapter isn't to add to your already overflowing list of potential library candidates. Instead, it provides you with a list of ten libraries that work on every platform and provide basic services that just about everyone will need. Think of this chapter as a source for a core group of libraries to use for your next coding adventure.

Developing a Secure Environment by Using PyCrypto

Data security is an essential part of any programming effort. The reason that applications are so valued is that they make it easy to manipulate and use data of all sorts. However, the application must protect the data or the efforts to work with it are lost. It's the data that is ultimately the valuable part of a business — the application is simply a tool. Part of protecting the data is to ensure that no one can steal it or use it in a manner that the originator didn't intend, which is where cryptographic libraries such as PyCrypto (https://www.dlitz.net/software/pycrypto/) come into play.

REMEMBER

The main purpose of this library is to turn your data into something that others can't read while it sits in permanent storage. The purposeful modification of data in this manner is called *encryption.* However, when you read the data into memory, a *decryption* routine takes the mangled data and turns it back into its original form so that the application can manage it. At the center of all this is the *key,* which is used to encrypt and decrypt the data. Ensuring that the key remains safe is part of your application coding as well. You can read the data because you have the key; no others can because they lack the key.

Interacting with Databases by Using SQLAlchemy

A *database* is essentially an organized manner of storing repetitive or structured data on disk. For example, customer *records* (individual entries in the database) are repetitive because each customer has the same sort of information requirements, such as name, address, and telephone number. The precise organization of the data determines the sort of database you're using. Some database products specialize in text organization, others in tabular information, and still others in random bits of data (such as readings taken from a scientific instrument). Databases can use a tree-like structure or a flat-file configuration to store data. You'll hear all sorts of odd terms when you start looking into DataBase Management System (DBMS) technology — most of which mean something only to a DataBase Administrator (DBA) and won't matter to you.

REMEMBER

The most common type of database is called a Relational DataBase Management System (RDBMS), which uses tables that are organized into records and fields (just like a table you might draw on a sheet of paper). Each *field* is part of a column of the same kind of information, such as the customer's name. Tables are related to each other in various ways, so creating complex relationships is possible. For example, each customer may have one or more entries in a purchase order table, and the customer table and the purchase order table are therefore related to each other.

An RDBMS relies on a special language called the Structured Query Language (SQL) to access the individual records inside. Of course, you need some means of interacting with both the RDBMS and SQL, which is where SQLAlchemy (http://www.sqlalchemy.org/) comes into play. This product reduces the amount of work needed to ask the database to perform tasks such as returning a specific customer record, creating a new customer record, updating an existing customer record, and deleting an old customer record.

Seeing the World by Using Google Maps

Geocoding (the finding of geographic coordinates, such as longitude and latitude from geographic data, such as address) has lots of uses in the world today. People use the information to do everything from finding a good restaurant to locating a lost hiker in the mountains. Getting from one place to another often revolves around geocoding today as well. Google Maps (https://pypi.python.org/pypi/googlemaps/) lets you add directional data to your applications.

In addition to getting from one point to another or finding a lost soul in the desert, Google Maps can also help in Geographic Information System (GIS) applications. The "Helping People Decide on Location" section of Chapter 19 describes this particular technology in more detail, but essentially, GIS is all about deciding on a location for something or determining why one location works better than another location for a particular task. In short, Google Maps presents your application with a look at the outside world that it can use to help your user make decisions.

Adding a Graphical User Interface by Using TkInter

Users respond to the Graphical User Interface (GUI) because it's friendlier and requires less thought than using a command-line interface. Many products out there can give your Python application a GUI. However, the most commonly used product is TkInter (https://wiki.python.org/moin/TkInter). Developers like it so much because TkInter keeps things simple. It's actually an interface for the Tool Command Language (Tcl)/Toolkit (Tk) found at http://www.tcl.tk/. A number of languages use Tcl/Tk as the basis for creating a GUI.

TIP

You might not relish the idea of adding a GUI to your application. Doing so tends to be time consuming and doesn't make the application any more functional (it also slows the application down in many cases). The point is that users like GUIs, and if you want your application to see strong use, you need to meet user requirements.

Providing a Nice Tabular Data Presentation by Using PrettyTable

Displaying tabular data in a manner the user can understand is important. From the examples you've seen throughout the book, you know that Python stores this type of data in a form that works best for programming needs. However, users need something that is organized in a manner that humans understand and that is visually appealing. The PrettyTable library (https://pypi.python.org/pypi/PrettyTable) makes it easy to add an appealing tabular presentation to your command-line application.

Enhancing Your Application with Sound by Using PyAudio

Sound is a useful way to convey certain types of information to the user. Of course, you have to be careful in using sound because special-needs users might not be able to hear it, and for those who can, using too much sound can interfere with normal business operations. However, sometimes audio is an important means of communicating supplementary information to users who can interact with it (or of simply adding a bit of pizzazz to make your application more interesting).

One of the better platform-independent libraries to make sound work with your Python application is PyAudio (http://people.csail.mit.edu/hubert/pyaudio/). This library makes it possible to record and play back sounds as needed (such as a user recording an audio note of tasks to perform later and then playing back the list of items as needed).

CLASSIFYING PYTHON SOUND TECHNOLOGIES

Realize that sound comes in many forms in computers. The basic multimedia services provided by Python (see the documentation at https://docs.python.org/3/library/mm.html) provide essential playback functionality. You can also write certain types of audio files, but the selection of file formats is limited. In addition, some packages, such as winsound (https://docs.python.org/3/library/winsound.html), are platform dependent, so you can't use them in an application designed to work everywhere. The standard Python offerings are designed to provide basic multimedia support for playing back system sounds.

The middle ground, augmented audio functionality designed to improve application usability, is covered by libraries such as PyAudio. You can see a list of these libraries at https://wiki.python.org/moin/Audio. However, these libraries usually focus on business needs, such as recording notes and playing them back later. Hi-fidelity output isn't part of the plan for these libraries.

Gamers need special audio support to ensure that they can hear special effects, such as a monster walking behind them. These needs are addressed by libraries such as PyGame (http://www.pygame.org/news.html). When using these libraries, you need higher-end equipment and have to plan to spend considerable time working on just the audio features of your application. You can see a list of these libraries at https://wiki.python.org/moin/PythonGameLibraries.

TIP

Working with sound on a computer always involves trade-offs. For example, a platform-independent library can't take advantage of special features that a particular platform might possess. In addition, it might not support all the file formats that a particular platform uses. The reason to use a platform-independent library is to ensure that your application provides basic sound support on all systems that it might interact with.

Manipulating Images by Using PyQtGraph

Humans are visually oriented. If you show someone a table of information and then show the same information as a graph, the graph is always the winner when it comes to conveying information. Graphs help people see trends and understand why the data has taken the course that it has. However, getting those pixels that represent the tabular information onscreen is difficult, which is why you need a library such as PyQtGraph (http://www.pyqtgraph.org/) to make things simpler.

Even though the library is designed around engineering, mathematical, and scientific requirements, you have no reason to avoid using it for other purposes. PyQtGraph supports both 2D and 3D displays, and you can use it to generate new graphics based on numeric input. The output is completely interactive, so a user can select image areas for enhancement or other sorts of manipulation. In addition, the library comes with a wealth of useful widgets (controls, such as buttons, that you can display onscreen) to make the coding process even easier.

REMEMBER

Unlike many of the offerings in this chapter, PyQtGraph isn't a free-standing library, which means that you must have other products installed to use it. This isn't unexpected because PyQtGraph is doing quite a lot of work. You need these items installed on your system to use it:

>> Python version 2.7 or above

>> PyQt version 4.8 or above (https://wiki.python.org/moin/PyQt) or PySide (https://wiki.python.org/moin/PySide)

>> numpy (http://www.numpy.org/)

>> scipy (http://www.scipy.org/)

>> PyOpenGL (http://pyopengl.sourceforge.net/)

Locating Your Information by Using IRLib

Finding your information can be difficult when the information grows to a certain size. Consider your hard drive as a large, free-form, tree-based database that lacks a useful index. Any time such a structure becomes large enough, data simply gets lost. (Just try to find those pictures you took last summer and you'll get the idea.) As a result, having some type of search capability built into your application is important so that users can find that lost file or other information.

WARNING

A number of search libraries are available for Python. The problem with most of them is that they are hard to install or don't provide consistent platform support. In fact, some of them work on only one or two platforms. However, IRLib (https://github.com/gr33ndata/irlib) is written in pure Python, which ensures that it works on every platform. If you find that IRLib doesn't meet your needs, make sure the product you do get will provide the required search functionality on all the platforms you select and that the installation requirements are within reason.

IRLab works by creating a search index of whatever information you want to work with. You can then save this index to disk for later use. The search mechanism works through the use of metrics — you locate one or more entries that provide a best fit for the search criteria.

Creating an Interoperable Java Environment by Using JPype

Python does provide access to a huge array of libraries, and you're really unlikely to use them all. However, you might be in a situation in which you find a Java library that is a perfect fit but can't use it from your Python application unless you're willing to jump through a whole bunch of hoops. The JPype library (http://jpype.sourceforge.net/) makes it possible to access most (but not all) of the Java libraries out there directly from Python. The library works by creating a bridge between the two languages at the byte-code level. Consequently, you don't have to do anything weird to get your Python application to work with Java.

WARNING

CONVERTING YOUR PYTHON APPLICATION TO JAVA

Many different ways exist to achieve interoperability between two languages. Creating a bridge between them, as JPype does, is one way. Another alternative is to convert the code created for one language into code for the other language. This is the approach used by Jython (https://wiki.python.org/jython/). This utility converts your Python code into Java code so that you can make full use of Java functionality in your application while maintaining the features that you like about Python.

You'll encounter trade-offs in language interoperability no matter which solution you use. In the case of JPype, you won't have access to some Java libraries. In addition, there is a speed penalty in using this approach because the JPype bridge is constantly converting calls and data. The problem with Jython is that you lose the ability to modify your code after conversion. Any changes that you make will create an incompatibility between the original Python code and its Java counterpart. In short, no perfect solutions exist for the problem of getting the best features of two languages into one application.

Accessing Local Network Resources by Using Twisted Matrix

Depending on your network setup, you may need access to files and other resources that you can't reach using the platform's native capabilities. In this case, you need a library that makes such access possible, such as Twisted Matrix (https://twistedmatrix.com/trac/). The basic idea behind this library is to provide you with the calls needed to establish a connection, no matter what sort of protocol is in use.

The feature that makes this library so useful is its event-driven nature. This means that your application need not get hung up while waiting for the network to respond. In addition, the use of an event-driven setup makes asynchronous communication (in which a request is sent by one routine and then handled by a completely separate routine) easy to implement.

Accessing Internet Resources by Using Libraries

Although products such as Twisted Matrix can handle online communication, getting a dedicated HTTP protocol library is often a better option when working with the Internet because a dedicated library is both faster and more feature complete. When you specifically need HTTP or HTTPS support, using a library such as httplib2 (https://github.com/jcgregorio/httplib2) is a good idea. This library is written in pure Python and makes handling HTTP-specific needs, such as setting a Keep-Alive value, relatively easy. (A *Keep-Alive* is a value that determines how long a port stays open waiting for a response so that the application doesn't have to continuously re-create the connection, wasting resources and time as a result.)

You can use httplib2 for any Internet-specific methodology — it provides full support for both the GET and POST request methods. This library also includes routines for standard Internet compression methods, such as deflate and gzip. It also supports a level of automation. For example, httplib2 adds ETags back into PUT requests when resources are already cached.

Index

Symbols

A

F

G

H

I

-i option, 40

IBM i (formerly Application System 400 or AS/400, iSeries, and System i) (platform), 22

icons, explained, 3

IDE (Integrated Development Environment), 2, 38, 55, 56–58, 83

IDE (Interactive Development Environment), 348, 366

identity operators, 116, 122

IDLE (Integrated DeveLopment Environment), 24, 31, 32, 35, 36, 38, 56, 348

IDLE (Interactive DeveLopment Environment), 28

IEEE Spectrum, 15

IEEE-754 standard, 108

if statement, 136–141, 143, 146–148

if.elif statement, 143–145, 146, 266, 270

if.else statement, 141–148

IfElse.py, 172

IIS (Internet Information Server), 355

images, manipulating of by using PyQtGraph, 375–376

imperative coding style, 45

import statement, 197, 202, 203–205

importing, 112, 197, 202–207

indentation, 75–77

index() function, 262

index(str, beg=0, end=len(string)) function, 237

information
    controlling how Python views data, 114–115
    creating and using functions, 123–132
    a.k.a. data, 113
    locating of by using IRLib, 376–377
    managing, 113–133
    storing, 104–105
    storing and modifying, 103–112
    working with operators, 115–123

inheritance, 283, 299

__init__() constructor, 289

initializing, 289

__initializing__ attribute, 216

Inkscape, 356

input() function, 132–133

Insert Cell Below icon, 90

insert() function, 250

insertion pointer, 229

install (pip command), 215

installation
    of Python, 24–31
    testing of, 35

instance, 283

instance method, 288

instance variable, 283, 290, 292–293

instantiate, 284

instantiation, 283

int() command, 111

int data type, 106

integers, 106–107, 108

Integrated Development Environment (IDE), 2, 38, 55, 56–58, 83

Integrated DeveLopment Environment (IDLE), 24, 31, 32, 35, 36, 38, 56, 348

Interactive Development Environment (IDE), 348, 366

Interactive DeveLopment Environment (IDLE), 28

interactive environment, 45, 368

Internet Information Server (IIS), 355

Interrupt (kernel-specific command), 94

Interrupt Kernel icon, 91

"Intro to Python & Automation for Network Engineers," 356

iPhone Operating System (iOS) (platform), 22

IPython, 96, 97, 98, 368

IRLib, 376–377

isalnum() function, 233

isalpha() function, 233

isdecimal() function, 233

isdigit() function, 233

islower() function, 233

isnumeric() function, 234

Isort, 369

isspace() function, 234

istitle() function, 234

isupper() function, 234

IT staff, as occupation that uses Python regularly, 355

iterable items, 279

J

Java (programming language), 14, 15, 18, 19, 377

JavaScript, 16

join(seq) function, 234

JPype, 377

--json flag, 211

P

About the Authors

John Mueller is a freelance author and technical editor. He has writing in his blood, having produced 104 books and more than 600 articles to date. The topics range from networking to artificial intelligence and from database management to heads-down programming. Some of his current books include discussions of data science, machine learning, and algorithms — all of which use Python as a demonstration language. His technical editing skills have helped more than 70 authors refine the content of their manuscripts. John has provided technical editing services to various magazines, performed various kinds of consulting, and he writes certification exams. Be sure to read his blog at http://blog.johnmuellerbooks.com/. You can reach him by email at John@JohnMuellerBooks.com. He also has a website at http://www.johnmuellerbooks.com/.

Dedication

This book is dedicated to the readers who take time to write me each day. Every morning I'm greeted by various emails — some with requests, a few with complaints, and then there are the very few that just say thank you. All these emails encourage and challenge me as an author — to better both my books and myself. Thank you!

Acknowledgments

Thanks to my wife, Rebecca. Even though she is gone now, her spirit is in every book I write, in every word that appears on the page. She believed in me when no one else would.

Russ Mullen deserves thanks for his technical edit of this book. He greatly added to the accuracy and depth of the material you see here. Russ is always providing me with great URLs for new products and ideas. However, it's the testing that Russ does that helps most. He's the sanity check for my work. Russ also has different computer equipment from mine, so he's able to point out flaws that I might not otherwise notice.

Matt Wagner, my agent, deserves credit for helping me get the contract in the first place and taking care of all the details that most authors don't really consider. I always appreciate his assistance. It's good to know that someone wants to help.

A number of people read all or part of this book to help me refine the approach, test the coding examples, and generally provide input that all readers wish they could have. These unpaid volunteers helped in ways too numerous to mention here. I especially appreciate the efforts of Eva Beattie, Glenn A. Russell, Col Onyebuche, Emanuel Jonas, Michael Sasseen, Osvaldo Téllez Almirall, and Thomas Zinckgraf, who provided general input, read the entire book, and selflessly devoted themselves to this project.

Finally, I would like to thank Katie Mohr, Susan Christophersen, and the rest of the editorial and production staff.

Publisher's Acknowledgments

Senior Acquisitions Editor: Katie Mohr

Project Manager and Copy Editor: Susan Christophersen

Technical Editor: Russ Mullen

Sr. Editorial Assistant: Cherie Case

Production Editor: Antony Sami

Cover Image: © Esin Deniz/Shutterstock